Diana:
A Commemorative Biography

1961 ~ 1997

Diana: A Commemorative Biography

**With Preface By
Dame Barbara Cartland**

Commonwealth
Publications Inc.

A Commonwealth Publications Paperback
DIANA: A COMMEMORATIVE BIOGRAPHY
First edition published 1997
by Commonwealth Publications Inc.
9764 - 45th Avenue,
Edmonton, AB, CANADA T6E 5C5
All rights reserved
Copyright © 1997

ISBN: 1-55197-846-6

Photographs used with the permission of
AP/Wide World Photos

Printed in Canada

*Dedicated to the memory of
England's Rose.*

Acknowledgements

Publisher: Donald T. Phelan
Executive Editor: Lyndon McLean
Senior Editor: Randy Epp
Design and Illustration: Patrick Earl
Layout and Typesetting: Ann Walsh

Researched and compiled by:

Emille Currie   Toni Owen
Randy Epp   Susan Owen-Routledge
James Gilhooly   Kathryn Ostlund
Vanessa Grange   Andrew Struthers
Lyndon McLean   Sophie Watson
Joan McManners   Joanne Wotypka

Preface: Dame Barbara Cartland

Special thanks to the management and staff of:
Bardes Press Ltd
Edmonton, Alberta
CANADA

The Spencer Family

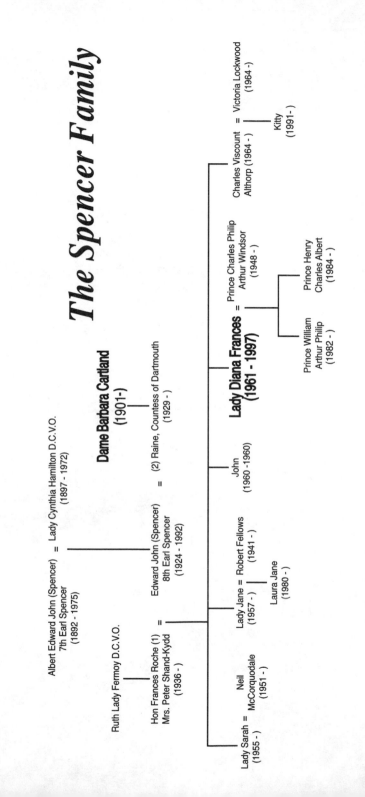

Albert Edward John (Spencer) = Lady Cynthia Hamilton D.C.V.O.
7th Earl Spencer   (1897 - 1972)
(1892 - 1975)

Dame Barbara Cartland
(1901-)

Ruth Lady Fermoy D.C.V.O.

Hon Frances Roche (1)   =   Edward John (Spencer)   =   (2) Raine, Countess of Dartmouth
Mrs. Peter Shand-Kydd   8th Earl Spencer   (1929 -)
(1936 -)   (1924 - 1992)

Lady Sarah = Neil McCorquodale
(1955 -)   (1951 -)

Lady Jane = Robert Fellows
(1957 -)   (1941 -)

Laura Jane
(1980 -)

John
(1960 -1960)

Lady Diana Frances
(1961 - 1997)   =   Prince Charles Philip Arthur Windsor
(1948 -)

Prince William Arthur Philip
(1982 -)

Prince Henry Charles Albert
(1984 -)

Charles Viscount   =   Victoria Lockwood
Althorp (1964 -)   (1964 -)

Kitty
(1991-)

Table of Contents

Preface 9
Chapter 1:A Silver Spoon; A Tarnished Childhood 17
Chapter 2:The School Years 41
Chapter 3:Diana: An Independent Young Lady 59
Chapter 4: A Fairy-tale Romance 79
Chapter 5: Wedding of the Century 96
Chapter 6: Wife, Mother, and Superstar 110
Chapter 7: Separate Ways 148
Chapter 8: Stepping Out 168
Chapter 9: The Divorce...and Life After 188
Chapter 10: The Tragedy 215
Chapter 11: Greater Causes 234
Chronology 253
Bibliography 273

Preface
by
Dame Barbara Cartland

It seems so extraordinary, in fact one can hardly believe it is true, that one young girl could change the whole of England, and indeed the whole world.

Diana Spencer was the daughter of the Earl Spencer.

She was, when she was growing up, very quiet, and people hardly seemed to notice her.

However, as she grew older and extremely pretty, there was no doubt that there was something about her which was very different from other girls.

Her father was a very important landowner and was also an aristocrat who was much respected.

He entertained at his stately home, Althorp, in the country, so Diana and her sisters grew up used to riding and country pursuits.

It was when their father was married for the second time to my daughter, Raine, that the girls felt isolated and not as important a part of the family as they had when their father was alone.

Diana was very pretty, but she was quiet and seldom talked about herself or her feelings to anyone.

It was her father who first gave her the books of Barbara Cartland which were about love and happy endings, of which she knew very little.

They were of love, and she found herself enjoying them more than anything she had read before.

She was, however, somewhat upset when her father married again.

She felt that the new addition to their family was somehow, in some way, keeping her father from her.

What her stepmother brought to the family was her son, who was only eleven at the time, but whom Diana thought was lonely and somewhat neglected by his older sister.

Diana took him to the Althorp swimming pool and found she could talk to him and make him happy.

It was the beginning of her being devoted to children and feeling that somehow, if they were neglected, she must make them happy.

She continued to read one Barbara Cartland book after another.

Because it amused her father to see his daughter reading, he took a photograph of her sitting on her bed with three Barbara Cartland books beside her.

What she learnt from them was that everyone wanted love, and to lose love left them miserable, lonely and almost wishing not to love any longer.

The more she read, the more she realized that the average person in the world was not particularly happy.

Some of them were silent and resentful if they were poor.

Others wanted the impossible and were miserable if they could not capture it for themselves.

"What they want is love," Diana reasoned to herself, and she felt she could give it to them.

The time in the country passed slowly and Diana and her sisters were not very fond of their stepmother.

Perhaps they were jealous that she attracted their father's attention more than they did.

As time passed, Diana became more and more interested in reading about love because she did not find it in her home.

When her father unexpectedly died, she came to London and for the first time discovered that there were numerous young children who were either ill or neglected by their parents.

She began to visit one or two hospitals and found there children without love, as well as older people nearing death who were lonely and had often been forgotten by their families and friends before they entered the hospital.

It was then, perhaps inspired by the books she had read on love, that she began to give love to those she visited.

From the first they were surprised and delighted when she appeared. They called to her and begged her to stay longer.

The more she thought about love, the more she was certain that people, especially children, thought of it as something they could not find in their own lives.

Therefore they sighed and tried to think about something else.

It was when she visited children that she talked to them about love, the love of God and his Angels, and made them feel that it was something they could have if they wanted it.

Of course they did want it.

It was the way Diana spoke which made them feel when she left that they had received something precious and wonderful which belonged to them, which was theirs forever.

Love, love, love was in her mind from early in the morning until she went to sleep at night.

She knew, in a way she could not explain in words, that she loved the children who suffered, who were alone and neglected.

Also those who were nearing death, who were suffering not only in their bodies, but also in their minds and souls, who felt they were not leaving behind anything of importance in the world where they had never known real happiness.

In some extraordinary way which is difficult to explain, she became more and more aware that she loved them all.

"I must make them happy," Diana said to herself.

Somehow she found that when she visited them and talked to them, and in many cases prayed with them, they were happy, where before they had been lonely and miserable.

All they wanted when she departed was that she should come again and make them as happy as they were when they said goodbye.

Diana knew herself that the feelings she had for the children and for those who were suffering came from God.

She, therefore, in her own heart, believed that God was showing her how to make the children happy and not be afraid of what would happen in the future.

To the older people she seemed to bring a happiness into their lives which had not been there before she arrived.

Many had been afraid of death, but after they had talked to Diana, they knew they were going to God, and God was love itself.

"I was miserable when you came," more than one person said to her when she went to a hospital, "but with your love, I can think of what you said to me. I feel happier than I have ever felt in my life before."

If time passed slowly for many people, for Diana it was often so demanding that she could not sleep.

One night after she had gone to bed, she thought of a man who was extremely ill and in hospital.

She felt in some strange way he was calling for her.

She got out of bed, dressed herself, went downstairs and, without anyone in the house knowing, went to her car and drove to the hospital.

When she told the nurse who opened the door why she had come, she went up to the ward where, as she expected, the man who was dying was moving restlessly in his bed.

He was alone with no one to speak to.

She took his hand, sat down and told him that he was going to Heaven and that it was a wonderful place.

She talked to him softly and quietly.

At the same time she poured out to him the love which was in her heart, which she knew instinctively was what he wanted.

When she left him, he thanked her from the bottom of his heart and told her that he would sleep now and think happily of the Heaven to which he was going.

Where Diana had told him he would find the happiness which he had never had in his life.

It would come to him now and he would be happy as he had never been happy before.

When he fell asleep, she drove home alone.

Fortunately, she was not robbed or kidnapped on the way.

It was then I told her that she must take more care of herself.

She promised me that she would be more careful in the future.

But I felt that with her concern for those who were suffering, who were calling silently for her in their hearts, she had to give them the magical love which came to her from Heaven, which, when they tried to explain it, they felt as a strange, unusual happiness they had never known before.

Love, love. It was love in the morning with the children and love in the evening with those who had no idea how to prepare themselves for death.

In fact, as one man said, "I did not know that Heaven had the love which I have always sought in my life but failed to find. But now I am certain that the love she has told me about is waiting for me. When I find it, I will be happier than I have ever been on earth."

It was that strange magic that Diana gave to everyone, young and old, with whom she came in contact.

It was a new love which came from her heart and her soul.

She would go on praying for them after she had left them.

She would be delighted when she learnt later that they had died with a smile on their lips and had not been afraid to leave the world behind.

It was somehow unbelievingly cruel that Diana's own life was not as happy and as wonderful as she made the lives of those she visited.

She was thrilled and delighted that she had two sons by the Prince of Wales.

But while she captured the hearts of·so many people, she did not manage to capture his.

Strangely, her Ladies-in-Waiting, who were friends, were taken away from her after the divorce. They could have stayed with her, to talk to her and prevent her from ever feeling lonely.

When she was not with her sons, whom she adored, she was often by herself.

The mere gloominess of it drove her hastily toward the children, who ran to her shouting with joy the moment she appeared.

And to the older people, who smiled with delight when they heard her voice at the door of the hospital ward.

Diana believed that the love she gave those who were dying came from Heaven itself.

The children she loved with her heart, giving them a happiness they had never known before they met her.

I have always thought of Diana as the Princess of Love.

It is love which I am certain carried her to Heaven.

It seems incredible that a young girl, by dying, should have alerted England and caused it to reach toward Heaven as it has never reached before.

How can it be possible that so many thousands of people should leave their homes so that they might see Diana's funeral cortege pass, bringing tears to the eyes of everyone who saw it?

How is it possible that in one day, so many people would think of

God the Father and of Jesus and be thankful that they themselves could feel the love that Diana had given them and which would eventually carry them to Heaven?

How was it possible that every street through which Diana passed to her burial was decorated with flowers?

That her passing should bring tears to the oldest as well as the youngest?

It would be impossible for anyone who saw London on that day to ever forget what they had seen and what they had felt.

It is that same love which Diana gave on earth which I am sure is coming down to us from the Heaven she has now reached and where we hope to join her.

It would be impossible to believe save for those of us who have known Diana and found her different in many ways which we will never forget.

But it seems almost incredible that one young English girl, who has not been applauded in any other way, should arouse the hearts of everyone she encountered.

Not toward herself, although she was extremely pretty and attractive, but toward something greater and more wonderful, which, to Diana, was Heaven itself.

That is what she has given us.

The love which comes from Heaven and from God, which can only come from our hearts.

There is no other way of reaching it.

How is it possible that Diana should give us the love which comes from Heaven, which is very different from the love which we accept so blindly as being required when we marry or when we find life on earth exceedingly difficult.

Only God Himself could have made the love which Diana gave from her heart and her soul to those who needed it.

Only God could have let her leave a memory amongst us which will sweep away much of the misery and the darkness which lie in so many people's hearts.

The flowers which filled the streets were flowers which must have come from Heaven itself.

Those who listened to the music in Westminster Abbey knew it was in many ways the music of the Angels.

Diana has shown us a way which has never been seen before to the happiness which comes from God Himself and the love which men and women hope and pray will be theirs.

It is the love which she gave from her heart and soul which aroused in those who received it a happiness which was not of this world.

But it came to us in a strange way, from a young girl who gave her heart and her soul to those who needed it.

It would be impossible for anyone who attended the funeral service for Diana at Westminster Abbey in London to forget that it was love which had brought them there.

Love which had made millions of people wait up all night just to see her cortege pass.

It was also the love which Diana created which has meant that while I write this, already £150 million has been collected for her memorial fund.

But the real memory which will remain forever in our lives, which will never be forgotten, is her love.

The love which comes from the heart and the soul, and from God Himself.

Dame Barbara Cartland
September 8, 1997
Camfield Place

Publishers note:

Related by marriage to the late Princess of Wales, Dame Barbara Cartland is the world's most published romance novelist, with over 600 titles to her credit.

Chapter 1

A Silver Spoon; A Tarnished Childhood

The tension that Saturday must have been intense. Frances, wife of Viscount Althorp, was ready to give birth to her fourth child. A son, John, the heir to the 500-year-old Spencer dynasty and fortune, had been born just eighteen months before, but had survived for only ten hours. Edward John Spencer, a tall, handsome English aristocrat with impeccable breeding, loved his two daughters, but the future of his family's title was at stake. Without a direct heir, the nearly two-hundred-year-old Spencer earldom would pass on to cousins, and along with it the wealth, possessions and 453-year-old ancestral estate of Althorp Park that are entailed exclusively on the title-holder.

Frances was in an upstairs bedroom attended by midwife Joy Hearn, Johnnie downstairs pacing the floor. The long July day crept past and evening shadows began lengthening on the tree-lined drive leading to Park House, the ten-bedroom Victorian home the Spencers rented from Queen Elizabeth II on her privately-owned Sandringham estate. No doubt all felt the anxiety-laced atmosphere: servants, apprehensive husband, 6-year-old Sarah and 4-year-old Jane alike.

Frances and Johnnie were so positive the baby would be the long-awaited heir, no female names had been chosen. Johnnie's father, the seventh Earl Spencer, stood ready in Northamptonshire to have his servants unfurl flags of celebration at Althorp while servants and employees in nearby Great Brington were equally ready to hoist a few pints at the Fox and Hounds to toast the new earl-to-be. Finally, at 7:45 p.m. on July 1, 1961, the Honourable Frances Spencer, Viscountess Althorp, herself the daughter of a baron, gave birth to a 7-pound, 12-ounce...girl.

The disappointment would have been palpable. Johnnie Spencer inspected the newborn and pronounced her at least a perfect physical specimen. It merited only a nine-word announcement in the *Times*: "Viscountess Althorp gave birth to a daughter on Saturday." In the rarefied world of nobility and aristocracy, the wait for an heir would go on.

Frances and Johnnie were at a loss for a name and it would be days before the local registrar, John Wilson, would record the Honourable Diana Frances Spencer on the birth certificate. Diana was a name steeped in Spencer tradition as well as the Roman virgin goddess of the luminous and changeable moon and of hunting, but the fair-haired, blue-eyed infant was not to grow up to be an aficionado of chasing foxes or shooting grouse, for her game was to be much more human, humane and humanitarian. She was an aristocrat from one of Britain's most noble families, but, like distant relations Winston Churchill and George Washington, she would be an aristocrat with a common touch.

But on that hot summer day all this was in the future and the world did not mark her arrival with pomp and ceremony, as it had marked, but 12 years earlier, the birth of the man who was to be her future prince, her nemesis, and the father of her children. Even her christening on August 30 at St. Mary Magdalene, the church at Sandringham, was perfunctory. While Sarah had merited Queen Elizabeth the Queen Mother as a godmother, and the Duke of Kent had been appointed Jane's godfather, Diana's godparents consisted of neighbors and businessmen.

Nearly three years later Althorp's flags would finally unfurl and cups would be raised when Lady Frances delivered a healthy heir. The names Charles Edward Maurice, held in reserve for so many long years, could at last be used. Charles would become Diana's companion, cohort and crusader, a role he was to reprise thirty-three years later before a grieving audience of millions.

Diana's childhood was a life of privilege, wealth and rank in an exclusive society in class-conscious England, but it was not royal, and her upbringing emphasized duty, decorum and demeanor. Although the Spencers's connection with royalty went back centuries (Diana's paternal grandmother, Countess Spencer, and her maternal grandmother, Ruth, Lady Fermoy, had served as ladies-in-waiting to the Queen Mother, and Diana's father acted as equerry to King George VI and Queen Elizabeth II), Diana's upbringing was vastly different from her royal neighbors half a mile away in the main house at Sandringham.

Quintessential English aristocrats, the Spencers could even boast of a grander and older lineage than the House of Windsor. The Spencers could trace their line back to Saxon and Tudor times, while the Windsors could only trace their German Saxe-Coburg line to the 18th century (the name of Windsor was adopted in 1917 after the first world war). Diana was, in fact, related to her royal Sandringham playmates, tracing a common lineage back to Henry VII and James I. Depending on the line traced, to the royal offspring Diana was either a sixteenth cousin once removed, an eleventh cousin once removed, or a seventh cousin once removed. Although the Spencers had impeccable and ancient breeding, none of them, through 500 years of wealth and nobility, had actually become a part of the Royal Family. It would take Diana—the disappointment, the superfluous girl, the three-is-a-crowd female child—to accomplish what 80 generations had not.

Diana was proud of her Spencer heritage. She once remarked to a friend that when challenged she would remind herself, "Diana, remember, you are a Spencer." The Spencer Motto is *Dieu defend le droit,* or "God defend the right". Diana's ancestry goes back to Geoffrey le Despencer, Justiciar to Edward II in the early fourteenth century. The Spencers have a long and distinguished record of service to the Crown, serving for centuries as courtiers as well as soldiers, merchants, naval officers and politicians.

The Spencer family seat, described as "stately" on the Queen's Webpage, is Althorp Park, a 15,000-acre estate in Central England that John Spencer, knighted by Henry VIII, first leased from the Abbot of Evesham in 1486. John Spencer bought it in 1508 and his grandson, Sir John, added wings to the forecourt of the moated, red brick manor in 1573.

Although the Spencers lived at Wormleighton in Warwickshire, they did not ignore their holding in Northamptonshire. In the 1670s, Robert, the second Earl of Sunderland, made further improvements and filled in the moat. Set in a park with ancient woods, exotic orchards and magnificent gardens in the English Midlands, the extensive, exquisitely-kept grounds included a canal and the original freestone manor house. By 1675, Althorp House was described by John Evelyn as "...a kind of modern...within most nobly furnished." The House itself had a gallery and vast hall, while lakes and waterways and gardens full of choice fruit could be found on the grounds.

Sir John's great-great-great-grandson's widow, Lady Dorothy Sidney, enclosed the central courtyard in the early 1700s to create a vast saloon and grand picture gallery. Connecting these rooms was a gleaming wooden staircase down which Diana would slide, centuries later, on a tea tray. In 1786, the second Earl Spencer, George, had the architect John Holland remodel Althorp. He covered the original red bricks with then-fashionable white tiles made in Ipswich and redesigned the interior to bring the state rooms down to the main level. He also had a landscape architect, the chief assistant of the renowned Capability Brown, improve the grounds and park.

The present gardens were designed in the 1860s by W. M. Teulon. One feature of the immaculate grounds is a man-made lake with a treed ornamental island at its center which would one day become the focus of a grieving world. A long winding drive flanked by ancient yews sweeps from the wrought iron gates through the grounds to Althorp House, which was described by Charles Kidd, co-editor of Debrett's Peerage, as, "A typical prestigious aristocratic seat, the very best, really."

When Diana was a child, Althorp contained one of the finest private art collections in Europe. The collection included Roman marbles recovered from the River Tiber, a pair of golden ice pails created for the first Duke of Marlborough in the late 1600s, gold and silver heirlooms, rare porcelain, fine furniture and treasures which belonged to Marie-Antoinette. The 115-foot-long picture gallery, used in the time of Queen Elizabeth I for walks on wet days, was the site of an elaborate reception for King William III in 1695, when the King slept in a bed covered in olive damask adorned with four ostrich plumes. The paintings in the gallery included masterpieces by Gainsborough, Sir Joshua Reynolds, Titian, Stubbs and Van Dyck as well as Spencer family portraits since the time of Queen Elizabeth I. The family's holdings in property, art and furnishings were estimated at $150 million.

The next renovation, in the 1980s and '90s, would see hundreds of precious objets d'art sold, sightseers trooping through the noble galleries, a gift shop, cafe and wine boutique opened on the ancient grounds, 40 cottages sold and the family in an uproar.

This imposing 80-room family seat was financed by a huge family fortune made from the wool trade. Robert, the first Lord Spencer, the great-great-grandson of the man who bought Althorp and fifth of the family to be knighted, was said to be the richest man in the kingdom at the time of the accession of James I in 1603. In 1603, the year she died,

Queen Elizabeth I was entertained at Althorp by a masquerade of lavish costumes, scenery, music and dancing produced by Ben Jonson. It was Queen Elizabeth I who elevated Sir Robert to Baron Spencer. The Baron Spencer spent most of his time at Wormleighton, as did all Spencers until 1643, tending his 19,000 sheep.

His son, William, the second Lord Spencer, was born at Althorp and built a racecourse on the grounds. William's eldest son, Henry, inherited the title at sixteen. In 1642 he joined the Royalists against Oliver Cromwell's Parliamentarian rebels when Civil War broke out. For his support (and his £10,000 contribution), King Charles I rewarded Henry with the title of Earl of Sunderland in 1643. A father of four at just twenty-three, Henry was killed during the Civil War shortly after receiving his title, and the manor at Wormleighton was burned by Royalists after the Battle of Edgehill to keep it from being used by Cromwell's forces. Henry's widow moved the family to Althorp, which became the Spencers's main residence.

Henry's eldest son, Robert, the second Earl of Sunderland, was an astute and devious manipulator and inveterate gambler who changed his allegiance, even his religion, to suit the political tides. After the restoration of the monarchy, Robert served as advisor to King Charles II, Catholic King James II and King William III. Under the reign of King Charles II, Robert was Ambassador to Paris, Madrid and Cologne in the 1670s and, while there, collected paintings and furniture from throughout Europe. He subsequently brought home these treasures to Althorp. In the 1680s he served as Secretary of State, Lord President of the Council, Lord Chamberlain and a Lord of Regency.

He was the first Spencer Knight of the Garter, the oldest and most desirable of honors monarchs can bestow on their subjects. Dating from 1349, the name stems from a contretemps by the attractive Countess of Salisbury. She was dancing with Edward III when her blue garter fell to the floor. When the King picked it up, he noticed the leers of fellow dancers and said, "*Honi soit qui mal y pense!*" meaning, "Shame on anyone who thinks bad thoughts," which became the motto of the order, "Evil to him who thinks evil." Originally limited to twenty-five members and since expanded, recipients of the Order of the Garter are personally selected by the monarch and invested in the Throne Room of Windsor Castle. Knights wear blue velvet robes, plumed hats and a large blue-and-gold insignia on the left breast.

Despite his numerous honors, Robert was dismissed from office in 1688 by the Catholic King James II when a male heir was born. The wily Earl went to Holland, bought Dutch masters and attended the Protestant church to gain favor with William of Orange, who would soon depose King James II to become King William III. By 1690, Robert and his paintings were back at Althorp, and within three years he became King William's chief political advisor.

Ever scheming, Robert tried to marry his own son Charles to Lady Anne Churchill, the daughter of the powerful Duke of Marlborough and the redoubtable Duchess Sarah. Despite the fact that Charles was a rabid Whig who, contended Jonathan Swift, insisted on being called plain Charles Spencer among friends and hoped to see an England devoid of titles, the match was made in 1699. He was not to be the last Spencer to eschew the confines of nobility and embrace the common touch.

When Charles's wife Anne died at thirty-two, she left five children, including the youngest, a six-year-old girl named Diana. Duchess Sarah, Anne's mother, took over the raising of this child. Two-and-a-half centuries later similar circumstances would strike another six-year-old Spencer named Diana. A thirty-two-year-old mother would also leave her husband and children, and this twentieth-century Diana would be brought up, to some extent, by her maternal grandmother, Lady Fermoy, lady-in-waiting to the Queen Mother. Many believe that this same Lady Fermoy, with help from the Queen Mother, promoted the marriage of the twentieth-century Diana to Charles, Prince of Wales.

Returning to the eighteenth century, the formidable Duchess Sarah also had her eye on the Prince of Wales as a bridegroom for her adored Diana. Nor was Diana the first in the Spencer family to have designs on a future king, other Spencer women had been royal mistresses. Sarah's designs were foiled, however, by the Prime Minister, Sir Robert Walpole, who had other plans for the impoverished prince. Diana married Lord John Russell and later became the Duchess of Bedford. She continued the close relationship with her grandmother, but died, childless, of galloping consumption in 1735.

Duchess Sarah had no sons and so, when her husband died in 1722, Diana's eldest brother, Charles, inherited the Marlborough title and Blenheim Palace. When Diana's father died, his second son, John, inherited the Spencer estates and Althorp, thus splitting the family. The Marlborough branch kept the name Spencer until 1817, when the 5th Duke added the name Churchill by royal licence.

The Duchess Sarah much preferred her grandson John to Charles, and left him her personal collection of priceless paintings, china and furniture in her will, all of which adorned Althorp. Sarah's considerable wealth also greatly enhanced the Spencers's fortunes and enabled them to build up a famous collection of art treasures.

In 1765, the Spencers moved up in the aristocracy when John's son, also named John, was created the first Earl Spencer by George III. He built Spencer House in London's Piccadilly, served as Member of Parliament for Warwick and was a patron of the arts. He was also a friend of Sir Joshua Reynolds and the actor David Garrick. The day after his twenty-first birthday, before he inherited his title, John slipped away from a house full of tea guests at Althorp, skipped upstairs to the Oak Room and was married by his former tutor to Georgiana Poyntz, a diplomat's daughter, while unsuspecting guests chatted downstairs. Their daughter, Georgiana, became known as the "Duchess of Dimples" and was the mistress of the Prince of Wales. She was also a mistress to Charles James Fox, a leading Whig. Georgiana traded kisses with Covent Garden tradesmen for votes for her lover in the Westminster elections of 1784.

Georgiana's brother, George, the second Earl Spencer, broke with family tradition and became a Tory supporter of William Pitt. George was First Lord of the Admiralty during the Battle of Trafalgar, personally knew Admiral Horatio Nelson and later became Secretary of State, but his career ceased with Pitt's death in 1806. Retiring to Althorp, George hired Henry Holland to finish the moat and remodel the interior of the house. Samuel Lapidge, Capability Brown's assistant, was, at the same time, improving the grounds, and George set about improving the agriculture of the region. George also actively sought to create one of the greatest libraries in Europe, which was sold ninety years later for £200,000. He was also a fashion leader, designing a tailless waistcoat dubbed a Spencer about the same time his friend the Earl of Sandwich invented a new dish.

The same year George left politics, his eldest son, twenty-four-year-old John, was elected Member of Parliament for Northamptonshire, a position he served for thirty years. Known as "Honest Jack Althorp," he was a large man, shy and awkward, who loved sports, horses, hunting and prize fights. Unlike his father, he preferred physical to intellectual pursuits. He married Esther Acklom when he was thirty-two and was devastated by her death in childbirth. He never remarried and plunged instead into politics, becoming Leader of the House of Commons and Chancellor of the Exchequer under Grey and Melbourne. He promoted the First Reform Bill. When he became the third Earl Spencer in 1834, he retired to Althorp and immersed himself in farming. He also founded the Royal Agricultural College at Cirencester, where Diana's father would study a century later.

When he died without issue, his brother, Frederick, succeeded him. A midshipman in the Napoleonic Wars, Frederick was a Whig Member of Parliament for ten years. Frederick also served as equerry to the Duchess of Kent, Queen Victoria's mother, and as a Privy Councillor, Lord Chamberlain, Rear Admiral and Lord Steward of the Household. He was made a Knight of the Garter in 1849. Frederick had learned stern discipline in the navy and applied it in his household, sometimes locking his daughter, Sarah, in a closet if she disobeyed. He married his second cousin, Elizabeth Poyntz, and their son, John Poyntz, succeeded him as fifth Earl in 1857.

Known as the "Red Earl" because of his beard, John was a consummate fox hunter, thrice Master of the Pytchley Hunt. He served as Liberal Member of Parliament for South Northamptonshire and became Groom of the Stole to the Prince Consort and then to the Prince of Wales, later King Edward VII. John was also Viceroy of Ireland twice, Lord Lieutenant of Northamptonshire, Lord President of the Council, First Lord of the Admiralty, Privy Seal to the Prince of Wales and a member of the Council of the Duchy of Cornwall. John married Charlotte Seymour, a woman famous for her beauty. They had no children and, when he died in 1910, the title went to his half-brother, Charles, the son of Frederick and his second wife.

Charles continued the family tradition, serving as Member of Parliament, Lord Lieutenant of Northamptonshire, Vice Chamberlain and Lord Chamberlain. Like George, Frederick and John, he was also a Knight of the Garter.

Charles's eldest son, Albert Edward John, was Diana's grandfather. Known as Jack, he was a godson of King Edward VII. Jack served in the First World War as a captain in the First Life Guards and, retired to Althorp after being wounded. In 1919, he married Cynthia Hamilton, the daughter of the third Duke of Abercorn, a beauty who had been pursued by the Prince of Wales. He became the seventh Earl in 1922.

Jack Althorp was a cultured man, slight of build, who dedicated his life to his estate and its contents. He loved art and created his own tapestries, some of which graced the chairs at Althorp. A curmudgeon, he seldom entertained except when necessary in his position as Lord Lieutenant of Northamptonshire. He closed many of the great rooms and allowed only selected visitors in. In contrast, his Countess was warm and friendly. Cynthia mixed easily with the locals, speaking to them with a natural concern and charm that foreshadowed that of her granddaughter.

Lady Cynthia and Lady Elizabeth Bowes-Lyon were friends before their marriages, and after Elizabeth became the Duchess of York, they continued to be close. When her husband became King George VI in 1936, Elizabeth had Cynthia appointed a Lady of the Bedchamber to the Queen. Cynthia then became a lady-in-waiting to the Queen and continued to serve her after she became the Queen Mother in 1952. Cynthia continued in this role until her own death in 1972.

Diana would not live at Althorp until she was fourteen. The seventh Earl died in 1975 and, after assuming his title, Diana's father moved the family from Park House in Norfolk to the imposing family estate. After the Spencers left, Park House was boarded up and remained empty. By all reports, except for tea tray sliding down the great stairs, Diana preferred the smaller and cozier Park House: it was home.

Great Brington and Little Brington lie just a few kilometers from Althorp. For five centuries, the residents there have worked for the Spencers as servants, tenants or for the family's tenant farmers. Once virtually owning the entire villages, the Spencer family began divesting itself of its holdings at the turn of the twentieth century. Well-to-do managers and professionals looking for an English country lifestyle were attracted to the pastoral hamlets' amenities. Great Brington, a one-hour train ride or 120 kilometers northwest of London, is set in lush rolling hills, has a population of 200 and contains a total of three streets, one pub dating from 1765, one church built by the Spencers in 1516, a post office and one phone booth. It is extraordinarily picturesque. The high street is flanked by sandstone houses roofed in slate or thatch surrounded by meticulously tended gardens. The historic, heavy brownstone St. Mary the Virgin Anglican Church contains the Spencer Chapel, where 20 generations have been buried under the stone floor beginning with John Spencer in 1522. It is a minor shrine that attracts a thousand visitors a year to see George Washington's great-great-great-great-grandfather's grave. The eighth Earl Spencer, Diana's father, would be buried there. It would not, however, be the final resting place of the most famous Spencer of all.

On the eve of the twenty-first century, Althorp would stand empty, its antiquity abandoned by the Spencers. Diana's sisters would be gone, and Charles, the ninth Earl Spencer, would have fled the baying hounds of the press to live in South Africa. Only Diana would remain.

Diana's maternal ancestors were less noble, but they added Scottish, Irish and American blood to her line, and, some say, Welsh as well, fitting for the future Princess of Wales. Her maternal grandfather, Maurice, the fourth Baron Fermoy, was a friend of the Duke of York, and, when the Duke became King George VI, the Fermoy's leased Park House on the King's Sandringham estate and the two became neighbors.

Diana's great-great-grandfather, Edmund Burke Roche, was Irish. The Member of Parliament for Cork from 1837 to 1855, he became Baron Fermoy in 1856. He was Lord Lieutenant of County Cork before he died, leaving his title to eldest son, Edward, who would die at the age of seventy and leave no heirs. Edmund's second son, James, then became the third Baron Fermoy at the age of sixty-eight.

The American connection came with James's wife, Frances Work, daughter of an illegitimate mother and a self-made Wall Street millionaire who rose from a clerk in Chillicothe, Ohio, to sell stocks to the likes of the Vanderbilts. Frank Work was an American xenophobe and threatened to disinherit any of his children who married European aristocracy. He was not pleased when Frances, known as Fanny, married Irish peer James Boothby Burke Roche. Fanny would inherit a title but no money.

Three children and eleven years later, the impetuous Fanny, tired of genteel poverty, left James and returned to New York to beg her father's forgiveness. Frank Work granted his forgiveness on the condition that Fanny stop using her title and resume her maiden name. He also insisted that neither she nor her children would ever return to Europe to live. Her children were forbidden from marrying Europeans. Her sons, twins Maurice, Diana's grandfather, and Francis, would receive an inheritance only if they became American citizens.

Fanny submissively settled in New York and the boys went on to Harvard. But when Frank died in 1911, she promptly married a Romanian and her sons sailed to England to take in the coronation of King George V. Then they returned and successfully fought to overturn the conditions of their grandfather's will. James became the third Baron in 1920, but died two months later. Maurice took his £600,000 and returned to England in 1921 to become the fourth Baron Fermoy.

Thirty-five and an Irish peer with money, Maurice stayed well clear of his native country's "troubles" and settled in Norfolk. Three years later he was elected Conservative Member of Parliament for King's Lynn, a seat he first held for eleven years, and again for two years during World War II. In 1931, he became Mayor of King's Lynn. In the same year he married, at forty-six, Ruth Silva Gill, who was twenty.

Ruth was a talented girl from Aberdeenshire studying to become a concert pianist at the Conservatoire in Paris when they met. The daughter of a colonel from Bieldside, her family tree contained no lords and one relation who was later to cause Diana concern. Ruth's great-great-grandfather, Theodore Forbes, had had a liaison with an Indian girl, Eliza Kewark, when he worked for the East India Company. They had an illegitimate daughter, Katherine, who was educated in Scotland and married locally, becoming the ancestor of Ruth Gill and Diana Spencer. It was not that Royals didn't also have ancestors born on the wrong side of the blanket, but, in Ruth's days, any taint of "native" or "colored" blood, as it was then called, disqualified gentry from marrying "white people."

Raised outside the rarefied circles of aristocracy, Ruth gave up her career as a pianist in order to marry Maurice, become Lady Fermoy and mix with Royals, a role she took on wholeheartedly. A strong character, she quickly learned the protocol of privilege and became very adept at it. Ruth played by the rules to the point that she would later denounce her own daughter, Frances. Ruth proved a powerful influence on her granddaughter Diana.

Maurice's Burke-Roche blood gave him abundant Irish charm, superb taste and good looks. Cahirguillamore and Kilshanning were the clan's superb ancestral homes. Once one of the richest families in Ireland, his father James had single-handedly rescued them from penury by his fortuitous marriage to Fanny.

Maurice and Ruth settled in Norfolk but didn't establish a permanent home until offered Park House on the Sandringham estate by King George V, Queen Elizabeth II's grandfather. Frances, Diana's mother, was born there the day King George V died in 1936, the second child of three. Mary was two years older, and Edmund, the heir, was born three years later.

Norfolk is variously described as windswept and remote. It is renowned for its hedgeless fields and woodlands and lies in the sunniest, driest part of the United Kingdom. Park House is one of several on the 20 000-acre royal Sandringham estate, one of two privately owned by the Crown, the other being Balmoral. Huge oaks planted by various sovereigns dot the grounds and the gardens are a blaze of azaleas and rhododendrons in season. It houses the royal stud where racehorses are stabled, the royal pigeon lofts and the royal kennels for pedigreed black Labradors. It is used by monarchs chiefly after Christmas for the shooting season, which runs from the twelfth of August to the end of February.

When in residence, the country quiet is broken by the retinue of Royals, private secretaries, equerries, officers of the guard, courtiers, dukes, duchesses, cousins, servants, retainers, guests and others. Those who rent homes on the estate are invited for tea and dinner or to shoot, and encounters with a Queen on horseback who stops to chat are not uncommon. All who inhabited Park House could not fail to learn the proper protocol, procedures and pomp associated with Royals. These inhabitants included Ruth, Frances and Diana.

The Fermoys continued to inhabit Park House after King George VI's accession to the throne. During the war, Maurice played ice hockey with the King on the estate's frozen lakes against American and Canadian troops, and the two enjoyed tennis in the summers. Lord Fermoy and the King went hare shooting the day before George died in 1952. Maurice died three years later, and Ruth became lady-in-waiting to her friend Queen Elizabeth, then the Queen Mother.

Maurice and Ruth's son, Edmund, inherited the title in 1955 when he was sixteen and still attending Eton. His sister Mary had married Anthony Berry, son of Viscount Kemsley, the previous year, the same year his sister Frances married Earl Spencer's son, John, Viscount Althorp.

John, Viscount Althorp, and Frances were Diana's parents.

Born in 1924 and educated at Eton and Sandhurst, Johnnie Spencer joined the Scots Greys when he was old enough to enlist and campaigned in northwest Europe. After the war, he went to Australia, where he served as aide-de-camp to Sir Willoughby Norrie, the Governor of South Australia. After returning to England, Johnnie became an equerry to Maurice Fermoy's friend, King George VI. After the King died in 1952, Johnnie was equerry to Queen Elizabeth II for the first two years of her reign, then resigned. Many eyebrows were raised when thirty-two-year-old Johnnie married eighteen-year-old Frances Roche.

Frances, with her siblings, had been tutored by a governess, Gertrude Allen, at Park House with selected children from the countryside. Besides reading and writing and English history, they learned manners: how to conduct themselves in different company and circumstances, and how to behave in public with restraint and decorum despite provocation. Ruth continued to be involved in music and exposed her children, and eventually her grandchildren, to a variety of artists and styles.

Frances was subsequently sent to Hertfordshire to the Downham School. She would later study art and languages in Paris and Italy. She met dashing, aristocratic Viscount Althorp in 1953 at her lavish coming-out ball in Londonderry House in Park Lane. She shared her debut with her sister, Mary. The Queen Mother was one of the guests.

Johnnie was a highly eligible bachelor: a peer, heir to a fortune, handsome, in service to the Queen. Frances was a beautiful, lively, fun-loving daughter of a Baron. It was kismet or fate.

But Johnnie was also unofficially engaged to Lady Anne Coke, eldest daughter of the Earl and Countess of Leicester, no mean catch herself. When Johnnie broke the engagement to be with the younger and lesser-born Frances, gossip tsked on well-bred tongues. The new Queen, Elizabeth II, asked Johnnie to accompany her and the Duke of Edinburgh on their Commonwealth Tour to Australia as an aide-de-camp for the Master of the Household. The tour was for six months, and the belief was that separation would cool things down.

It didn't.

Despite their fourteen-year age difference, Frances and Johnnie wrote to each other every day, and, by the time the tour reached Tobruk, Johnnie was granted permission to marry her. Their wedding, held at Westminster Abbey, had a guest list of 1500, including the Queen, Queen Mother, Prince Phillip and Princess Margaret. Dressed in a dazzling white gown of faille with embroidery of diamante, sequins and rhinestones, Frances was the youngest bride in the twentieth century to be married in the venerable cathedral. Her bridesmaids wore white hailstone muslin and her pages wore blue-sashed white satin suits, replicas of a costume worn by the young Lord Althorp when he was painted by Sir Joshua Reynolds, a portrait displayed in the Marlborough Room at Althorp House. At the recessional, The Royal Scots Greys, dressed in their ceremonial best, honored their former comrade with lifted swords as he passed under with his new bride. Then the newlyweds left for a magnificent reception for 700 guests at St. James's Palace. It was an extraordinary wedding, the society event of the year, with pomp and ceremony that would presage another spectacular Spencer nuptial just twenty-seven years in the future.

Johnnie and Frances began married life far from the sophistication of London, in a rented house at Rodmarton. Johnnie was studying at the Royal Agricultural College at Cirencester and Frances was pregnant with their first child. Sarah was born in March of 1955, nine months after the wedding. The couple returned to Westminster Abbey to christen their daughter three months later. The Queen Mother was one of the godparents at the ceremony in St. Faith's Chapel. They had by then moved to the Althorp estate, to Orchard Manor at Little Creaton.

But Johnnie and his father locked horns. More easy-going than the irascible Earl, Johnnie preferred farming to art and the outdoors to creating tapestries. He liked the company of people where his father emphatically did not. Lacking both his father's intellectual bent and love of fox hunting, Johnnie preferred shooting. When the Earl's foxes devoured Johnnie's pheasant chicks, the two were destined to discord.

And Frances proved not to be the oil that would soothe them. Unlike Lady Cynthia, she did not humor Jack or put up with his abominable manners. The patriarch, in turn, disliked Frances's high spirits. It was Lady Cynthia who broke the impasse when, after the death of Lord Fermoy late that year, she suggested the new parents take over Park House on the royal Sandringham estate. Located on the west coast of Norfolk, Park House was built in the 19th century by the Prince of Wales, later King Edward VII, after he bought the estate in 1861.

At the end of a gravel drive, the house is flanked by clipped lawns dotted with venerable trees and shrubs which screen the house from the public road. It commands a sweeping view of Sandringham's expansive parks and cricket pitch. Constructed of brick faced with dark, rough local carrstone, the house itself is large and bleak from the outside. One of several homes on the grounds, Park House was originally intended as accommodation for the Prince's guests and staff. The Duke and Duchess of York, the future King George VI and Queen Elizabeth, used York Cottage, a similar house on the grounds, when they stayed at Sandringham.

Despite its dreary facade, Park House is warm and comfortable inside. There are ten bedrooms plus the quarters of the servants and the garages. Unfortunately, Johnnie Althorp did not find West Norfolk nearly as suitable. He needed something to do.

He found a 250-acre farm at Ingoldisthorpe, close to Sandringham, and bought it to raise beef cattle. A year later Frances bought an additional 236 acres at Snettisham. After adding adjoining land at Heacham, Johnnie had 650 acres to keep him occupied.

Jane was born in 1957 in the Queen Elizabeth Maternity Home in King's Lynn. The Duke of Kent was her godfather. Two years later, on January 12, 1960, Frances delivered a boy in her bedroom at Park House. Elated at finally producing the Spencer heir, they called him John. But the baby lived only ten hours. He is buried next to his grandfather Maurice in the west corner of the churchyard at Sandringham. They, in turn, were to be joined by Elizabeth Roche, another grandchild, who lived just six days in March, 1966.

After three babies in six years, and one tragic death, Frances, now twenty-four, felt disillusioned with her dream marriage. The once dashing and sophisticated Johnnie was comfortably settled into farming and rural pursuits and fast approaching forty. Known by the locals as a nice, mild-mannered man, Johnnie Althorp showed a different face to his young wife. But it was 1960, and Frances, being a proper wife, dutifully became pregnant again, hoping to give him the heir he so desperately wanted. Just eighteen months later, on July 1, 1961, she delivered Diana.

The new baby stayed with midwife Joy Hearn for a month before the new nanny, Judith, hired just three months before, took her to her cream colored nursery overlooking the drive. On August 30, she was christened by the Right Reverend Percy Herbert in front of the solid silver altar in St. Mary Magdalene church at Sandringham.

Sandringham church has been blessed by the many monarchs who have worshipped there. Extensively restored in 1857, it contains an organ donated by King Edward VII, a nave roof given by King George V and a folding lectern from King George VI. American Rodman Wanamaker contributed the stunning solid silver altar, a jewelled Bible, reredos first presented to Queen Alexandra in 1911, and the processional crosses which commemorate the dead of the two world wars. A brass cross set into the floor of the chancel marks the place where the Royal coffins rest before being buried at Windsor. By tradition, no one walks on it.

Amid St. Mary's richly colored windows, walls and vaults, in the baptistry at the base of the tower, surrounded by gilded angels and the colors of the Royal York Regiment, over the Florentine marble font donated by King Edward VII, Diana was dedicated to God, the only Spencer child to have no royal godparents. Of course she did have godparents. Her parents asked John Floyd, a friend of Johnnie's from Eton and Sandhurst, and later chairman of Christie's auction house, and Johnnie's first cousin, Alexander Gilmour, to serve as godfathers. Her godmothers were Lady Mary Colman, a relative of the Queen Mother, and neighbors Sarah Pratt and Carol Fox.

When Frances grew up at Park House, her family had employed a full complement of servants for grand entertainments, but with Maurice's egalitarian Irish/American upbringing and Ruth's celebrated musical friends, they were less formal than many noble homes. Frances and Johnnie did not have the social obligations of Baron Fermoy and reduced the staff accordingly to six, including a full-time cook. Frances was lively and fun-loving and Johnnie was a man of the land, able to chat with servants and sovereigns with equal ease. With Johnnie immersed in farming, sports and local matters, their entertaining was primarily for friends and for local occasions. Consequently, the house was even less formal when Diana was born.

Nonetheless, Diana had a very traditional English upper class upbringing. Lunch was frequently pheasant and the children lived in the nursery. The nursery had three bedrooms, a bathroom and a large playroom. It was above the butler's pantry on the main floor in a separate wing from the rooms of their parents and from the rest of the house.

They were attended by nannies. They learned to eat what they were given, never to interrupt, to sit up straight and not to speak with their mouths full, to smile and to be polite to everyone, to shake hands when being introduced, to play quietly, to talk nicely and to keep the nursery tidy. Like children everywhere, this last item proved to be a sticking point and Diana's nanny, Janet Thompson, who cared for the Spencer children from the time Diana was three to almost six, said their beds were never made and their bedrooms were a mess.

As the third daughter, Diana held no special place. She wasn't first or even second, and it would be three years before another child came along. As is often the case with younger siblings, she could not hope to keep up with her older, more mature and accomplished sisters. Raised in their shadow, Diana had the choices of all latter-born children: outrageous acts to attract attention or pleasing behavior to gain approval. As Viscount Althorp was unlikely to approve rebellion, Diana chose the latter, pleasing behavior, a choice which shaped her personality but never obscured her strong will and desire to count for something. Relegated to relative oblivion, then, she grew up shy and unprepossessing, a dutiful daughter who adored her parents and trailed after Sarah and Jane.

Even as a newborn, she did not cause the midwife to get up at night for the first month she stayed in her room. It would form her character, this inferiority in the face of more powerful elders, and create a penchant for identifying with simpler, more common folk, with whom she was able to feel at ease. In the insular and remote Spencer household (Diana had never been to a circus or a zoo until she took her own children) there were few outside playmates and Diana spent more time with servants than her parents.

She learned empathy and compassion, especially toward those younger then herself and, unlike her royal neighbors, would stand in line to buy things, play with the neighborhood children and mix with a variety of people. Her upbringing would give Diana a common touch that marked her as different and set her apart from her aristocratic peers. It was this touch that would one day earn her the name " the People's Princess".

She was not without love. Her sisters, her nanny, her vibrant young mother, her father, all cared for the new baby. Sarah and Jane treated her like a doll: fussing over her, helping to bathe and dress her. But mornings, when Sarah and Jane trooped downstairs for their lessons, Diana was left alone with the nanny in the nursery.

When her brother Charles, the long-awaited heir who must have elicited sighs of relief from the entire household, was born three years later at the London Clinic, Diana was delighted. He was someone younger to love, someone to care for and instruct. Charles was to say thirty-three years later that Diana mothered him and that the two spent an enormous amount of time together as the family's youngest siblings. It was fortunate for both; Diana had a role to play as mother/sister and Charles had an older sister who doted on him. The seed of caring, of reaching out to touch others, was planted in the young Diana the day her mother brought Charles home. It was to serve her well in later years.

And she had a strong will. She was firm with Charles, directing that he do his duties promptly.

The royal connection also grew. Johnnie Spencer was not involved in politics, but he was close to the Royal Family. He viewed Queen Elizabeth II as his godmother, and Diana's sister Jane would marry the Queen's private secretary, Sir Robert Fellowes. Diana would make her own royal connection as she grew up, becoming friends with Andrew and Edward, the Queen's younger sons. If she and Charles, Prince of Wales, met at this time, he would hardly have noticed the chubby young toddler.

She loved parties. When she was five, she dressed in a new frock, took her brother Charles by the hand and trooped to the "big house" at Sandringham for tea with Prince Andrew and Prince Edward. She was later found by her nanny playing hide-and-seek with Andrew—and the Queen.

This was no fairy tale princess bereft of parents, scrubbing floors and awaiting her prince. This was a modern child of privilege, a child who possessed all the trappings of nobility, including royal playmates, especially Prince Andrew. Prince Andrew's remote and reserved big brother even then loomed large in her life, as he would years later.

Sarah and Jane spent the mornings downstairs for lessons, but after lunch they would walk with Diana either riding in her pram or toddling after them. These walks would be headed by their nanny, Judith, or by their mother, Frances. As Diana grew and became more able to keep up with her active sisters, they would include her in their games. She was cheerful and determined, with a quick sense of humor.

Warm and affectionate Lady Althorp, who was friendly with the servants and locals, would stop on their walks to chat. She spent a lot of time in the nursery, reading bedtime stories and cuddling. The girls were considered perky and pretty as they played on the estate, and they would climb trees, ride ponies, scooters and bikes and slide on tea trays down the stone steps.

The grounds of Sandringham are a walker's heaven, with some 20000 acres of woods, lawns, gardens, farmland and parks crisscrossed with wide paths for walking and riding and with carpets of heather. Diana would grow up with horses and ponies and a variety of pets including rabbits, hamsters, a springer spaniel named Jill and a cat Diana called Marmalade. There is a photo of her cuddling a guinea pig, chin already tucked, eyes slanting up at the camera from under long bangs.

Sandringham is the great royal hunting estate, and walkers are on notice during the six-month pheasant season. Johnnie was an avid hunter and his gun room at Park House was forbidden to his children. He kept his gun dogs in outside kennels; they were definitely not pets or welcome in the house. When the Royal Family spent the hunting season and New Years at Sandringham, the Queen would stop to chat if she was out for a ride. The children of both families would have tea with each other, particularly Prince Andrew, Prince Edward and Princess Margaret's children. After Johnnie built a heated pool at Park House, the younger Royals would often come over to swim and Diana would become a good swimmer.

But the Royals, who were seldom in residence, were not the closest neighbors of the Spencers on the vast estate. The Reverend Patrick Ashton moved his family into the rectory next door when Diana was small.

He had a daughter Diana's age. The land agent at Sandringham, Julian Lloyd, lived in Laycocks across the park, and his daughter, Alexandra, was close to Diana's age. Diana, Alexandra and Penelope Ashton were playmates.

Diana's maternal grandmother, Ruth, who had given up her promising career as a pianist to become Lady Fermoy, used her energy and talent to foster music in West Norfolk. After the war, Ruth organized lunchtime concerts in King's Lynn, sometimes playing the piano herself. In 1950, she played a Schumann piano concerto for the Queen Mother at the Royal Albert Concert Hall, and the next year she launched the King's Lynn Music Festival after the restoration of St. George's Guildhall. It attracted luminaries like Benjamin Britten and Peter Pears. The Queen Mother was its patron for twenty-five years and Ruth its chairman. Lady Fermoy was made a Freeman of the Borough of King's Lynn for her work in 1963. She was a strong influence in her granddaughter's taste in music.

When Diana was nearly three, Frances at last delivered the heir Johnnie wanted. It was May, 1964, ten years and five children after their marriage. She was twenty-eight, Johnnie forty-two. She went to the London Clinic for the delivery and, when the phone call came announcing the news, Park House was exultant. Rejoicing servants at Althorp unfurled flags to announce the heir, who was, thank heavens, healthy.

Two months later, the boy was christened Charles with great ceremony at Westminster Abbey. His family and godmother, Queen Elizabeth II, were all gathered, but three-year-old Diana was left home. She had struck her head on a stone step the previous day and had a nasty bruise on her forehead.

She did get to dress up in a new coat and straw hat for the wedding of her Uncle Edmund, her mother's younger brother, soon after. The fifth Lord Fermoy married Lavinia Pitman at the Guard's Chapel at Wellington Barracks in London.

Displaced as baby of the family, Diana was sent downstairs each morning for sessions with Gertrude Allen, who taught her the same things she had taught her mother. Called Gert by Frances, she had become Ally by the time Diana toddled into her care. Miss Allen taught a select coterie of children in West Norfolk for decades and prepared them for entrance for major public and preparatory schools throughout England. During the summer, they would hold their lessons on the grounds around Park House. Four-year-old Diana worked at her own pace, as did all the children, but showed a certain interest in history. She also liked painting, cutting out and gluing paper more than the times tables being rattled off by her older sisters. She was later to show an interest in the history of the Tudors and Stuarts.

Snettisham was the nearest village with interesting shops, and Diana and her sisters would go there after school with their mother. Diana undoubtedly liked to go in order to buy her favorite chocolates. Other times the girls would go into King's Lynn, which was farther away, or to Johnnie's farm to see the cattle. One of their favorite summertime expeditions was to Brancaster, a twenty-minute drive to the north coast and the sea, where the family had a beach hut. Special trips would include a picnic lunch and a whole day of sand, sun and swimming, a recreation Diana would love all her life. Their only trips to Althorp were rare ones when Frances took them to see the Earl. Johnnie refused to see his father, and Jack never came to Park House. Cynthia would visit when Johnnie played in the annual cricket match with Julian Lloyd's President's XI against the local club and when she attended the Queen Mother during her stays at York Cottage.

York Cottage was the honeymoon home of King George V and Queen Mary when they were the Duke and Duchess of York. Built by Edward when he was Prince of Wales, they made it their principal country home until 1925, when they moved to Sandringham House for the extra room. Thereafter other Royals, including the Queen Mother, used it when at Sandringham.

Sarah and Jane had a pony named Romany, but he was bad tempered and inclined to bite the tiny hands that fed him sugar lumps. They all rode bicycles on the endless park paths. Their birthdays were always celebrated with parties with their friends and the Spencer fireworks on November 5, Guy Fawkes day, were a popular annual event. Johnnie would set off the Catherine wheels, bangers, squibs and whizzers while local children, dressed in scarves and woolen hats and full of hot sausages, oohed and aahed.

It was an idyllic, aristocratic, but normal childhood. Until 1967. Diana was six, Charles, three-and-a-half. In September, Sarah and Jane went off to boarding school at West Heath in Kent, leaving a large empty space in the nursery.

Then, Frances, too, left. Scandal was about to descend on Park House.

Despite what went on behind the closed doors of Park House, Frances and Johnnie kept up appearances until the day she walked out, when the newspapers trumpeted the disgrace in headlines. Frances was vilified as the unfaithful wife and negligent mother; Johnnie was portrayed as the wronged husband and deserted father. But, like all human stories, in particular one which was to follow with even more fanfare and glaring press coverage twenty-five years later, there were two sides.

Frances had been unhappy for years. Johnnie, kind and dull, was gentle with the children and affable in public, but displayed his own father's cruel temper in private. Frances was no Lady Cynthia, who put up with the bad-tempered Earl. In love at sixteen, married at eighteen, Frances was still a young and attractive thirty. After producing the requisite heir, she started going to London to seek livelier companions in the more stimulating social swirl of the "Swinging London" of the sixties. Then she fell in love with another man, Peter Shand Kydd. He was wealthy, debonair and witty, a contrast in every way to her pedantic, proper and pedestrian husband.

She met Peter Shand Kydd at a dinner party in London in 1966. She was with Johnnie and he was with his artist wife, Janet Munro Kerr. They all got along and went skiing together. When they returned, Peter moved out. Janet let him go, believing he would "get it out of his system." He didn't.

Peter was then forty-two and Frances thirty-one. He had been married for sixteen years. Described as a gypsy, he had moved around frequently; the family had just returned from Australia. He had inherited the family wallpaper business and was wealthy, but no businessman. Educated at Marlborough College and Edinburgh University, he was in the navy during the war. After becoming enchanted with Australia while visiting on a business trip, he resigned from the Shand Kydd board and emigrated to farm a 500-acre sheep station in New South Wales. He was not very successful and returned to England after three years. He dabbled in other things, including pottery. The fact that he was married and the father of three fed the frenzied press, disapproving peers and a public hungry for scandal in high places.

Frances and Peter saw each other for a year, until September 1967, when Sarah and Jane went to boarding school in West Heath. Shortly after, Frances and Johnnie had a huge fight at a party. She packed her bags the next day and left. Feeling it was better for the children to see her happy than to see their parents fight constantly, she moved into Cadogan Place, close to Sloane Square, one of the smartest areas of London. She announced to the press, "I am living apart from my husband now. It is very unfortunate. I don't know if there will be a reconciliation." The day after her departure, Johnnie sent Diana and Charles to London with their nanny. Frances enrolled Diana in a day school and Charles in kindergarten. Violet Collinson, a housemaid from Park House, was her cook. Frances had no intention of leaving her children, but she was determined to leave her empty marriage. She had explained this to each of her children before she left, anxious that they understand. But Charles was three-and-a-half, Diana, six. How much they understood is debatable.

In the 1960s it was practically unheard of for a father to gain custody of his children, especially young children, and then only after the mother had been portrayed as irredeemably wicked and unfit in court. By all accounts, including the warm relationship Frances maintained with all her children, she was a passionate and devoted mother. Diana and Charles seemed to take the change as an adventure; Sarah and Jane were devastated. Frances dutifully took Diana and Charles back to Park House for the Christmas holidays. But Johnnie, who had said that both her departure and her sensational announcement in the press had come as a "thunderbolt," had come to accept that the "trial separation" was permanent and that Frances had no intention of returning to him. She wanted a divorce. His temper flared.

Johnnie refused to let Frances take the children back to London. Frances pleaded to no avail and then accepted the arrangement. After all, Diana and Charles were at home at Park House and they adored their father, who doted on them. Frances knew they would be well looked after, in familiar surroundings and life would go on, as she put it, without a hiccup. She returned to London alone, totally unaware it would be permanent.

Not everyone was surprised at the break up. Certainly the staff was aware of the couple's troubles, and the children could not have missed it, either. In a year of departures, more were to hit Diana and Charles. Marmalade the cat died and their governess, Ally, who had been with them for years, left after Christmas. The aftermath of all this began to affect Diana and Charles. Bereft of their sisters, mother and nanny, they clung to each other.

Johnnie, who had perhaps kept the children hoping that Frances would come to her senses, had to face the fact that she would not be back.

No longer protected by Johnnie's noble standing, Frances was condemned for "bolting" and leaving her young children. Her own mother, the correct and ultra-proper Ruth, would denounce her actions. Protective of her privileged position, Lady Fermoy would disapprove loudly and publicly and would not speak to her daughter for years. Other acquaintances in Norfolk turned their backs on her as well. Frances, unhappy at being so far from her children and stymied by a stubborn Johnnie, petitioned for custody and the dissolution of the marriage.

Frances was young, beautiful and fun-loving, but she also had a strong will and determination. Johnnie was sweet and kind as a father and nice gentleman to his neighbors, but older and settled and, as Frances charged in her petition for divorce, cruel.

If she had won her case, she would have gotten the children, but Johnnie contested it, and he would call in character witnesses from the highest realms in the land. Her case would be dismissed amid a storm of juicy gossip and sensational press coverage, a situation her daughter would face years later. The press hounded the Spencers, spreading their acrimonious divorce across the headlines each day, greedily repeating every rumor, every juicy tidbit of this trouble in aristocratic paradise. It was a dark cloud that was to trouble Diana again.

Frances would marry Peter and later divorce him, again foreshadowing her daughter's life. Diana faced all this with remarkable aplomb but was not unaffected. She learned to face misfortune with fortitude, a trait she would return to again and again in the years to come. Her friends all knew her mother had left, but what this meant to six-year-olds before divorce became commonplace is uncertain. Diana displayed an occasional flare of temper or crying jags, but both were unusual. The adults in her life strived to keep her busy. Both grandmothers stepped in, just as their maternal ancestors had, much to Johnnie's relief. Sarah and Jane helped with Diana and Charles that Christmas. With invitations from everyone designed to keep the family occupied and the house full again, the holidays were as close to normal as possible. But in January, Sarah and Jane again packed their trunks and left for school and Frances returned to London without them.

Fortunately, Diana and Charles got a new nanny, Sally. Diana took on the task of instructing Sally how to run the nursery, where everything in her bedroom belonged and how much sugar they were allowed in their tea. Diana became a tidy girl, with everything in her room in its place, even the teddy bear and all her stuffed animals lined up just so.

Socks were not left on the floor, and her toys were neatly stored in cupboards or on shelves. At six, Diana was constantly on the go, never playing at anything too long. It may have been her method of dealing with everything, but she was exhausting for others to be with, talking more than at any other time in her life. She became obstinate, sulking and struggling when her hair was washed, and played tricks on the maids. She did not acknowledge her mother's absence, but chattered nonstop about everything else.

One distraction she welcomed was school. Johnnie, depressed and steeped in self-pity at Frances's desertion, decided Diana and Charles would be better off in school, away from the sad memories of Park House. Early in January of 1968, they were enrolled in day school at King's Lynn, seven miles from Sandringham, to be with other children in a happier atmosphere. Diana was to later say she adored her days there.

Whatever the truth of his relationship with Frances, Johnnie seldom used the children as weapons against Frances. He allowed her to see them and have them for weekends both before and after the divorce. Years later, Charles, the ninth Earl Spencer, was to recall those long train trips with Diana between the houses of their parents when he addressed a world in mourning.

Chapter 2

The School Years

As the third daughter of Johnnie and Frances it was understandable that the Spencers had been hoping for a son and an heir when Diana was born. As Penny Junor wrote in her book *Diana, Princess of Wales,* when Charles was born, "The entire household had been waiting with bated breath, terrified that the new baby would prove to be another girl. But no, at last a boy, an heir and a healthy one. The flags flew that day at Althorp." It is unknown if Diana felt the subtle sense of disappointment after her birth, but she appeared to display a desperate need to be reassured that she was loved and needed, which continued to manifest itself throughout her tragic life. Diana's need to be loved and wanted seemed to carry through into her later life when she immersed herself in charitable causes in a very personal and endearing manner, receiving, from a much larger populace, the love and nurturing that she missed after her mother left.

Up to the age of six years, Diana had lived what appeared to be an ideal childhood at Park House on the Sandringham Estate. Park House, Diana's primary residence, is deep in the Norfolk countryside. Sandringham, which reportedly is not large for a King's home, has a few imposing rooms and many small, cozy ones. It is a good place for small groupings, teas, card games and jigsaw puzzles, for both children and adults. The grounds are landscaped with huge oaks planted by various Royals beginning with Queen Victoria, and wonderful gardens created by King George VI. Almost fairy tale in its elegance, Diana and her siblings spent some very happy years at this childhood home, including rumors of the ghost of a troubled young page who went around snuffing out lighted candles.

Reports from one of Diana's earliest nannies affirm that Diana was very much a normal child during the early part of her childhood. "Diana was not a difficult child, but she could be obstinate," Janet Thompson revealed. "She didn't like walks, wouldn't eat the crusts of her bread. She wasn't keen on horses and wouldn't fuss over our two dogs. She was very fond of pretty clothes and keeping them neat." Diana loved flowered dresses and even as a child had a passion for sweets, especially Smarties, Kit Kats, Swiss Lindt chocolate and fruit pastilles.

In 1967 Diana's life changed forever. The course of events that followed affected and influenced how she would relate to others for the rest of her life.

In September 1967, Sarah and Jane left home for the first time, departing for boarding school at West Heath in Kent, southeast of London. For Diana and Charles, they left a large, seemingly empty house.

Then in the autumn of 1967, although there had been rumors of infidelities about both of Diana's parents, it came as a huge shock to Diana and the rest of the Spencer family when Frances Spencer, Diana's mother, moved out of the family home. Johnnie Spencer, Diana's father, described Frances's decision as totally unexpected. He had been, he said, unaware of any problems and assumed the marriage was as healthy and happy as any other.

Unsatisfied in the marriage, Frances Spencer filed for divorce early in 1968, petitioning for custody of her children on the grounds of cruelty. What followed was a lengthy, bitter and much publicized custody battle that ultimately resulted in Earl Spencer being awarded custody of all four children. The bitterness between Johnnie and Frances took its toll on the Spencer children, and Diana in particular. "I'll never marry unless I really love, someone," Diana told her favorite nanny, as reported in the *DailyMail*. "If you're not really sure you love someone, then you might get divorced."

To add to the confusion and distress being suffered by Diana and her siblings, Ruth, Lady Fermoy, Diana's maternal grandmother and lady-in-waiting to the Queen Mother at the time, testified in court against her daughter, Diana's mother. Diana is said to never have forgiven her grandmother for this betrayal of the mother-daughter relationship. Diana's older sister, Sarah McCorquodale, was twelve; her other sister, Jane, now the wife of the Queen's private secretary, Robert Fellowes, was ten years old at the time; Charles, Diana's younger brother, would have been three years old.

Frances's divorce became final in 1969 after nearly three years of bitter wrangling. She and Peter Shand Kydd, who had divorced his wife and lost custody of his own three children, were married quietly. They alternated their time between a sheep farm in Australia and a remote 1000-acre estate on the Isle of Seil, in Argyllshire, off the west coast of Scotland near Oban. Frances's children visited her on holidays, which were spent in London or at one of the country homes. The children soon learned to like Peter Shand Kydd as much as their mother did, but it was a whole different story when Johnnie Spencer decided to remarry.

As Frances herself later acknowledged, the sensational split between her and her husband, took an immense toll on her children. "It would be ridiculous to pretend that it was anything other than traumatic," she said. Years later, Charles, Diana's younger brother, would recall in his eulogy how he and Diana, "…endured those long train journeys between our parents' homes at weekends."

After the divorce of her parents, Diana formed a close attachment to her father, Johnnie. In spite of his apparent self-imposed emotional distance from his children, Diana's display of outward affection toward her father, although not the norm for his children, endeared Diana to her father and a close bond developed between father and daughter.

Because the Spencer children were raised by nannies who made sure they "visited" with their father at set times each day, Diana lacked the spontaneity of a loving family life. Pursuits such as going to the movies, McDonald's, amusement parks or theater, which were taken for granted by most of her peers, were outings that never happened for young Diana.

The emotional trauma of the effect of her parents' divorce, and the decision of her mother to leave her husband and home behind for Peter Shand Kydd, seemed to leave Diana with a strong need for acceptance and affection. This happened in spite of efforts by her father and family to try to ensure she lived as "normal" a life as possible in the aftermath of her parents' divorce. In fact, Johnnie Spencer went out of his way to ensure that Diana, especially, did not feel neglected.

Her father displayed this close bond with his third daughter when he surprised her on her seventh birthday. Johnnie had persuaded officials at the Dudley Zoo to lend him a camel for the afternoon, and the twenty-plus friends of Diana were awed and delighted when they were allowed to mount and ride "Bert" the camel around the grounds under the watchful eye of his keeper.

However, no amount of presents or gifts could ever take the place of a mother, and Diana's own poignant words later expressed her confusion and distress over her mother leaving the family home. At a speech Diana gave to the European Society for Child and Adolescent Psychiatry in September 1991, she stated, "Parents sometimes desert families, leaving their children bewildered and bereft with no explanation, let alone the opportunity or encouragement to express their feelings."

In early 1968, when Diana was six years old, after the unsuccessful trial separation of her parents and a particularly stressful Christmas, she and Charles were sent to Silfield School in King's Lynn. Diana received a lot of individualized attention, Silfield being a small family school. The school emphasized old-fashioned discipline and offered plenty of outdoor activities and games which took place on the tennis court and in the garden at the back of the house. The headmistress of Silfield at the time, Jean Lowe, recalled that Diana was a fluent reader in her first term and had good, clear handwriting. Miss Lowe was also immensely impressed by how Johnnie Spencer dealt with his children. He made every effort to be supportive and encouraging of both his younger children, in spite of his numerous other duties. Penny Junor, who wrote her biography of Diana in 1982, described her as "perhaps quieter than most of the children to begin with, but then she had lived a very cocooned existence up to that point. She had never been amongst strangers, never been into a building on her own that didn't belong to either a friend or a relation, never played team games, and never been exposed to the boisterousness of gangs of little girls and boys, and the teasing and the jokes." Thankfully, however, Diana adapted quickly and enjoyed the spirit of teamwork encouraged at Silfield School. It is not known whether the loss of a stable, consistent and available maternal figure affected Diana's school aptitude, but she never excelled at her academics. It was noted that she was a well-mannered, amazingly neat and sensible sort of child. She was also reportedly cheerful, bright and mischievous at times. This was confirmed by Mary Clarke, Diana's nanny from 1971 to 1973, who reported that, although by no means docile, Diana was "very, very caring but...an ordinary child too. She had a lovely, sunny disposition."

Even at that early age Diana displayed qualities that she carried with her throughout her life, namely her interest in younger children. Penny Junor reports that Diana "used to enjoy going into the nursery class and helping with the little ones at Silfield and she was always like a mother hen with Charles." Although Diana learned that her mother was not returning to Park House, she would still dedicate her school paintings and drawings to "Mummy and Daddy," to the concern of some of her teachers who felt she had not yet accepted the divorce of her parents.

In the absence of her mother, Diana became very close to her somewhat reserved father and would worry when he was late returning home. The apparent confidence and outgoing personality which Diana displayed at six years seemed to desert her as she grew older. She became shy and reticent, especially in her adolescence and early teens. At the age of seven Diana spent the first of many summers to come, divided between two homes, her mother's and Park House, which she still regarded as "home". In 1969 Frances and Peter Shand Kydd bought a house with a big garden at Itchenor on the West Sussex coast, and that summer Diana enjoyed herself there, swimming, boating and playing lawn games, as well as readying herself for her new school, Riddlesworth Hall.

It was felt that at the age of nine Diana might do better both emotionally and academically at a boarding school such as Riddlesworth Hall. Diana already knew some relatives and acquaintances at the Hall, so she wouldn't be totally isolated in these new surroundings. Riddlesworth was a fairly small school, with approximately one hundred and twenty girls between seven and thirteen years old, and was only a two-hour drive from Park House. Since the Hall was still in the Norfolk countryside, it was hoped Diana would soon feel at home there.

The school prospectus read, "The basis of a good education has always been the family, and a boarding school should provide a stable family atmosphere in which a child can develop naturally and happily. Where individual freedom and the discipline of a community are in easy balance, a sense of security can be achieved and every child will have the opportunity to be good at something."

Although homesick initially, within weeks of arriving at Riddlesworth Hall, Diana began to enjoy herself. As past students have claimed, "you couldn't not be happy at Riddlesworth: it's just like one big happy family." Although Riddlesworth Hall, like Silfield School, was based on a house system for competitive purposes, and teaching methods were also formal and traditional, the similarities ended there. Riddlesworth Hall, which is still in operation as one of Britain's more prestigious schools for girls, was, and still is, one of the best money could buy. Present-day fees are listed at £2940 for a full boarding student. The school prides itself on good facilities, qualified and enthusiastic staff and, reportedly, an impressive success rate at Common Entrance for public schools like Benenden, Wycombe Abbey, Felixstowe and West Heath. the last of which Diana subsequently attended.

The day at Riddlesworth Hall began with the rising bell at 7:30 a.m. Once the girls were dressed, those with long hair, including Diana, had to line up to have it tied back by the matron. This was followed by breakfast at 8:00 a.m., after which everyone had to return to their dorms and make their beds before returning to a common room for morning prayers. Lessons took up the entire morning, with the exception of a half-hour midday break for milk and cookies, as well as time to feed the pets they were encouraged to bring along with them to the school. The headmistress strongly believed that allowing the girls to continue their connection to their pets from home was therapeutic. Care of the menagerie was left entirely up to the students and anyone who neglected their pet had it returned home. Diana's contribution to Pet's Corner was her guinea pig named Peanuts. She was quite fond of the rodent and was as meticulous about keeping Peanuts's living quarters clean as she was about her own living quarters. As one parent learned, responsibility was only one outcome of encouraging the girls to care for their pets; another was a roundabout way of introducing the young students to the "facts of life," as Penny Junor put it. In addition to academics, the students learned arts and crafts, including pottery, weaving and basketwork, as well as drawing and painting.

The lunch break was followed by a mandatory imposed period of bed rest for forty minutes. More often than not the forty minutes was interspersed with giggling, whispering and notes surreptitiously passed to each other. Diana, who was by no means a "goody-goody," was full of energy and somewhat of an instigator, making her peers burst into giggles at the most inappropriate moments.

The afternoon lessons were interrupted by hockey and netball in winter, tennis and swimming in summer, and another half hour to look after their pets before tea and vespers. Although it was mandatory to have a bath every other night, supervised by the matrons, Diana tended to err on the side of caution and bathed and washed her hair almost every day, sometimes in the dark and against the rules. She was unusually clean and meticulously tidy for a girl her age.

On Saturdays there were some lessons in the morning, followed by hymn practice for the next day. Then they were free until lunchtime to take their pets out on the lawn of the school, climb trees or visit "Frog's Alley" outside the gym. The high point, however, without any doubt, was the chance to dig into their tuck boxes, which contained sweets and candies. This occurred after lunch on Sundays as well, and the distribution of the candies was carefully supervised and regulated by the matron. Of course, those who had been disciplined during the week went without sweets on the weekend——a true deterrent to bad behavior. The rest of Saturday afternoons were free for the students to spend at their discretion.

Diana was a keen swimmer, winning team trophies for the school. She also was a passionate dancer and dreamed of becoming a ballet dancer until she grew too tall and turned to tap dancing instead. Since extra ballet lessons effectively prevented Diana from taking up riding, which was offered at the same time, she never became as keen an equestrian as her sisters. Of course the fact that she broke her hand falling off a horse at around ten years of age may have had something to do with her lack of enthusiasm for riding.

On Sundays the girls slept in until 8:15 a.m. and went down for one of their favorite breakfasts of sausages. Church followed in St. Peter's across the courtyard. The girls had to don their Sunday best, including their heavy walking shoes, which they all hated, and were given a fixed amount by the matron to put in the collection plate.

Diana's parents took turns at visiting her at Riddlesworth, careful not to cross paths and thus cause any awkwardness which might distress their daughter. It was difficult for those around Diana to gauge if she suffered adversely from the divorce of her parents as she apparently never was the kind of child to be openly emotional. She was always very controlled and was never likely to cry or show emotion in public under any circumstances. On Sundays Diana regularly used allocated time to write to both of her parents. The contents of her letters were never known, as letters to parents were never checked by staff; only those written to friends. During the late afternoon the girls swarmed around on the heath behind the school for half an hour, supervised by the matron. They revelled in the natural paradise of Riddlesworth's grounds and the heath behind it. The children were allowed to climb trees, since they would have done so unsupervised anyway.

As Penny Junor reports, Diana seemed happy and soon reverted to her old self, alive and full of go, always wanting to dash on to the next thing. However, Diana was never seen as a leader. She was satisfied with fitting in with the status quo and displayed a need to be liked. Even in those early days, this need was very much in evidence, with Diana winning the Legatt Cup for helpfulness, for volunteering to do things around the school. Diana was extremely surprised at winning the Cup for actions which seemed second nature to her, but it also foreshadowed what one of her strongest traits was to be.

During the autumn of 1972, Diana's paternal grandmother, Cynthia Spencer, died. Diana had always been fond of her grandmother and appeared to have inherited many of her qualities including her ease with children. Diana was quite upset at her grandmother's death and was given time off from school to attend the official memorial service in London.

In the summer of 1973, Diana took her Common Entrance exams and was accepted by West Heath School, a small, select boarding school for girls near Sevenoaks in Kent. Her two older sisters had already attended West Heath, and Jane was still a student when Diana arrived. Jane was a prefect and was doing well academically as well as in other areas. However, Sarah had been expelled for misdemeanors, even though academically she had been doing very well.

The present West Heath is a magnificent country house on thirty-two acres of farm and woodland near Sevenoaks. Girls applying for acceptance at West Heath have to sit the Common Entrance exam. However, there is no pass or fail mark. The only required qualification, besides the ability to pay the fees is an ability to express themselves neatly and tidily in writing, all the old-fashioned things, as the principal says, which go with a willingness to share what they have.

Diana appeared to settle in well at West Heath, enjoying the added advantage of having both her sister, Jane, and her cousin, Diana Wake-Walker, among her contemporaries. Boarding school held no great fears for Diana at this time, with the experience of Riddlesworth behind her.

Penny Junor details, "Diana started off in a form called Poplar. Girls were put into forms according to age, but were then put into divisions for work according to ability. So it was not impossible to be in a division for a subject you were good at with girls two forms above, and, for a subject you were weak at, with girls from forms below. There were usually no more than eight people in each division."

However, unlike her sisters, Diana did not excel academically here, either. After four years and one term she had absolutely no exam passes whatsoever. However, Diana's friends say the real reason she failed was sheer laziness and the fact that she was never pushed. As one of her friends claimed in Penny Junor's book, "We just used to spend all our time reading Barbara Cartland books...when we were supposed to be doing prep... We read hundreds of them. We had a craze on them. We all used to buy as many as we could in the holidays and sneak them back in, and we'd swap them around."

According to Miss Rudge, the principal at West Heath, "The training in the art of living together is the most important part of school life: the endless variety of experiences, including squabbles, accusations, sharing or lack of sharing, clashes of personalities, together with much mutual joy and helpfulness between those of the same and of different generations are the experiences that form attitudes and judgments, and teach tolerance or leave us with a sense of frustration that will affect our lives and our relationships with others far more than the acquisition of three 'A' levels and six 'O' levels. I am sure that in the long run, it is one's own consciousness of the dignity and the importance of oneself to others and the awareness of others as individuals with problems similar to one's own, and the knowledge of how to cope with oneself and with others in the endless variety of situations in which one finds oneself, that are of prime importance in living. This I hope we are learning here, and if so our existence is justified."

Although Diana did not excel academically, she seemed to have admirably met some of the other requirements that Miss Rudge espoused, presumably equipping her to cope with many of the trials and tribulations of her later life.

Diana did much better at sports, which were played every afternoon from 2:00 till 3:00 p.m. and included lacrosse, hockey and netball in winter, tennis and swimming in summer. Diana's strongest suit was her swimming; the experience of having a swimming pool at Park House while she was a child contributed greatly to her love of water sports. In *Diana, Princess of Wales*, it is reported that "In her first summer she won the Junior Swimming Cup, in her third year she got her colors and won the Senior Swimming Cup and a Diving Cup, and in her last summer she had her colors renewed." Being totally at home in the water, Diana even responded to a dare by her fellow students during a cold afternoon in November, when she climbed in among the tires into the green, slimy pool and swam two widths. The tires were put there during the winter to prevent ice from forming and cracking the walls.

During summer Diana also displayed a love for tennis and played in the evenings and on her own time, in addition to lessons. West Heath boasted four hard courts and eight grass courts.

Since Diana spent much of her adolescence and early teenage years attending West Heath, it is probable that the education and grounding she received there had a huge bearing on how she conducted herself in the future. Although best friends were not encouraged, Diana made several close friends at West Heath and kept in touch with them throughout her life. It is notable, too, that the helpfulness and the grace which Diana later displayed in her many personal contacts with patients, children and old people was encouraged and cultivated at West Heath, where every other afternoon during her last year, she and another student would visit an old lady living near Sevenoaks. They spent a couple of hours with the old lady, chatting, making tea and helping her with anything she could not accomplish herself. She also volunteered often at a nearby home for handicapped children.

Details of Diana's life at West Heath reveal that she never slept with any stuffed animals on her bed as many of the other girls did. However, she sported an array of photographs of her family, her animals and Park House on her chest of drawers by her bed. Here again, Diana's meticulousness did not escape unnoticed. She was a compulsive washer; not just herself, but her clothing as well, seeking permission more than most to do extra washing. Diana was entitled to two weekends off each term in addition to a half-term break of four days. On the weekends Diana generally would stay with either Sarah, once Sarah returned from finishing school in Switzerland, or with Jane, once Jane had graduated. As an "old girl" of West Heath, although not one of their most notable, Sarah was allowed to take Diana out to lunch or tea on any Saturday or Sunday. Normally friends and relatives could only do so on a set number of days, if they weren't alumni of the school. When visiting her sisters, Diana apparently did their washing for them and cleaned up their flats, both being chores which she seemed to take pleasure in. When Diana's parents visited, they visited separately. The only exception was later, at Diana's confirmation.

The weekends at West Heath, far from being boring, were filled with potential activities for all those who so desired. School outings to exhibitions, concerts, museums, theater or the ballet, provided some of the extracurricular activities offered by the school. Diana adored ballet and would always put her name down for outings to the ballet, with the result that she saw *Swan Lake* at least four times, as well as numerous other well-known ballets. Diana's dreams of becoming a professional ballet dancer herself, dashed when she grew too tall, never negated her love for it. Diana took ballroom and tap-dancing lessons, working hard at practicing, sometimes before breakfast. She was rewarded for her perseverance when she won the school dancing competition at the end of the spring term in 1976. Diana also took up piano at West Heath, starting at fourteen. Although Diana never achieved any grades, it was said that she displayed "phenomenal progress" and talent in the little time that she actually devoted to playing.

At West Heath Diana did not display any of the later problems she encountered with eating disorders, even though anorexia was a noted concern at West Heath, as it apparently was at most other boarding schools for girls at the time. If anything, Diana ate too much at West Heath. Penny Junor states, "She loved food, particularly baked beans, and she'd help herself to anything up to four bowls of All Bran every morning. But she did put on weight easily and periodically had to slow down on the baked beans." Diana often supplemented her meals at West Heath with snacks purchased in nearby Sevenoaks, cream eggs being her passion.

After breakfast a school prefect would bring the girls' personal letters around. Most of Diana's letters were from her family. Penny Junor confirms, "Prince Andrew never wrote to her, as people have suggested." The letters were brought around at the same time as the local newspaper and Diana couldn't wait to get her hands on it, delving into the Court Circular and the fashion pages in particular.

On weekends spent at West Heath, the girls were allowed to wear their home clothes. In *Diana, Princess of Wales*, the school Principal, Miss Rudge, noted that "the way (Diana) dresses now is just an extension of the way she dressed here. She had a sense of color. She was meticulous about the way she looked. It was natural to her—she's a neat, tidy person, and simple. She always dressed simply, but there was a bit of distinction about her even if she was wearing jeans and doing the weeding." Penny Junor further reveals, "The weeding was the Principal's pet punishment, inflicted on anyone caught talking after lights out, running in the passageway past the kitchens or storing chocolate in their sock drawers." Diana reportedly did her share of weeding along with all the other miscreants.

Although close friendships were not encouraged at West Heath, Diana managed to form friendships with Caroline Harbord-Hammond, a former Riddlesworth contact, Theresa Mowbray, her mother's goddaughter, Mary-Ann Stewart-Richardson, who also lived at Norfolk, and Sarah Robeson, who shared her interest in children. Reportedly both Sarah Robeson and Diana planned to work with children upon graduation, and both went on to do so. While at West Heath they used to babysit the English master's children during their free time.

At nearby Sevenoaks, Diana got her ears pierced, and although jewellery was not encouraged, it was not prohibited. So on one of Diana's birthdays on July 1st, which always fell during school term, she received a necklace with the letter D on it from her fellow students, who chipped in to finance the birthday gift. Diana wore the necklace faithfully right through the time she worked in a kindergarten after she finished with school.

Sarah Robeson and Diana used to help Barbara, who worked in the pantry, to set the tables at suppertime. This wasn't from a love of either food or work. There was a method to their madness. This way at supper they got seats close to the door so that they could get out the dining room quickly after the weekend meals and get the most comfortable chairs in the common room to watch television. On Sunday afternoon they watched old films, and Diana, in particular, was reported to love anything romantic. Additionally, Diana and the television were inseparable during Wimbledon days, during which her mother always obtained tickets for her for the first Saturday's play.

Sundays at West Heath were similar to those at Riddlesworth. Church was held at St. Mary's in Kippington, one-and-a-half miles down the road. Of the two services at 8 a.m. and 11 a.m., Diana went to the latter, until she was confirmed on March 12, 1976, when she was fifteen. It was the only time when her parents attended together, along with her sisters and godparents. The distinct advantage of going to the later service was that the girls got to sleep in. A special Sunday breakfast of hot rolls, boiled eggs and coffee was served at 9 a.m., giving the older girls a chance to return from the early service. After her confirmation, Diana went to the early service and spent the remainder of the morning reading the newspapers and Barbara Cartland novels, writing letters home or doing her washing.

Some of the compulsory subjects at West Heath were needlework, mathematics and French. Apparently Diana was never very good at needlework and worse still in the other two. Unlike many of the other girls, Diana was at a disadvantage when it came to her French. When the term was over, she never went abroad for holidays, summer or winter. All her holidays were divided between her father's and her mother's homes. Soon after the Countess Spencer's death, Diana's mother and stepfather moved hundreds of miles away to Scotland, off the west coast, creating yet another "home" for her to get used to. Diana, however, loved the windy, rainy working farmhouse and often used to invite her school friends over during holidays. Diana spent her days there walking on the island, helping her stepfather with his fishing or simply accompanying him, and assisting her mother with her show Shetland ponies and in the shop she operated. Occasionally, she even braved the frigid waters for a dip. Unfortunately, Diana was never around long enough to form any real friendships in these places. She still regarded Park House at Sandringham as her real home, complete with her animals, the grounds and most importantly her long-standing friends nearby.

Diana's lack of motivation and panic when faced with exams caused her to fail her exams in English Language, English Literature, Art and Geography, which she took in June 1977. Although some of her friends who had failed left at the end of summer and went on to take their exams over elsewhere, Diana stayed on at West Heath and sat for her exams again in the autumn, but she failed again and finally left West Heath at Christmas of 1977.

Although it was unusual for anyone leaving at Christmas to be made a prefect, Diana was one of the exceptions, entitling her to move out of the main building at West Heath and sleep in the post-"O" level study sleeping area known as the "Cowsheds" for obvious reasons. As Penny Junor describes, "The dormitory consisted of one long corridor with partitions on either side, each one housing a bed, a desk and a chest of drawers. But there was a kitchenette at one end and a certain amount of privacy and independence." During that last term at West Heath, Diana also was awarded the Miss Clark Lawrence Award for service to the school. The award was not always granted and was for service and helpfulness to the school, above and beyond the call of duty, as explained by the School Principal, Miss Rudge. Apparently Diana was surprised and delighted at this parting acknowledgment of her value to the school.

Diana seemed to have been adapting well to school life, and that roughly ten-year period might also have been the happiest time of her life. Three years after the death of her paternal grandmother, Cynthia Spencer, her grandfather Spencer died on June 9, 1975, at the age of eighty-three. Diana was upset, not only at the actual death of her grandfather, but also at the manner in which she had the news broken to her. After prayers one morning her cousin, Diana Wake-Walker, informed her of her grandfather's death. Diana was reportedly hurt that her own father had not been the person to contact her with the sad news.

With the death of the old Earl, Diana's life and, indeed, the lives of all the Spencers changed irrevocably. Her father, Johnnie, became the 8th Earl and inherited Althorp; Diana and both her sisters became Ladies while Charles was titled as Viscount Althorp at the age of eleven. The endowment of titles was accompanied by a move from Park House to Althorp. Diana arrived home from school at the end of the summer in 1975 to be confronted by the move in progress. Depressed and upset, Diana apparently called up a friend, Alex Loyd, and they departed to the Spencers's beach hut at Brancaster for the day. She never went there again.

As related by Penny Junor, "Althorp was a vast, stately home, steeped in family history and containing one of the finest art collections in Europe." Diana's memory of the house was very slight since only her mother had ever taken her to Althorp when Diana had been quite young. Of course when her mother left home in 1969, Diana stopped visiting Althorp altogether, as her father rarely set foot in the family home.

Park House, although big by most standards, was nevertheless a cozy family residence. Althorp, on the other hand, was an enormous, stately home, resplendent with high molded ceilings, chandeliers, marble floors, fireplaces, antique furniture, priceless paintings and much more. The house contains one of the finest private art collections in Europe, including items that once belonged to the first Duke of Marlborough. Some of the priceless items include Roman marble figures rescued from the River Tiber and given to the Duke by his brother, and paintings by Thomas Gainsborough and Sir Joshua Reynolds. In the Picture Gallery, which is reported to be thirty-five meters long, hang portraits of each generation of the family since the time of Elizabeth I, when the gallery was used by the household and their guests for walks on wet days. Since then it has seen many presentations, banquets and, in 1695, a reception for King William III.

Althorp is a rich treasure house of history, a record of the service given to their country by the Spencer family. Some of the furnishings should hold a particular appeal to future generations of Spencers, as the tapestry chair covers on many of the chairs at Althorp were embroidered by the late seventh Earl of Spencer, Diana's paternal grandfather, who was a very skilled upholsterer and reported that he found embroidery relaxing.

Unfortunately, Diana had no friends in Northampton, the site of Althorp, and although there was a tennis court, there was no swimming pool at the time. Additionally, it was a great distance from the ocean. Diana never grew fond of Althorp. This may, however, have had something to do with some of the other events which occurred at the same time in Diana's life.

Just prior to the old Earl's death, Johnnie had been working with Raine, the daughter of well-known author, Barbara Cartland. Raine was writing a book called *What Is Our Heritage?* for the Greater London Council, and she commissioned Johnnie, always a keen photographer, to take pictures for the book. During the course of this project, they fell in love. Although Raine was already married to the Earl of Dartmouth at the time and had four children by him, she divorced him and lost custody of her four children. To make matters worse, Raine's soon-to-be ex-husband had, at one time, been a close friend of Johnnie's at Eton.

The Spencer children were horrified, as was Raine's husband. As Penny Junor writes, "Raine, whose maiden name had been McCorquodale, had been in the public eye for years. She was seldom out of the gossip columns. As Lady Lewisham she had been a forceful member of the Westminster City Council, the London County Council and the Greater London Council, and was constantly sounding off about any controversial subject from refuse collection to cracked cups at London Airport and smutty films...But she was also a clever woman...It has to be said to her credit...that the only reason the estate is a going concern today is because of Raine's business sense." Several sources have expressed their belief that had Raine not taken a very forceful hand and brought a touch of brutal but much needed reality into the running of the house, it would likely have been taken over by the National Trust years before. There were crippling duties to pay after the 7th Earl died, and the general belief was that Johnnie wouldn't have known where to begin on his own.

Johnnie, married Raine on July 14, 1976, in London, and while he remained devoted to her for sixteen years until his sudden death in

April, 1992, his children shunned Raine, and Diana and her siblings even bestowed her with the moniker "Acid Raine."

Raine came across as a dominating and forceful woman who obviously alienated her stepchildren to the extent that Sarah and Jane chose to stay away from both Althorp and their father. They resented having to share their father's attention with Raine and hated having to acknowledge Raine as having authority over things they had long taken for granted, such as giving orders to the servants. No longer could they seek their father's advice in confidence around the dinner table. The ever-present Raine was a very visible presence and a thorn in the sides of the Spencer children, who after eight years of not having a mother around, had to get used to Raine, who was anything but a motherly figure. An article in *People Weekly* reported that "the Spencer children's loathing for Raine was unanimous and instant the moment she entered their father's life...Raine was everything their mother wasn't. She's bossy, showy, brassy. She's businesslike and unsympathetic."

Raine's plans to make Althorp pay for itself included opening the house to the paying public. The stable block was converted into a tea-room, a souvenir shop and a wine shop. The old staff were retired in favor of new staff, but only the barest minimum: a cook, a housemaid, a butler and a ladies' maid. Only the west wing was used solely by the family. The rest of the house was put on display for the benefit of the curious and paying public. All the Spencer household pets from Park House, including Marmalade the cat, a dog, another gitshound named Gitsy, Diana's hamster, Hammy, and a collection of Charles's Java sparrows, were banned from Althorp by Raine.

Searching for a more homey feel, Diana would often visit the kitchen and chat with the staff and delivery persons; in fact, she would search for anyone who was willing to chat with her. Unlike Raine, who insisted on dressing formally whenever she exited her bedroom, Diana would dress in jeans, do her own as well as her brother's washing and ironing, and never acted as if she expected anyone to treat her as a Lady. She was warm, friendly and chatty, wore no make-up and spent her days swimming (in summer), walking in the park and dancing on the black-and-white marbled floor of Wootton Hall, the Althorp entrance hall, prior to the arrival of the public.

Diana's stepmother's lifestyle was as opposite to Diana's as black is to white. Raine disliked the country and preferred to spend her time in the Spencer flat in London or at her flat in Brighton. When she was at

Althorp, she spent her mornings in bed, completing her work for the day. The bedclothes would be strewn with her paperwork until she was awake and ready to emerge, always dressed immaculately, as befitted her role as Countess. In the evenings she would dress for dinner in a long gown, even if she and her husband were the only ones at dinner. She made it clear to Diana that she was expected to follow suit during the evenings, although she was allowed to dress more or less as she pleased during the day. It was noted that in spite of the Spencer children's unanimous distaste for their stepmother, Diana was always very kind to Raine's younger children when they came to visit their mother. Charlotte, the older of the two, was fourteen when Diana's father married Raine, and Henry was eight at the time.

At sixteen, Diana was still a shy, quiet young woman, but she slowly began to come into her own with her gradual independence. A description by her nanny, Mary Clarke, that Diana was "every bit an actress, astute, devious, nonetheless sympathetic, genuine and sensitive," seemed to sum up Diana's complex personality.

Around this time as well, when Diana was writing her "O" level exams in June of 1977, her elder sister Sarah unwittingly began to map the future for her. Sarah had met Prince Charles at Ascot and the two had become good friends. Inevitably, Sarah was touted by the press as the possible future bride to Prince Charles. During Prince Charles's friendship with Sarah, he spent a night at Althorp (as Sarah's guest) to shoot on the estate the following day. It was then that Sarah introduced Prince Charles to Diana for the first time. The background was, as far as anyone could remember, Nobottle Woods, in the middle of a ploughed field. Diana was only sixteen then and home from school for the weekend. No one gave it any more thought at the time. However, unknown to most, the Queen, Prince Phillip and Ruth Fermoy, the Queen's lady-in-waiting at the time and Diana's maternal grandmother, had been planning Prince Charles's marriage for him. Fearful that Charles would have exhausted every eligible opportunity available, the Queen and Ruth, Lady Fermoy, had done everything in their power to ensure that the friendship between Sarah Spencer and Prince Charles would develop into something lasting. However, Sarah had other ideas and, in typical Spencer style, declared she was not in love with Prince Charles and would only marry for love.

The Queen and Lady Fermoy, not to be deterred, began to fuel a long-range plan to encourage the friendship between Diana and Prince Charles, even though Diana was only sixteen at the time (thirteen years younger than the Prince). Obviously, discretion dictated that further plans be put on hold, at least until Diana finished her formal schooling. However, the seeds had been sown, and slowly but surely they began to take root from that point on.

After Christmas of 1977, after failing her second try at her "O" level exams at West Heath, Diana left for finishing school in Switzerland. She was unfortunate to start school some time after the regular start of the school year, which ran from September to July. Most of the girls already knew each other and although Sarah had attended the same school, Diana, understandably, did not fit in. It was the first time she had been so isolated from all her friends and her family: it was Diana's first time on an airplane and her first trip abroad. All these firsts at the same time were somewhat overwhelming for Diana. To compound matters, out of a group of sixty students, only nine were English speaking, and the school rules insisted that she speak French. Diana's French, however, had never been good and she quickly made friends with the English girls, in particular Sophie Kimball, who remained Diana's close friend. Despite the rules, Diana spoke English almost exclusively.

Her subjects were domestic science (in particular dressmaking and cooking), business and French. In actuality, she took a Pitman's correspondence and typing course, spoke French and learned to ski and dress well.

Bitterly homesick, Diana returned home after six weeks and refused to return. Her mother was sympathetic, with the result that Diana moved to a large three bedroom flat in South Kensington and decided to try her hand at working. The flat was owned by her father and Diana lived in it with two roommates, also her friends. It was from this location that she traveled to her first jobs in child care.

Chapter 3

Diana: An Independent Young Lady

Always a girl who knew her own mind and relied on her stubborn streak to see her through challenges, Diana was not one to stay in a situation that was not to her liking. Being forced to speak French and coping with homesickness were definitely not to her taste. She packed in the Institut Alpin Videmanette, the finishing school at Chateau d'Oex near Gstaad, and headed back to England.

Upon her return from Switzerland in March 1978, four months away from her seventeenth birthday, Diana needed to make some personal decisions. Unsettled and without direction, she went to London to stay with her mother. Like any parent of an ambivalent teenager, Frances Shand Kydd must have felt some concern for her normally cheerful daughter, who had returned to England despondent and at odds with her life and the world. Frances offered Diana a haven in London in her spacious four-story flat at Cadogan Place. Diana preferred the company of her mother and the excitement that London offered over the option of returning to her father and Raine at Althorp. Since her mother only came in for occasional weekends, Diana was largely on her own in the Cadogan house until she followed her mother's advice to share it with friends and invited Carolyn Grieg to room with her.

Meanwhile, the Spencer family was preparing for Jane's twenty-first birthday and spring wedding. The second oldest in the family,

Jane was most like Diana in temperament and manner, and the two got along well. Unlike Diana, Jane graduated from West Heath. Following graduation, Jane went to Florence, Italy, for six months to study art and art history, much like the Grand Tours that upper class Britons would embark on in earlier centuries. After finishing her studies in Italy, and with an eye to establishing a career, Jane took a secretarial course. That training and her social network helped her land a job as an editorial assistant at the prestigious fashion magazine *Vogue*. The connections she made there would be of immense help to Diana when she made her transformation from dowdy nanny to fashion superstar a few years later.

On April 21, 1978, Lady Jane Spencer married Robert Fellowes. Fellowes was the son of Sir William and Lady Fellowes of Flitcham House, Norfolk. Sir William Fellowes had been the Queen's land agent at Sandringham. Robert was fifteen years Jane's senior, so they had not been childhood friends. Their families would have known each other, particularly as they would have been in such close proximity to each other when the Spencers lived at Park House on the Sandringham Estate. Robert Fellowes is a permanent member of the Queen's staff. His present position is assistant private secretary to the Queen. Illuminating his feelings and loyalties in the present tensions between the Windsors and the Spencers, Robert has said, "I love my wife but I worship my monarch."

Lady Jane and Robert's wedding ceremony on that warm and sunny April day took place in the Guard Chapel at Wellington Barracks in London. The service was followed by a lavish reception at St. James's Palace. Among the guests were the Queen, the Queen Mother and other members of the extended Royal Family. Diana was maid-of-honor. The other attendants were children, all of them dressed in quaint country-style wedding wear. The boys wore knickerbockers, and the girls were dressed in pinafores that matched the cummerbunds of the boys. Diana was dressed to match. Such traditionally sweet clothing would have suited her taste at the time. The Queen, Robert's "boss", must have been pleased with Lady Jane's wedding bouquet; she chose lilies of the valley, freesia, and stephanotis—all white, the Queen's favorite flower color. After returning from their honeymoon, the Fellowes moved into Kensington Palace in London, living rent-free in a "grace and favor" apartment granted them by the Queen.

The hopes and aspirations of Britain were turning to the uncertain prospects of another more auspicious marriage. Prince Charles had turned thirty in 1978, and he himself had once said that thirty would be a good age to get married. The nation was getting anxious. Since his Cambridge days, the press had been hot on his trail whenever they caught the whiff of a possible romance. Every romance was a lead-in to a potential wedding, every date, a potential queen. Charles was feeling the pressure not just from the press and the public, but most certainly from his family. Prince Philip in particular was maintaining a campaign to bully Charles to settle on a wife. Yet Charles was heeding Lord Mountbatten's advice to "sow his wild oats and have as many affairs as he can before settling down," before choosing for his wife a girl who is "suitable, attractive and sweet-charactered" and to get her "before she has met anyone else she might fall for...I think it is disturbing for women to have experience if they have to remain on a pedestal after marriage." The world's most eligible bachelor, Charles was the object of both the ambitions and affections of many women, commoner and royal. Lord Mountbatten had his own designs in that regard as well. He would have liked to have seen his granddaughter, Lady Amanda Knatchbull, strengthen the ties between the houses of Windsor and Mountbatten. The difficulty with that was that although Charles and Amanda did spend time together, even holidaying in the Bahamas with her parents, they had been too familiar with one another and saw their relationship as more filial than passionate. Besides, the Queen Mother did not approve of the choice.

While Charles was enjoying his bachelorhood and putting off the inevitable, his aunt, Princess Margaret, was in the midst of divorcing her husband, Lord Snowdon.

At one time the Queen would not even allow divorcees into her Royal Enclosure at Ascot, and now there was one in her immediate family. The Royals were having to adapt to changing times. The path for the Snowdon's divorce had been cleared in 1967 by the Earl of Harewood, the Queen's cousin, who divorced his wife in the midst of an adultery scandal—he lived with his secretary, with whom he had had a son. Then when the Earl wished to remarry, the Queen was put in an impossible position: as head of the Anglican Church she could not condone divorce and consent to the second marriage (which under the Royal Marriages Act was necessary), and yet how could she not give consent when the same thing was happening all around the nation? How could she balance her role as keeper of tradition with staying in step with the times? British Prime Minister Harold Wilson took it on his shoulders by making it a cabinet decision and not a Church of England matter. By doing so it became just another act of Parliament that the Queen gave her consent to, and it technically did not involve the church at all. Her roles stayed balanced. Consequently, when her own sister and Lord Snowdon went through the divorce, the Queen, being fond of Snowdon, continued to involve him in family events and the whole matter was handled compassionately and adroitly. It was a sign of the times, but it was not a path that would be possible for Charles. As potential Supreme Governor of the Church of England, divorce would be unheard of and a second marriage impossible.

Strings of women had been linked to Charles. One woman in particular had captured his heart: Camilla Shand. They had met in the early 1970s and had a great deal in common. They both loved horses, polo, outdoor activities and painting. Camilla was fun and lively with a strong personality and commanding presence. She was his intellectual match and emotional sanctuary. Not particularly attractive or stylish, Camilla Shand did have that certain earthy sexiness not evident in pictures but tangible in person. Many a girlfriend of hers, possibly more pretty and demure, were confounded by the net of attraction that Camilla could cast over the young men with whom she came into contact. She certainly snared Charles. But he did not play his hand quickly enough, and soon after their romance began, his duties in the Royal Navy took precedence. While Charles was away on a long assignment, Camilla met and fell in love with Andrew Parker-Bowles, and before Charles knew it, Camilla, the love of his life, had married someone else. They remained good friends up to and throughout his marriage, a friendship that later Charles confessed had deepened into a love affair. Camilla's influence over Charles is evident, even when it came to choosing a wife. He consulted Camilla, who advised him, perhaps in an attempt to secure her own place in his affections, that Diana would be a good choice. Camilla must have known that there were certain needs that she alone could fill and that she sensed Diana couldn't. In bringing in Diana, Camilla must have hoped that Diana would prove to be too vapid in the end and that Charles would still need her own continued friendship and support. Her ancestress, Alice Keppel, had been the mistress of another married Prince of Wales, Edward VIII, and Camilla must have taken some delight in the parallels drawn down through the generations. The ties were strong: Charles was the godfather to their son Thomas, as he is to children of many of his old flames, and Highgrove, the house he bought the year before his marriage, is just a scant ten miles from the Parker-Bowles residence, a convenient situation for the two of them in the years that followed. The future of Charles and Camilla's present relationship is the subject of a great deal of speculation in light of Diana's death. Marriage at this point is not possible in the foreseeable future.

As for Diana, her sister Sarah, six years her senior and the eldest in the family, was an enormous influence on the choices Diana would come to make in the next few crucial years. The name of Spencer was not new to the world when the cameras first caught Diana in their glare, for years earlier her sister Sarah had been linked to Prince Charles and indeed was seen as a possible and probable wife for him. Charles first met Sarah when she was the guest of the Queen at Windsor for the 1977 running of the Royal Ascot. Camilla had been married for four years by then, and her star was fading while the Spencer's star was rising. Sarah, afflicted with anorexia nervosa at the time, spent much of the seven months she was involved with Charles fighting the disease. It is said that Charles helped her through it. It seems ironic that his experience in helping the older sister could not have transferred to the younger sister when she, too, was suffering from eating disorders.

Sarah was a spirited, wilful young woman, given to pranks and unabashedly standing her ground and speaking her mind. Indeed, it was from Sevenoaks, the exclusive boarding school that Lady Diana attended, that Sarah was expelled for numerous misdemeanors. Sarah displayed many of the attributes typical of first-born girls: independent, intelligent leaders and achievers. Jane, on the other hand, was more conservative, more likely to toe the line and do what was proper.

Sarah and Charles were linked repeatedly from the summer of 1977 until the following February, when Sarah, fed up with the attention and the misrepresentation of what was essentially only a mild flirtation and friendship, told *Women's Own* magazine, among other things, that she "wouldn't marry anyone I didn't love, whether it was the dustman or the King of England. If he asked me I would turn him down."

It was during this period that Sarah set herself up as Cupid and introduced Charles and Diana. It was in November of 1977, and Charles was in Althorp for a weekend of pheasant hunting. Diana had been present the evening before in the "ploughed field" for one of the Althorp's renowned dinners. As was typical of Diana, she felt no snobbishness toward the house staff and went into the kitchen first to show off her gown. It is said they were astonished by the metamorphosis from girl to young lady that they saw in her that evening; perhaps Charles thought so as well. Charles said during their engagement interview what a "jolly and attractive sixteen year old he thought her to be" at that meeting. As for her side of it,

Diana was reportedly more interested in Prince Andrew than his older brother. Rose Ellis, the family cook at Althorp, speaking with Diana while driving in for groceries one afternoon, told Diana that she was keeping newspaper cuttings about Lady Sarah and Prince Charles. Diana had laughed that it would probably be the closest her sister would get to the Prince. And when the cook teased Diana about not having a steady boyfriend of her own, Diana laughed and said, "I'm saving myself for Prince Andrew." If she thought about it realistically, it would have been plausible to set her sights on Andrew. That didn't mean she couldn't indulge in a schoolgirl crush on Charles. Apparently she was smitten with him from that November on and is rumoured to have kept his picture under her pillow.

In the early spring of 1978, amidst the larger picture of the nation's interest in Charles's love life and her family's preoccupation with her sister's wedding, Diana began sketching out for herself a life in London. Diana lived close to Sloane Square, alive with its unique shops, cozy bistros and expensive houses. The smartest of the smart set drove Range Rovers, the world's first high quality sports vehicle. Two social satirists, Ann Barr and Peter York, noticed the upsurge of a certain type of titled, conventional young woman living near or in the area. They also noted that they tended to drive Range Rovers, dress in expensive but frumpy fashions and that they were virtually the opposite of the extreme "punk" scene that was also emerging. Many of them went so far as to ape the Royals' headdress—Hermes headscarves made of fabric printed with the requisite horse or hunting theme. Barr and York coined the phrase "Sloane Ranger" to describe these politically unaware, non-intellectual, conventional young women. Essentially these were former private school girls ("public school" as it is called in Britain), children of titled or moneyed parents with homes in the country as well as apartments, or "flats," in London. They "loved jokes, didn't use big words, were sexually innocent and regarded Sloane Square as the centre of the modern world." Jane Austen's main character in *Emma* would have understood these young women well because they shared the same values and expectations for their lives. Their goals in life were to be passingly domestic, a little artistic, able to dance when required, slightly well-traveled (as long as it didn't involve anything too exotic) and, in the end, well-married. In Ralph Martin's book *Charles and Diana,* he quotes the rules of behavior as outlined in *The Offical Handbook of the Sloane Ranger* :

"One must not think too hard or it would disturb people. One must use understatements so as not to bore or whine. One must use all the right words in the right voice. Sloane Rangers love the past. All the good things have been going on for ages. That means old houses, old furniture, old clothes, old wine, old families, old money."

Besides an obsession with being in the right family, having the right address and wearing the right clothes, a Sloane Ranger valued her friends, she considered her mother as one of her best friends, and she clung to her virginity until marriage. The time between school and wedding was a mere waiting period, a time to work at odd jobs and to socialize, with little real thought put into making or maintaining a long-term career. They lived in their own privileged, insulated world, which made them the objects of scorn for some and envy for others. All around them, women were caught in the fight to be recognized as more than consumers, wives and baby machines, and these Sloane Rangers seemed to be totally oblivious to the issues, social forces, political conditions and economic realities swirling around them. On the surface, there was little need to rebel in their lives, and these girls seemed to slip from childhood into adulthood with little muss, fuss or bad behaviour. Diana has been labelled "Supersloane" because she fit the mold almost perfectly.

In most ways Diana was interchangeable with her friends: they liked the same music (Sting, Duran Duran, Phil Collins), read the same books (romance, particularly Barbara Cartland) and went to the same hair dresser, Kevin Shanley of Headlines, who was creator of the famous "Lady Diana cut" that she wore at the time of her engagement.

In other ways, Diana was very different. On the surface, it looked as if all was well, but it has since been revealed that Diana harbored self-destructive feelings stemming from the traumas of her childhood. She did not take the usual teenage route of rejecting the lifestyle and values of her parents. Had she done so, it might have helped her develop a healthier adult self more quickly. She was on her own at seventeen and had all the amenities and luxuries of life given to her without the bother of a lot of parental involvement. It looked ideal on the surface—she went from one phase of her life to another without taking the opportunity to examine deeper issues and concerns until they flared up in her marriage and manifested themselves in her bulimia.

Lady Colin Campbell, in her book *Diana in Private*, reports Dr. Gloria Litman of the Institute of Psychiatry of the Maudsley Hospital in

London confirming that children of the aristocracy sometimes have difficulty coping once the firm boundaries of childhood are loosened. According to her, being "well-behaved, polite, achieving and maintaining the peak of social perfection can result in an underlying frustration and a suppressed rage that everything has been mapped out for you to the exclusion of your natural inclinations. If these conflicts between what the family expects of you and what you want to do are not resolved, the result can be alcoholism, drug addiction, melancholia" and other emotional difficulties, including eating disorders.

Nonetheless, for the time being life was sweet on the surface for Diana. Her two roommates and two sisters provided her with the connections for a full and lively, if not sophisticated, social life.

Diana and her girlfriends would spend evenings at each other's apartments chatting about prospective husbands, the latest film gossip, or eating pasta in front of the television. Other entertainment included hanging out in the cheaper bistros or catching a movie. Occasionally there would be trips to see stage productions or the ballet, a particular passion of Diana's. Tickets for these outings were often arranged by Lady Fermoy, Diana's maternal grandmother, with whom she visited often and is said to have had a strong relationship. It has been said that Lady Fermoy was more of a mother to Diana and that Frances, in typical Sloane Ranger form, was more of a friend.

Diana's main group of girlfriends included those she knew from Norfolk and West Heath: Alexandra Lloyd, Caroline Harbord-Hammond, Mary-Ann Stewart Richardson, Natalia Phillips and Theresa Mowbray. The boys who hovered around the edges of their lives came from families that were familiar with each other. The boys were usually graduates of Eton, the most prestigious of England's "public" schools, and had gone on to join the army or work in their family businesses or, in the rare case, join the professions. Shoots at Althorp would have provided additional acquaintances. Chief among these boys were Humphrey Butler, Rory Scott, Simon Berry, James Boughey and Harry Herbert. It was a stable, insular group. They had no need or interest in meeting new friends and inviting them into their circle; few left, fewer entered.

Diana spent most weekends in the country at house parties, visiting friends on her own or occasionally going to Althorp to visit her father. Rarely would she stay at the main house. Her sister Jane and her husband had a cozier, smaller house on the grounds, and Diana was more comfortable and felt more welcome there.

Within her social group, Diana was lively and loved attention. And she received plenty of attention from the boys around her. The family butler, Ainsly Pendry, told the story of one party: "Towards the end of evening, after everyone had gotten a little merry, some of the boys grabbed Lady Diana and threw her into the pool. But instead of getting out, Lady Diana threw off most of her clothes and swam around, laughing. The boys were applauding and enjoying every moment of it. Lady Diana's a lovely looking girl, and it was all innocent fun. Then she asked for her bikini and put it on before she got out of the water."

She was shy with strangers, but with people she knew, Diana could be boisterous and almost brazen. The butler also remembers another of Diana's visits to Althorp, "a time when an older man had arrived at Althop for a family visit. Diana had been swimming in the pool. She was just getting her robe on when the man complimented Diana on her tan. She smilingly opened her robe for his full view of her bikini, then calmly walked away, leaving the old man spluttering, 'If only I was fifty years younger!'"

As preoccupied with her social life as she was, that was not all that kept Diana busy. The spring of 1978 saw Diana at sixteen, close to seventeen, take her first paid position as a nanny for Alexandra, the baby daughter of Major Jeremy Whitaker and his wife Phillipa. Diana lived with the family at their estate, The Land of Nod, in Hampshire. She cared for the baby and generally made herself useful being that rare breed of person who noticed things that needed doing and did them. Her employers appreciated her conscientiousness and enthusiasm for her duties. "She was also a great help around the house, " said Mrs. Whitaker. "If there were strawberries to pick, she would help. Or meals to be fixed. She didn't mind work at all. If there was a job to be done, she did it." Diana's wide network of connections and family friends helped her land the position. Phillipa's brothers knew Diana through weekend shoots at Althorp, and when the Whitakers needed someone to help her out, he recommended Diana. She spent three months with them and returned in the summer of 1978 to her mother's house in London, where she stayed for the next year.

Back in London, Diana registered with employment agencies specializing in domestic help. Many of her friends worked in trendy boutiques or in office positions, but such positions held no appeal for Diana. She loved children and had a special talent with them that she wanted to put to use. The two agencies she signed with were Knightsbridge Nannies, which provided temporary babysitting jobs, and Solve Your

Problems, where she was offered a variety of assignments from shopping to cleaning to errand-running. Diana loved this sort of work.

By this time, Diana had asked Sophie Kimball to join her and Laura Grieg at her mother's home. Sophie had been the one who brightened Diana's life in Switzerland, as she was someone with whom Diana could speak English. The two girls also shared a love of skiing. Sophie became the source of many of Diana's enduring friendships. Laura was a cookery student at the Cordon Bleu school and treated her flatmates to the benefits of her daily lessons. It was she who got Diana interested in, and signed up for, a cookery course that September at Elizabeth Russell's in Wimbledon.

Diana had always been good in the kitchen and had absorbed cookery skills from hanging around the kitchen and whipping up snacks. Now she wanted to add professional credentials to her name and expand her employment possibilities. She took the underground daily from Sloane Square to Wimbledon, and at the end of the three-month course, she added catering to her roster of assignments at the employment agencies. She signed up with Lumleys, an employment agency specializing in catering, and worked cocktail parties making and serving snacks; her sister Sarah was among her customers.

That fall, life was simple and satisfying for Diana; and then adversity struck.

The Earl Spencer collapsed at Althorp with a cerebral hemorrhage. He was taken, unconscious, to the local Northampton General and then to the National Hospital in London. The Earl remained unconscious and in a coma for the next six agonizing weeks, and the doctors gave little hope for his survival. The only person who held faith was his wife, Raine. The rest of the family had all but lost hope for his recovery. Everyone now believes that without Raine's strength of will and round-the-clock ministrations, he would have died. She was ferociously protective of him to the point of barring his children from visiting. There are reports that the Spencer children would wait outside in the evening until Raine left, and then they would sneak in the back way to see their father.

In an interview with the *Daily Express,* Raine said, "I'm a survivor, and people forget that at their peril. There's pure steel up my backbone. Nobody destroys me, and nobody was going to destroy Johnnie, so long as I could sit by his bed—some of his family tried to stop me—and will my life force into him." Raine heard of a new drug developed in Germany, Aslocillin, that was not yet available in Britain. She persuaded her

friend Lord William Cavendish-Bentinck, chairman of the British sub-
sidiary of Bayer Chemicals, to get some for Johnnie. The drug was effective. It is said that he finally came to and "was back" while Raine was
playing him "Madame Butterfly" on a portable tape recorder in his room
one afternoon in November. He stayed in the hospital until January, and
then he and Raine stayed at the Dorset House in London until February. It
was reported that the cost of his stay and subsequent recovery at the Dorset House amounted to £60 000. His recovery was almost complete, except that he suffered from a slight speech impairment and a general slow-
ing down. He also took to repeating back to the speaker what was, and he
was forced to give up many of his activities in the country. The Earl of
Spencer paid tribute to his wife's devotion, as recorded in Ralph Martin's
book *Charles & Diana*: "Without Raine, I wouldn't be here...I'd be dead.
Raine saved my life by sheer willpower. The doctors had me on the death
list eight times, and they kept at her to order a coffin. They said I'd need a
miracle to survive. Raine was my miracle. It's entirely due to her—her
love for me, her determination not to let me go—that I'm still around. I
couldn't talk to her, but I knew she was there, hour after hour, week after
week, holding my hand and talking about our holidays and my photography—things she knew I liked."

The Queen, knowing of the plight of the Spencers, invited Diana
and Sarah to Sandringham for a shooting weekend in January, to help
ease their stress from their father's illness. The girls escaped for a much
needed weekend away as the Earl was finally returning home from the
hospital.

Charles and Diana were reacquainted with each other that blustery
January 1979 weekend in the country. In these familiar and cherished
surroundings, they were both relaxed, cheerful and wonderfully open to
each other.

Diana was only one of many there that weekend, and any special
attention Charles conferred on her was no more than he gave to others.
Besides, at that point, other than a wholesome, healthy attractiveness, she
wouldn't have been much to look at in comparison to some of the glamorous women with whom he had recently been. Her hair was shoulder length
and mousy brown, not styled in a distinctive or particularly appealing
"do". She was a conservative but expensive dresser, still sporting clothes
that her mother picked out for her: demure sweater sets with knee-length
tartan skirts and corduroy pants. That said, her more important qualities
must have caught his eye. Diana's quick wit, joyful laugh and easy

manner made an impression on Charles, and he apparently enjoyed her fresh, naïve and undemanding company. Charles began to see a lot of Diana, relying on her to be a complete-the-numbers for a party to the opera, perhaps, or some other occasion. She was no girlfriend at this time, however, and was seemingly no threat to be one. Diana was fun, though; she was someone with whom the Prince could relax.

At the end of January, Diana's mother, once again concerned with the lack of career direction in her daughter's life, suggested that she combine the two things she loved best, children and dancing, and train to become a dance teacher. Acting on her mother's suggestion, Diana wrote to Betty Vacani, who had been running a school for the children of the upper classes for the past fifty years. Not surprisingly, among Betty's past students were Prince Charles and Diana's stepmother, Raine. A Vacani teacher at West Heath had taught Diana, and she had won a prize in an end-of-term competition that Miss Vacani had judged. Betty Vacani has no recollection of Diana at that time. Diana later reminded Betty that she had taken care of her Pekinese dog while that competition had been in progress. Perhaps it was that, along with her performance in competition and passion for ballet, that made Betty Vacani agree to take Diana on for the tuition of £100 a year, even though she was short on the qualifications. Diana loved ballet so much that as a young girl she had waited outside Covent Garden in the rain to get Mikhail Bariyshnikov's autograph—a fact she surprised him with at a formal dinner in Washington twenty years later.

At Vacani's, Diana was enrolled in a program to become a certified Cecchetti Method dance teacher. The program would take her a minimum of three years to complete. She started assisting in the youngest class, working with students between ten and twenty-two. Her job was to round up the little ones and get them ready for the main part of the lesson by playing movement and rhyming games like "Ring Around the Roses" and "Hickory Dickory Dock". The children brought their own mice to class for a rousing finale, releasing the mice at the end "when the mouse ran down". It was a raucous activity that the children loved but Diana found stressful, not the least because she had to act like a clown and be silly. For a shy girl to act foolish was difficult enough, but having the children's nannies and mothers in eagle-eyed attendance made it absolutely excruciating for her. Diana must have had to steel her nerves every morning as she road her bicycle through Kensington, preparing herself for the onslaught of another day.

She was also involved with older groups of children learning more formal skills; she joined the higher classes as a student and also participated with the mothers' ballet group. She enjoyed being a student of these classes far more than teaching, but in the end it became evident that she did not have what it would take to become a professional dancer, nor did she have the drive to stay the course to become a teacher. Diana did what she had always done when a situation became uncomfortable: she quit.

A major factor in her decision to leave was that she was uneasy and out of her element with the other student teachers, who were likely bound for the stage and much more sophisticated and worldly than she. Diana was, at heart, a country girl, wearing no makeup and mummy's choice of clothing. Never one to be comfortable with people outside her own social set, Diana didn't fit in at the dance school, and neither did she try. A sign of her inherent strength of character was that, rather than trying to adapt to new situations and possibly compromising herself in the process, Diana would leave.

"She tried it for a term, but she realized that you've got to be absolutely dedicated, and she had a rather full social life," said Miss Vacani. "But the ballet helped her posture."

Diana, saying that she had hurt her foot, simply quit going, thereby freeing herself from an awkward and, to her thinking, unnecessary situation. The injury to Diana's foot couldn't have been too serious, because she promptly left for a skiing trip to the French Alps with a dozen or more of her friends in March 1979.

Friends who were with her on that trip said they were struck by her domesticity and good humor. Simon Berry tells the story: "One day she had a slight injury and stayed behind while the rest of us went skiing. With eighteen people living in the chalet, we had dishes piled up in the sink, and there was clothing scattered everywhere. Diana washed up all the dirty dishes, swept the floor and tidied it up to such an extent the place was immaculate."

He goes on to illuminate Diana's appeal. "There was nothing hoity-toity about Diana," said Berry. "She had this wonderful gift of getting on well with everybody. You know, she has broken the hearts of dozens of young men. Chaps would meet Diana and fall instantly in love." Perhaps it was the blue eyes, the hearty laugh, the blush or her sweet nature. Maybe it was her naturalness and joy for life.

"I was skiing down an icy slope," recalled Berry, "and suddenly I heard the strident tones of Miss Piggy in my left ear, informing me,

'You're treading on thin ice, frog.' In the next instant, Diana went hurtling past me, with a big grin on her face. She's a great mimic."

Following that trip to France, Diana continued to take on temporary cleaning, cooking and babysitting assignments. She even worked for her sister, cleaning her flat once a week for two hours.

Independence took on a new meaning for Diana in July 1979. She was eighteen and received the money left to her in trust by her American grandmother, Frances Work.

Frances Work was a headstrong and self-willed daughter of a millionaire New York stockbroker. She enraged her father, who detested foreigners, when she married the third Baron Fermoy, then the James Roche. Frances, or Fanny, as she was called, eventually left her husband and returned home to the States and papa. In order to be reinstated into his will, her father, Frank Work, forbade her to use her married name and title, and she had to agree never to return to Europe. He forced the same conditions on her twin sons, Maurice (Diana's grandfather) and Francis. They were entitled to his fortune only if they became American citizens and renounced their British ties completely. Fanny and her boys complied while Frank lived, but once he died they had his will overturned and returned to Britain. Frances's grandchildren were the inheritors of her stubbornness and her considerable fortune.

Frances Shand Kydd once again stepped in as advisor, and she encouraged Diana to buy her own flat like her sisters had done. Sarah had bought a flat on Elm Park Lane, and Jane had bought hers in Warwick Square in Pimlico. Diana launched into the project with enthusiasm and bought the flat at 60 Coleherne Court in Fulham for £50 000. Sarah had found it through her employer, Saville's, an upper-end real estate agent in Berkeley Square, and Frances handled the legal end of things.

Diana dedicated the remainder of that spring to decorating, shopping for paint, wallpaper, furnishings and artwork. Diana had always had an appreciation for beautiful surroundings, and she was used to an aesthetically pleasing environment. For the first time in her life, she had free reign to make her own decorating choices and to feather her nest according to her own taste, although she did check with both her mother and her roommates before making final decisions on her purchases. She chose wallpapers, accessories and comfortable modern furniture, from upscale shops and dealers, to help her once again have a cozy home. Hers was a roomy apartment, complete with high ceilings, wall-to-wall carpeting and three bedrooms, all housed in a nondescript four-story mansion on the corner of the Old Brompton Road. Diana's neighborhood was on the edge of a more bohemian district, and she enjoyed the closeness to the variety of shops and restaurants. Coleherne Court had the added benefit of being close to both her sisters.

Sophie Kimball and Phillipa Coaker, a domestic science college friend of Sophie's, moved in with Diana.

Frances, having no further need for her large house in Cadogan Place, took over Jane's flat in Warwick Square, which Jane had not been using since her marriage a year earlier.

Diana was spending less time at Althorp, perhaps finally getting fed up with Raine's rules and dominance. The family butler at Althorp tells how "Lady Diana got very angry because she wasn't allowed to use the stereo record system which was in the house. So she took up all the floorboards in the room and disconnected the wiring, so no one could use it."

Among her social life, her new apartment and her work, Diana's life was continuing on a steady if unremarkable path. However, tragedy struck again during this relatively peaceful period, although this time it was not so personally connected to Diana. Just as the Royal family retreat to their Balmoral estate in Scotland every year for six weeks, for intimate and relaxed family time, so, too, did Prince Charles's favorite uncle, Lord Louis Mountbatten go to his own retreat. Mountbatten went to his estate, Classiebawn, on the Irish coast. Because of the Irish troubles and ongoing IRA threats to members of the Royal family, Mountbatten knew he was risking death with each visit. He considered, however, the pleasure of being surrounded by family, and a few of his closest friends, at his favorite spot on Earth, well worth the risk. On August 27, 1979, on their way to check the lobster pots late in the morning, Lord Mountbatten, his son-in-law Nicholas Knatchbull (Amanda's brother) and a local Irish boy, Paul Maxwell, were killed instantly when a fifty-pound bomb exploded underneath them. Knatchbull's mother died the next day. Other people on the boat were seriously injured. In explaining the assassination, the IRA said, "it had been a discriminate operation to bring to the attention of the English people the continuing occupation of our country. Mountbatten's execution was a way of bringing emotionally home to the English ruling-class and its working-class slaves...that their government's war on us is going to cost them as well....We will tear out their sentimental, imperialist heart."

Prince Charles was devastated at the news of his uncle's death, and the nation was rocked by the horror of it. In his funeral service, which he had planned years earlier, Mountbatten chose the hymn "I Vow My Country To Thee." Charles lost his strongest support and his greatest friend when he lost Mountbatten. Bereft with grief and loneliness, among those who offered Charles support and helped him to cope with his grief was Camilla Parker-Bowles. It was at this time that Charles and Camilla renewed their relationship, and that autumn, he bought Highgrove in Gloucestershire, an estate close to his sister, Princess Anne, and the Parker-Bowles.

Meanwhile, Diana had gone to Scotland to visit with her mother and then gone over to Balmoral to stay with her sister Jane. Robert Fellowes was obligated to travel with the Queen because of his position of assistant private secretary, so when the Royals were in Balmoral, so, too, were the Fellowes. Charles was in seclusion at Balmoral with his cousin, Norton Knatchbull, trying to come to terms with Mountbatten's death and working through his grief. It is unlikely that he and Diana saw each other at all during this time.

That fall, Diana began one of the most pivotal years in her life, and the last time of prolonged happiness for her. Life took on more of a settled air for Diana after she finally found a permanent, though not full-time, position as a helper at Young England Kindergarten in St. George's Square, Pimlico. Again her sisters had a hand in her fate. The kindergarten was run by Victoria Wilson and Kay Seth-Smith, whose sister Janie had been at West Heath with Diana's sister Jane. Jane had been on the lookout for jobs for Diana and asked Janie if she might have an opening for Diana. With her background, personality and knack with children, Diana turned out to be exactly what they were looking for in a kindergarten worker. Starting with the new afternoon playgroup, Diana soon became so popular with the children and so adept at handling their squabbles, their tears and their discipline that she was first offered mornings and then offered full days. Her easygoing manner and joy for life were well matched by the emphasis at the school on love over discipline. However, Diana was able to handle her charges with firmness as well as affection. One young boy, Alexander Stevens, remembers the time that "Miss Diana" surprised him and another boy in the bathroom. They had been goofing around, seeing who could pee the farthest, when Diana's surprise appearance in the bathroom so startled them, they turned in shock and peed across her shins. She reprimanded them for their naughtiness and informed their parents that it had been dealt with and nothing further need be done. She was firm but fun-loving—just what the children needed and what their parents appreciated. These were privileged children of Britain's upper crust and they included Sir Winston Churchill's great-great-granddaughter, as well as grandchildren and children of government and society people. Diana had, at last, found her niche.

While at Betty Vacani's, Diana had to deal with children in a large, unruly group, trying to keep their attention focused on learning dance and its discipline; at the kindergarten, however, Diana only dealt with small groups of five children, all under the age of five. She was able to give them the one-on-one attention she later became so renowned for giving to others in her later, more public activities. Neither did Diana any longer have to carry out her duties under the critical eye of nannies and mummies. There were fifty children in all at the kindergarten, and ten teachers. Diana's main duties were to organize their art activities, which meant putting out the supplies, supervising their messy creations, and cleaning up afterward. Diana loved her work. Over early morning chats at tea or flopped on the couch at the end of the day, she frequently regaled her roommates with uproarious stories of the children's antics of the day. This was heaven. She loved her work and she gained confidence through her ability to meet the children's dependence, need and affection.

Not only was Diana working three days a week at Young England Kindergarten, but Knightsbridge Nannies also gave her an on-call job looking after a one-year-old American boy, Patrick Robertson, the son of an oil company executive. She adored Patrick and looked after him as if he was her own, taking him back to her apartment on long walks, playing with him for hours and shopping at Harrods while he slept in his stroller. It was a relaxed and satisfying situation. Her employers had simply hired her as Diana Spencer, and they knew nothing of her family connections.

According to Mrs. Robertson, "This charming girl reported for duty, and she was so refined and well-educated that we knew she must be somebody special. All I can say is that Lady Diana was wonderful with children." It was not until the photographers appeared a year later, lying in wait for Diana at their door, that the Robertsons had any idea of just how special their nanny was.

Wanting to stay busy and continue to develop her dancing abilities, Diana enrolled at another dance school, the Dance Center in Covent Garden where, during her free time, she took jazz, tap and keep-fit classes. As well, she kept up her other agency work, cleaning or babysitting as the need arose. Diana was also indulging her passion for shopping, especially at Harrods and Harvey Nichols. With her growing sense of contentment and self-confidence, she began to develop a more individual mode of fashion, catering less to her mother's taste and more to her friends', and her own, sense of style. The young ladies at 60 Coleherne Court were similar in size and generous in nature; if one bought an outfit, the others, of course, shared it. Diana once told a friend that her idea of heaven was shopping at Harrods; how ironic, in looking back, that statement would prove.

Living in a flat with a series of roommates held its joys and tribulations. According to reports, the apartment had the look one would expect from a group of girls living the carefree life. The front hallway was an obstacle course of bicycles—they couldn't risk them being stolen by leaving them outside—and jumbles of sporting equipment. Makeup, magazines and articles of clothing would be strewn blithely about, and music played continuously. Of course, when things got a little too disheveled, Diana would be the first to jump in and create order out of the chaos.

Soon after the Christmas of 1979, there were changes in the flat; Virginia Coaker decided to go traveling and was replaced by another girl, Virginia Pitman, a friend of Sophie's from Eggleston Hall, the domestic science school. Soon after Virginia arrived, Sophie decided to move out. In her place came Carolyn Pride, a friend of Diana's from West Heath school. Carolyn was studying music at the Royal College of Music, and along with her horsemanship trophies, she brought her piano. A fourth roommate was added, Ann Bolton, who was a friend of a friend of Diana's. Diana and Ann had met on the skiing trip to France the winter before. Ann, a practical and somewhat bossy young woman, was also a co-worker of Diana's sister, Sarah. These young women paid their rent, shared other common expenses, pooled their clothing and contributed to the life and liveliness of the apartment. They had, however, one strict rule about boys they might be interested in: "no poaching."

Diana was driving her own car by this time, her skills greatly improved in the time since she had barely passed her driver's test on the second go-round. Her mother had bought Diana her first car, a Honda Civic, and her second as well, a blue VW Polo, which Diana promptly crashed in a minor accident. Frances, always generous with her children (she'd paid for both Sarah and Jane's weddings) replaced the Polo with the famous red Mini Metro.

Life was sociable and busy, but for all that Diana didn't enjoy parties much unless they were gatherings of her own group. She had no interest in meeting new people. She particularly didn't like the discomfort of night-clubs—flamboyant, sophisticated people made her feel insecure. One of the more exciting times would be when Prince Charles would phone Diana to round out a party, but he was never a visitor at her flat.

Within her own circle, Diana was a treasured friend and a good person to have around. "What all her friends loved most about her," said Theresa Mowbray, who knew Diana since childhood, "was her great sense of humor. She loved a joke and had a tremendously hearty laugh that was really infectious."

Invitations to parties were commonplace, but there were few steady boyfriends. According to the Queen's stable manager, Harry Herbert, Diana "never dated; she used to go out with friends in groups." A true romantic, she was a virgin and was determined to save herself for marriage. She had the interest of various young men, but when she ventured out, the girls often clustered on one side of the room, eyeing and being eyed by, the boys on the other side. It was a year of chummy relationships with the young men: maybe a mild flirtation or two, but certainly no passion.

That spring brought another family wedding. On May 17, 1980, Diana's sister Lady Sarah Spencer wed Neil McCorquodale, stockbroker and only son of the Alastair McCorquodales of Little Ponton Hall, Grantham, Lincolnshire. It was a far less ostentatious affair than her sister Jane's wedding. The couple was married at the local church—St. Mary's at Great Brington, Northampton—on a warm and sunny day. The reception was held at Althorp. Although attended by many wealthy and close friends, there were no senior members of the Royal Family as guests. The most pre-eminent Royal was Lady Sarah Armstrong-Jones, who was one of the bridesmaids. Even though Diana did not play an official role in this sister's wedding, she must have made an impression on Sarah Armstrong-Jones, for not long after the wedding, Diana received a series of special invitations from the Royal quarter. The day was noteworthy for one other reason: the old Earl's ghost was reported as being present, silent but smiling, in the drawing room during the reception.

Wedding pressure continued to build for Charles, and he felt it within himself, too. The time was rapidly approaching, he knew, when he would have to steel himself and make his choice. Charles had trusted accomplices in this pursuit—his grandmother and her lady-in-waiting,

Lady Fermoy, Diana's grandmother. The two elderly matchmakers had been firm friends since before King George VI, Charles's grandfather, had ascended to the throne in 1936. When Diana's mother left the Earl of Spencer for Peter Shand Kydd, Lady Fermoy, Frances's mother, had been appalled and had turned her back on Frances in favor of her son-in-law. Her loyalty to the Earl had been one of the factors that led to Diana's father winning custody of the children in the subsequent divorce suit. The sordidness of the divorce left Lady Fermoy determined to resurrect the family reputation and find suitable matches for her granddaughters. Who would be a more suitable groom than the grandson of old friends and the next King of England? It was perhaps their subtle suggestions that led to Diana's being invited by Sarah Armstrong-Jones, the daughter of Princess Margaret, to join the Royal Family aboard their yacht off the Isle of Wight during Cowes week in July of 1980.

Joining in with some of Charles's parties, as she had occasionally been doing for the previous few months, and her recent invitations to join the Royal family, gave Diana the opportunity to show herself to Charles as an independent young woman. She was more than the baby sister of an old girlfriend; yet, because of her age and family connections, his attentions toward her remained well-masked and were allowed to develop relatively unnoticed by others, particularly the press…at least for a while.

In June of 1980, Jane Fellowes gave birth to their daughter, Laura, and the Fellowes followed the Royals to Balmoral for the yearly holiday. Diana visited her sister there, ostensibly to help with the new baby. It proved to be a convenient set-up. When Charles was in residence, Diana and Charles got to know each other under relaxed and relatively uncontrolled circumstances. The surrounding secluded moors provided many opportunities for the outdoor pursuits that Charles loved. Diana, reportedly in love with Charles from the time she first met him when she was sixteen, more than likely enjoyed the headiness of having him to herself, with no other glamorous women about to grab his attention. By the time the first photograph was taken of Diana and Charles, where she lay on the bank, watching him fish for salmon in the River Dee, the couple had both realized that there was, indeed, "something in it."

Diana's return to London was heralded with a headline, "He's in Love Again," and so was heralded the new path Diana was to start down, a path from which there would be no respite, and no return.

Chapter 4

A Fairy-tale Romance

By the summer of 1980, Prince Charles and Diana were frequently at the same social events. In September of that year, Diana was a houseguest at Balmoral for one of the Royal house parties. This seemed to be a pivotal point in their relationship. The media were just beginning to speculate on the nature of their friendship, and according to Prince Charles's valet at the time, this was when the Royal staff began to suspect that something was on the horizon for these two.

As Diana was once quoted as saying, the fact that she ended up being the chosen one had a lot to do with the fact that she was in the right place at the right time. There was a lot of pressure at this time for Charles to marry and produce an heir. By the summer of 1980, Charles was taking this marriage pressure seriously. Diana had all the right characteristics, and she was British. Her British blood was to be a key element in her popularity—it had been at least 300 years since the heir to the throne had married a British subject. Apparently, Charles had once said that when you marry someone you are forming a partnership that should ultimately last a long time. This being the case, Charles said that he'd like to marry someone whose interests he could share.

Prince Charles's romantic past was full of adventure. The only woman who met his standards and was deemed worthy of marriage was Anna Wallace, or "Whiplash, " as she was later nicknamed. According to James

Whitaker, in his book *Settling Down*, the list of Charles's lovers was long and varied. Whitaker had apparently been on Charles's trail for years, and he had managed to thoroughly document many of the Prince's romantic goings-on. The Prince's first public date was with his cousin Marilyn Wills when he was fourteen. Apparently they did not even hold hands. Charles always had a detective around him, which was clearly not conducive to romance. Some of Charles's ex-girlfriends have said that it is intimidating enough to date the heir to the throne, let alone deal with a chaperone. Charles was reportedly a romantic wooer: he brought flowers, favored candlelight, and liked holding hands.

Charles first actually fell in love with Lady Jane Wellesley, the daughter of the Duke of Wellington. Jane was considered to be a very suitable match for Charles. Whitaker wrote that Jane was pretty, intelligent and well-versed in the ways of court life. She also had the approval of the Queen. It was 1973 and Whitaker was under the impression that had it been years later, their relationship would likely have flourished. At this time, however, Charles had to consider his naval career, while Jane had ambitions to be a journalist. Unfortunately, their relationship finally dissolved under the pressure from the media, and Jane reportedly did not want to give up her independence in order to perhaps one day marry Charles. Though the romantic part of their relationship came to an end, their friendship survived.

Charles's relationship with Anna Wallace was feisty, sensuous, dramatic and tempestuous. The Prince apparently proposed to Anna but she rejected him, perhaps suspecting she would never be fully accepted because she didn't have the right character to marry into the Royal Family. Anna admitted to having past lovers, as well as having too willful a personality to ever become part of the Royal Family. She also apparently knew that the Queen was not too fond of her, nor had Fleet Street shown her in a positive light.

Whitaker states that when Charles proposed, Anna was confused because she knew she could not marry him. Charles then decided to take her to Balmoral to try to convince her of marriage. Whitaker was on the scene and saw Charles lying on a blanket beside Anna. This was apparently uncharacteristic behavior for Charles, normally he would have been fishing. Clearly, this visit to Balmoral did nothing to persuade Anna to accept Charles, but, instead, the pressure became so great that, according to Whitaker, an explosion of emotions took place.

This so-called explosion took place over the course of two nights. The problems came to light at the Queen Mother's eightieth birthday celebration. Charles, with so many people to talk to, was so busy that he ended up neglecting Anna, and she was not the least bit pleased. It was later reported that Anna complained loudly and bitterly about having been ignored. Furthermore, Anna warned Charles never to do it again. The second part of the explosive breakup took place at Stowell Park. Charles apparently danced numerous dances with his favorite female friends, while Anna looked on in fury as the evening dragged on and she was ignored once again. Upset at this repetition of Charles's dismissive behavior, Anna left in a huff and the two never exchanged tender words again. Many sources agree that the bitter end to this tumultuous relationship was traumatic for both Charles and Anna. Their relationship had lasted from November 1979 until July 1980. Shortly after this, Diana came onto the scene.

According to Charles, a woman marries not only a man, she also marries his job and his way of life. Therefore, it was necessary the woman he marry would have some knowledge of what, and not just who, she would be marrying. Charles was looking for a woman who had a certain familiarity with the royal scene. He went on to say that marriage should be like a very strong friendship. And perhaps most importantly, Charles had to consider the fact that the woman he chose to marry could very possibly become Queen one day.

Diana was definitely part of the right social circle. Her sister Sarah had briefly dated the Prince in the seventies. Her other sister Jane is married to the Queen's private secretary. Clearly these kinds of links helped to promote a familiarity between Charles and Diana.

Having Diana at Balmoral allowed Charles the chance to better acquaint himself with her. She apparently brought her needlepoint and a couple of Mills and Boon romance novels with her. During the day, Diana and the other women socialized while the men were out shooting. At lunch the women would wander across the moors to join the men for tea. During the evening there was a lot of dancing. Some sources suggest that Charles's serious girlfriends were put through what was referred to as the "Craigowan Test," which entailed sitting around in the house all day or traipsing around the moors, and just generally watching Charles from the sidelines while he engaged in outdoor activities. It has been suggested that Charles figured that because these outings were so important to him, his girlfriends must be willing to partake in the activities, if only in the role of spectator. Diana obviously passed the test because the invitations continued. Charles reportedly became aware that Diana was no longer the amusing, bouncy sixteen year old he remembered. She was now a fully grown woman with whom he could enjoy himself.

Diana was finally invited to Balmoral. The first view the press had of Diana as a potential romantic interest of the Prince's came when Whitaker spotted them together in the countryside. Whitaker came upon the scene to see Charles fishing in the River Dee for salmon and Diana standing on the riverbank watching him. She in turn spotted Whitaker and was cunning enough to hold a small hand mirror so that he and his photographer would not be able to get a clear look at her face. Apparently he took it upon himself to evaluate the Prince's choices in women, and in some cases he had been quite critical. Whitaker apparently from the start liked Diana much better than Charles's other girlfriends. For a girl that many people described as being unsophisticated and innocent, Diana actually had a few tricks up her sleeve, and Whitaker noticed this right away. She wrapped her hair in a head scarf and put on a cap—her identity was an enigma for a short while.

Whitaker confessed that he was very impressed that Diana had outwitted him and his photographers. Apparently, during the whole incident, Charles feigned ignorance of the photographer's presence until Diana walked up the hill. He then followed her to his parked car and then he turned around and looked through his binoculars to determine who was stalking them. Charles left with his mystery girl. The question of this girl's identity, though, was soon answered. One of Whitaker's colleagues had found both her name and her address from a mutual contact and for a while the *Daily Star* was the only Fleet Street paper to have her address.

The first really big clue that something was going on was a bouquet of roses, with a handwritten note from the Prince that arrived at Diana's flat. Though there were no other overt clues or hard evidence of a seriously budding romance at this point, the notion persisted among the media that she was "the One". Why did the press and many others feel that Diana could be the chosen one? There were many points in her favor. First of all, Charles was at the marrying age. Not only was Diana charming, sweet and innocent, she was also well groomed and a member of the British aristocracy. Short of a princess—and there were no available British princesses at the time—Diana was the perfect match. She was not especially career driven, like some of Charles's previous girlfriends, and her employment working with children indicated she had maternal capabilities. It was said that Diana's aspirations revolved around getting married and having a family—this was certainly very compatible with the Prince's agenda.

After the seeds of romance were sown in the late summer of 1980, Charles had to be careful about how he was going to court Lady Diana; he did not want to scare her off as he had others before her. Diana was also very young and shy, so pursuing her would have to be a delicate affair. Charles knew there was sure to be rampant media interest in Diana, and this would almost certainly cause her stress and unease.

During the early days of their courtship, Diana tried to pay very little attention to the media. She managed successfully to evade questions about the nature of her relationship with the Prince. Usually she answered such questions by saying that the reporter knew that she was not at liberty to discuss the Prince or her relationship with him. This ambiguity did nothing but confirm that there was definitely something going on. Diana, however, tried to carry on with her life as normally as possible. She still worked at the kindergarten and still shopped at the supermarket.

Diana went to Scotland again the following month, but this time she went to Birkhall to stay with the Queen Mother. Birkhall is actually next door to Balmoral. Soon after this visit, in late October, Prince Charles and Lady Diana arranged to go to Highgrove, which was his new home in Gloucestershire. Apparently Diana visited Highgrove three times during the autumn of 1980 but she supposedly never spent the night. Charles hunted and Diana spent time strolling around the house and the gardens. They often enjoyed having tea together alone. According to the valet, they usually had a very simple dinner—egg dishes were a favorite. In the early evening the Prince would drive Diana back to London.

Charles sought approval for Diana from his mother and from Camilla Parker-Bowles. Clearly he had to make a careful choice of a life partner, but he felt reassured by everyone's approval. It has been said that Diana was a favorite of Queen Elizabeth. This was crucial, because under the Royal Marriages Act of 1772 the Prince was required to get consent for his marriage from the Sovereign. Charles also sought the approval of the Queen Mother, who reportedly arranged occasions for the couple to spend time together.

Many sources agree that it is highly likely that the Queen Mother and Diana's grandmother, the Queen Mother's lady-in-waiting, had a role in the matchmaking of Charles and Diana. Diana's grandmother had always wanted her family to marry well, and the Queen Mother naturally took a major interest in the future of her favorite grandson. It was likely that, over the years, the ladies had spent time discussing the possibilities of future spouses for their grandchildren.

The first major public appearance of Charles and Diana took place at Ludlow, in Shropshire, where Charles was racing his horse, Alibar. Diana reportedly had bet money on him. She watched the race and cheered happily while he rode. During the race, Diana sat with Camilla and Judy Gaselee, the trainer's wife. After the race, the media who were at the event, started to realize that Diana was there, and that her being there was very meaningful. Upon realizing these two facts, chaos broke out among the press as they tried to get a picture of Diana, who apparently hid out in the lavatory for quite a while. Following the race, Charles and Diana left in separate vehicles and headed toward the residence of the Parker-Bowles.

Camilla Parker-Bowles apparently wholeheartedly encouraged Charles's courtship of Diana. Diana and Camilla spent some time together at social occasions, such as after the Ludlow race. On other occasions, Charles and Andrew Parker-Bowles went clubbing and Diana and Camilla stayed home. The following weekend Charles and Diana returned to the Parker-Bowles' residence once again. Camilla had apparently not approved of some of the Prince's former girlfriends, but Diana had her blessing. It was later reported that it was in the cabbage patch of Camilla's garden that Charles first spoke of the possibility of marriage to Diana.

Soon after the race at Ludlow, Charles and Diana were together again publicly at the Ritz Hotel, where they celebrated Princess Margaret's fiftieth birthday. It was now becoming clear that they were indeed a romantic item. During this time, the Prince was involved in his official duties and Diana was working at the Pimlico kindergarten.

Prince Charles's trusted valet became invaluable during the courtship period. Being very much in the public eye was a hazard and something which both Charles and Diana sought to avoid. The pervasiveness of the British press produced a climate that was not conducive to clandestine meetings between public figures; the two had to tread carefully. Organizing their private meetings was no easy feat. Charles's valet was often called upon to pick up Diana at various different locations. In his memoirs, the valet told of his whisking Diana away from the ubiquitous reporters who were on a never-ending vigil, scouting her every move. It took a lot of scheming to pick her up without the reporters noticing. Apparently the Prince would first phone his servant to prepare him for Diana's call. Often she called from her grandmother's or sister's house where she had arrived by taxi, frequently eluding press with this anonymous form of transportation. The valet would then pick her up at one of these different locations, and off they would go to meet Charles.

The valet's descriptions of their escape missions shed a very flattering light on Diana. He described her as being friendly, talkative and having a penchant for sweets. Apparently she often got into the car sporting a bag of toffees or a Yorkie bar which she always offered him. Her generosity also extended toward Charles, and she frequently brought gifts for him. The valet told Diana that Charles's favorite color was blue, and the following week Diana showed up with a blue pullover for him. She seemed to derive a lot of pleasure from bringing the Prince little gifts, and in the valet's opinion she actually helped to spruce up Charles's wardrobe.

Though the courtship period was filled with happy times, it was also the beginning of a very persistent media presence. Diana was clearly a novice in dealing with the frantic photographers. Trying to appease the ravenous journalists on September 18, she agreed to let them photograph her at the Pimlico kindergarten. Apparently she insisted that two of the children be in the photograph as well; perhaps the children made her feel safe and more secure. The children's names were not mentioned in the caption because their parents had not been consulted—the photo was clearly a spontaneous decision on her part. She bargained with the reporters, getting them to agree to leave her alone if she posed for the photo. The pictures that were taken on that day became among the most famous of her. Unfortunately, while the pictures were being taken, the light was behind her and so her skirt became quite transparent on film. A very clear silhouette of her thighs was strikingly noticeable, and it contrasted with the very endearing image of her holding young children. Needless to say the demand for that photograph fueled the ambitions of the merciless photographers who hounded this young and vulnerable potential Princess.

Diana was said to have been very embarrassed by the picture. She is remembered as saying that she did not want to be remembered for not having a petticoat. Charles was reportedly amused. One source reported that Charles said, "I knew your legs were good, but I didn't realize they were that spectacular. But did you have to show them to everybody?" It also presented to the world a picture of Diana that showed her to be skilled and comfortable with children. This would be a strong selling point in considering her as a future Queen and mother of the Heir to the British throne.

At the time, Diana's flat at Coleherne Court literally came under siege. From the first sighting of Diana with Charles, to the engagement five months later, reporters and photographers were present around the clock. Until Diana was officially engaged, she was pretty much on her own in dealing with the press. She was in the papers almost daily and the reporters resorted to using the most minor events to try to make a news story. She was seen stalling her Mini Metro car, and even this made the papers. On November 26 in a *Times* article, Diana allegedly told a journalist, who was living in the same block of flats, that she felt the whole thing was slightly out of control. She was no longer able to go shopping, or to a restaurant, or anywhere at all without being followed and having her photograph taken. Diana clearly objected to the blatant aggression of the reporters who interrogated her anywhere they could— on the street, in her car, even on park benches.

Despite her frustration, Diana managed to maintain a strong sense of poise throughout the harassment, a skill she needed to continue her blossoming relationship with Charles. Though she was inexperienced with the press, she managed throughout their pursuit to prove to be a worthy candidate. By being painstakingly polite at all times, no matter the strain, smiling easily and sometimes even remembering a name, Diana succeeded in winning over the press, and they generally cast her in a favorable light. She went out of her way to try to deal with them in a friendly way, and she would often crack jokes. The press could not help but be enamored by her charm. The persona that they created was a sure sell to the general public. She was the proof that living fairy tales existed; little girls everywhere saw that a girl could indeed meet a Prince, fall in love and live happily ever after. There were so many pictures taken of Diana that her face was very familiar. Women all over England tried to emulate the way she looked, and there was an extreme fascination with her glamour. All over England hair salons had pictures of her charmingly feathered famous blond hair and a wave of Diana hairdos swept the nation.

The media also hyped the angle that Diana was an ordinary woman, one who shopped the sales, took the public transportation system and even did her own laundry. These elements were probably true, but the media exaggerated this as an example of just how much she was just like the girl-next-door. The truth was that while she was the girl-next-door, her neighborhood was exceptionally posh. Still the down-to-earth image that the press focused on was not pure fabrication; Diana did try to lead as regular a lifestyle as her background permitted. Ironically, the image presented by the press that so endeared her to all also led to her being more hounded than ever, and eventually it stopped her from living an ordinary life. Normalcy was soon to be a thing of the past.

The strain on Diana was immense and many wondered how much this nineteen year old could handle, particularly when the *Sunday Mirror* article was published. The article reported that on the nights of November 5 and 6, Diana had crept aboard the Royal train to be with Prince Charles, and they had enjoyed some time together while the train was stopped. According to the article, after driving down from London, Diana had been allowed past the police checkpoint and escorted aboard the train. Apparently, she spent some time with Charles on the train and then slipped away and drove home. Everybody that was questioned about the validity of the article denied that there was any truth at all in it. The tawdry implications of the article disturbed Diana and her family a great deal. So great was the affront to Diana's mother that she took it upon herself to write a letter to the *Times* criticizing the editors of Fleet Street for their harassment and lies about her daughter. She attacked the editors for abusing the freedom of the press in their merciless pursuit of Diana. According to Diana's mother, fanciful speculation, if done in proper taste, was tolerable, but lies, on the other hand, were inexcusable.

Charles was also very upset with the article. He told his valet that it was rubbish and it put Diana in a very bad light. Apparently he was also angry because the British public owns the Royal train, and Charles has strong convictions about not using public-owned property for his own pleasure.

The article outraged Lady Diana. It was her first major encounter with the pain the press could inflict. Charles was in India when the scandal reached its peak and Diana had to deal with it by herself. She went on record to say that the story was unequivocally false. Diana emphasized that she had never even seen the Royal train, that she had no idea what it even looked like. It was clear that she objected strongly to the innuendo in the article. Diana was also upset because she knew that people often believe what they read.

Even the Queen was seemingly angry about the article. At her request, her private press secretary demanded a retraction from the tabloid. This unprecedented action from Buckingham palace was a huge reinforcement that Diana must indeed be the chosen one. The Palace's obvious efforts to preserve Diana's reputation, and the strength of their denial fueled the belief that an engagement was on the way. The press had been fooled earlier when Buckingham Palace had vehemently denied an imminent engagement between Mark Phillips and Princess Anne—two weeks later their engagement was official.

The press's reaction to the criticism of the *Sunday Mirror* was mixed. The editor of the *Mirror* refused to retract the article. Other newspapers took on a more self-righteous attitude, saying that the *Mirror* had given journalists a bad name and that that kind of reporting brought disrepute to the whole industry. One editor is remembered as saying that maybe they should leave the sweet nineteen year old alone until more significant events actually took place. John Witherow, in the *Times* on Wednesday, November 26, stated that though there was sympathy among members of the media for Diana, the general feeling was that because she was now a public figure she should expect copious amounts of attention. As a result of all the fuss made over the notorious article, sixty Members of Parliament tabled a motion in the House of Commons that strongly criticized the press's treatment of Lady Diana. They also objected to the invasion of her privacy by the media. Some of the Fleet Street editors reportedly met with the senior members of the Press Council to review the matter. Unfortunately, these events had little if any impact on the actions of the press, and the harassment of Diana continued as ferociously as ever.

Though the Royal Family was used to being in the public eye, no member had ever endured the extent of media attention that Diana had; it was unprecedented. It was no wonder, then, that she became quite frightened at times and was reduced to tears on a few occasions. To go from being relatively anonymous, to being someone whom the whole world was interested in was bound to be a very trying transition, but Diana managed to keep herself together smashingly well.

Perhaps the most interesting thing that surfaced out of the whole Royal train incident is the blatant, and age-old, double standard that exists for men and women. It was generally perceived to be okay if Charles had a past history of being a philanderer. He was a self-confessed romantic who had admitted to falling in love regularly. The Royal Family's massive outrage at the sullying of Diana's reputation clearly showed the expectation that Diana be virginal, or at least seem to be. This shows that the courtship had to include the very important dynamic of public relations. It was essential that the public perceive Diana as impeccable—she could be the future Queen after all. Nobody required that a future King be a virgin, but it was imperative that a future Queen have a spotless past.

Though Diana could not stop the press from printing falsehoods about her, she did learn various tricks to elude the press along the way. On one occasion Diana even resorted to escaping via the fire exit of a department store. This meant climbing over dustbins to avoid photographers. In December of 1980, Diana apparently packed up her car, parked outside her home, with an overnight bag and a pair of Wellington boots. It appeared as if she were planning a trip. Then she locked up her car and headed to the nearby shops. The press took her bait and lost her trail, waiting for her departure and assuming she would be driving to her destination. Diana was on her way to Scotland before the reporters realized they had been duped. She was going to spend a weekend with Charles at Birkhall.

Apart from the occasional clandestine trips to Scotland, Diana would also see Charles at polo matches and other social activities where they were both under heavy public scrutiny.

Though the rumors persisted, still no engagement announcement came forth. There was a lot of pressure on the Prince to choose a marriage partner before he ran out of suitable candidates. Apparently the royal staff was curious as to what the Prince was waiting for. Their perception of Diana was that she was beautiful, had an impeccable reputation, a charming disposition and no known previous lovers—surely she was his perfect match.

In an article in the *Guardian* on November 29, 1980, Diana answered speculative questions with vague answers. When asked if she would be a married woman by the same time next year, she replied, "Who knows?"

Her deliberate ambiguousness did nothing to subdue the reporters' marriage fever. She was also quoted as saying, "I'd like to marry soon. What woman doesn't want to marry eventually? I don't think 19 is too young—it depends on the person." This was taken to be a strong indication that a marriage proposal was, or would be, on the way. Both Charles and Diana seemed ready for the decision to marry.

November 14 marked Charles's thirty-second birthday. A small family gathering took place in Norfolk at Wood Farm. The Queen,

Prince Philip, Prince Charles and Lady Diana were all there. The press anticipated that this would be a pivotal event. According to Prince Charles's valet, the family had originally planned a four-day weekend but their plans were thwarted by the hordes of reporters who were staked out. There was no possibility of privacy, no possibility of even going for a walk. Supposedly the Duke of Edinburgh was furious because the hunting had to be curtailed. It was thus decided that Lady Diana should go back to London earlier than planned. The valet described his role as that of a decoy. While Charles's valet drove down the drive and into the fields, Charles and Diana left in another vehicle. The decoy plan worked and Diana was not spotted again until she arrived back at her flat in London. The valet described the Princess as being visibly depressed by the unfortunate turn of events; the end of the weekend had been spoiled.

The press had anticipated that there would be an engagement announcement on his birthday, but this was not to be the case, perhaps because of the media's obnoxious intrusion on the family's weekend. In the *Guardian* on November 15, 1980, Paul Keel wrote that the court circular that issued from Buckingham Palace came as a huge disappointment because it did not contain any engagement announcement. The day before the *Daily Express* had proclaimed Diana to be "Fit For a Queen." The media did not know quite what to think about the lack of the announcement, yet nobody could deny that indeed a romance was going on.

It was widely thought that Diana was a romantic. Her step-grandmother, Barbara Cartland, is a world-renowned romance novelist and Diana had read a great deal of her stories. Charles and Diana's relationship has even been compared to the fairy-tale-like romances of Dame Cartland's novels. One can imagine that Lady Diana was the perfect Cartland heroine: beautiful, pure and shy yet confident. Wealthy, worldly and handsome, Prince Charles met the criteria for a Cartland romance hero. The most notable difference between Charles and Diana's romantic relationship and the couples in Cartland's books is that her fictional characters do not have to undergo the unbearable scrutiny of the media and, by extension, the general public. Since Charles's birth, there had been speculation about who would be his Queen.

Christmas of 1980 was uneventful for the gossipmongers. Lady Diana and Prince Charles spent the holiday season with their respective families: Diana at Althorp, Charles at Windsor and Sandringham. It was at this point that the Royal Family themselves was subjected to the same kind of treatment from the press that Diana had endured all fall. The Queen even reportedly told some reporters to go away in a most unregal manner. Someone apparently even fired a shotgun over a photographer's head from twenty yards away. It was then that Charles uttered his famous quote, "I should like to take this opportunity to wish you all a very happy New Year and your editors a particularly nasty one."

It was not until January that the reporters picked up the trail once again. The Royal Family was in Sandringham, and Lady Diana was their weekend guest. The easy access to the Sandringham estate meant that once again the Royals were inundated with media attention. Diana's movements were thus heavily restricted. During this visit she met more of the staff while waiting inside for the Prince to come back from hunting. The valet stated in his book that the Prince expressed feelings of frustration over the stifling and restrictive effect the press was having on his personal life. Moreover, the Prince apparently felt terribly bad for everyone else in the house whose holidays were also ruined by the press's obsession with his romance. He decided that he and Lady Diana could no longer rendezvous at Sandringham. Instead they would go to Highgrove, even though it was still under renovation. This was a clear indication that the pressure was becoming unbearable. The couple would now rather go to a construction site than be subjected to the pushy press.

In order to have some privacy at Highgrove, the Prince created a decoy. He organized a hunting party in Leicester. Then he ensured that there would be a back route to the house. He left the party and met Diana at Highgrove. The plan worked. The construction crew was not there and they spent some time alone—in a mess but out of the spotlight. This hiatus lasted until the following dawn. Diana had gone to the Berkshire Downs to watch Charles exercise his horse, but Whitaker was once again on her trail. Clearly the fact that such trouble was being taken in order to keep seeing each other was proof that they had a strong affection for each other. Otherwise they surely would not even have attempted to try to withstand the immense pressure being put on them. The difficulty of having a courtship under the scrutiny of the media and the world must have been overwhelming. To be interrogated at every opportunity about your intentions is bound to set up an unnatural element to the normal evolution of a relationship. For the time being, Charles and Diana had passed the test and survived the pressure of being under an ever-present microscope. Some sources suggest that in fact what Diana had had to undergo was just that—a test. The reasoning goes that because the

Palace only stepped in after the Royal train incident, and that, for the most part, they deliberately left Diana to deal with the press on her own they were testing her to see how well she would handle the pressure. Did Diana have the strength of character to withstand the glare of the ever-present flash bulbs? The answer was yes.

According to all accounts, Diana was clearly in love with Charles. She was readily available whenever he called, and, she always accommodated his plans. In the opinion of Charles's valet, Diana visibly adored being with the Prince. In January of 1981, the Prince supposedly wrote a memo to his office that they should brief Diana of his whereabouts at all times. This was apparently an unprecedented move on the Prince's part. Harry Herbert has been quoted as saying that Diana was very definitely head over heels in love. Herbert goes on to explain why Diana was an ideal match. Before Charles, she had apparently never dated but rather went out with friends in groups. Herbert's father managed the Queen's stables and so Harry used to spend time with Diana and her friends when they were teenagers. According to Herbert, Prince Charles was the first man that Diana really dated.

Some sources suggest that Diana had had no previous romantic relationships because she had set her sights on the Prince of Wales from the age of sixteen. According to Penny Junor, Diana watched from the sidelines as glamorous and tempestuous women came and went. Her patience clearly paid off, and by the time she was old enough the pressure on Charles to marry was at a peak. He started to pay new attention to his friend Diana. From this perspective their relationship seems to have evolved very naturally and positively—they grew into their romance. The other dynamic in their relationship was that while the Prince had had numerous relationships and had supposedly fallen in love a few times, Diana had no experience and so her affection for Charles was full of the intensity of a first love and characterized by a schoolgirl passion. She was, after all, only nineteen. Furthermore, if the notion that she had carried a torch for three years was true, then her feelings must have reached a very profound level.

Diana was quoted as saying that because she was only nineteen and he was thirty-two she had not expected Charles to notice her. At that time he had reportedly found her to be delightful company. Junor states that the Prince thought that Diana was bright and witty and easy to be with. Diana always laughed at his jokes and made him feel good.

In order to leave Highgrove that fateful weekend, the valet and the couple organized what they referred to as the "dawn dash." The valet remembers Diana as being particularly happy that morning. He suspects that the Prince had perhaps proposed to her the previous evening. The official story is that Charles proposed to Diana over a private dinner in Buckingham Palace. But by his valet's estimation, the Highgrove weekend was more probable since they had had little else in the way of private time together. The valet was not sure whether or not she said yes right away, but he is fairly sure the Prince probably told Diana to think about it. Apparently the Prince always advised everybody to "think about it" when faced with an important decision. The official story is that Charles proposed over a bottle of champagne. Diana apparently had no doubts and wanted to say yes immediately. Charles advised her to think about it during her trip to Australia. Diana told the valet, on the morning of the "dawn dash," that she was planning a three-week trip to Australia with her mother. Even though their engagement was not official, apparently Sarah did not need to be told because as soon as she saw Diana's face, she knew. Diana looked jubilant. The uninformed press speculated that this Australia trip was to provide the necessary breathing room for both Charles and Diana to decide, for certain whether or not they would make their relationship permanent.

During this time apart they spoke to each other regularly on the phone. While in Australia, Diana was reportedly inseparable from her mother. According to Junor, once Diana was in Australia, Buckingham Palace began the preparations to the as yet unannounced wedding. There was to be an enormous amount of preparation. Junor goes on to say that Diana had already made up her mind and that she remained unwavering while she was in Australia; she was determined to marry Charles. She had been warned of all the ramifications of being married into royalty and was willing to take on the challenge. The general speculation among the press was that Diana must have said yes to Charles's proposal because she cut her trip short by a week to return home.

Once Diana was home, Charles sent her a lavish bouquet of flowers. He put a royal aide on the case. The aide then managed to get a florist to deliver the flowers. Unfortunately the florist was unable to deliver the flowers at first because there was no response at Diana's doorbell. The florist then contacted the aide, who then decided to call Diana. She was apparently most gracious, and she immediately arranged for the caretaker to open the main door. The surprise was ruined, but the welcome home bouquet was stunning.

Charles also tried to arrange a private weekend together at Highgrove before the announcement was made official. It was to be Diana's last weekend as a private citizen and not a person officially affiliated with the Royals. Before the announcement was made official, Charles broke the news to his valet that Diana had indeed said yes. On the weekend of Diana's return from Australia, Charles had been hunting at Highgrove. When he and the valet returned to Buckingham Palace, Charles rang for the valet to come into his study and then he broke the news. According to the valet, the Prince was in an exceptionally good mood. When he teasingly asked the Prince whether or not he had proposed on both knees, the Prince laughed and said, "neither."

Soon after, the couple drove to Nick Gaselee's stables in the countryside. The Prince had his heart set on riding his favorite horse, Alibar. Charles rode a quick seven miles and then went back to join Diana. On his way, he realized that something was amiss. Moments after Charles dismounted, the horse rolled over and died from a heart attack. Diana was reportedly in tears and she tried to comfort the stoic, but deeply disturbed Charles. The Prince had to go off to a commitment in the West Country, but before going he urged the staff to look after Diana while he was away.

Lady Diana had dinner with the Queen on that Sunday night and it was then that she chose the ring. Diana told Charles's valet that there was a whole tray of rings from the royal jewelers and that the Queen's eyes had popped when Diana chose the largest one. The ring had a sapphire in the middle surrounded by diamonds. Diana fell in love with it. What Diana didn't know was the furor that surrounded the purchase of the ring. As it turned out, upon approval of the ring, the Queen learned that the ring was not specially designed, as she had expected, but rather it was an ordinary ring from Garrard, the crown jewelers, and was available to anyone with £24 000. Garrard's jeweler, a Mr. Summers, was apparently called to the Palace and reprimanded by Prince Charles's private secretary, Edward Adeane. It was apparent that he was venting anger on behalf of the Queen. She would have preferred to give Diana one of her antique rings, but by that time it was too late; Diana needed a ring to show at the official announcement and the one she had, the one she wanted and loved, was the one she showed the world. Diana was never told of the jeweler's faux pas.

The following day, February 23, the eve of the engagement, she went to the palace with her sister, Jane. This was the night of the pre-engagement party and Lord and Lady Spencer had been invited. It was a fairly subdued affair and everybody left relatively early. The next day, however, was much more exciting. February 24 marked the official announcement of the engagement and the atmosphere at the palace was electric. The news was spreading fast among the staff members. Cases of champagne were already chilling. The staff was all called to a meeting in the morning where the Prince introduced Diana as his future wife.

When Diana was older, she said during a BBC interview that at nineteen years old "You think you are mature enough to handle anything," but in retrospect it was a very daunting future that she faced. However, Diana also explained during the interview that when someone comes from a broken home like she had, "You try even harder to make it work." Most importantly, Diana said she desperately loved Charles. Hers was a love that had to survive a lot of strain in the years to come.

Chapter 5

Wedding of the Century

"It is with greatest pleasure that Her Majesty, the Queen, and the Duke of Edinburgh, announce the betrothal of their beloved son, the Prince of Wales, to Lady Diana, daughter of the Earl Spencer and the Honorable Mrs. Shand Kydd."

The official announcement of the upcoming wedding was made at 11:00 a.m. on the morning of February 24, amid some degree of pomp and circumstance. It came from the Lord Chamberlain, Lord Maclean, at a routine investiture at Buckingham Palace.

That afternoon, the Prince and Lady Diana went for lunch with the Queen. By that point in the day, flowers had started arriving from all over the world. There were so many flowers it was difficult to know where to put them all. Telegrams also arrived en masse. Outside, Lady Diana and Charles spent the afternoon posing for photographers and finally satiating the inquisitive reporters. Diana appeared radiant as she showed off her gorgeous engagement ring. She smiled as they snapped photograph after photograph, her bashful air as enchanting as usual. Diana's life had changed dramatically overnight. Normally she would leave and have to deal with the hordes of photographers by herself, but now that the announcement was official, she was to be escorted by two plainclothes policemen. From now on she could expect more protection.

Later on that same day, Charles was quoted as saying, "I feel positively delighted and frankly amazed that Diana is prepared to take me on." When asked how she felt to be engaged, Diana replied that she was "blissfully happy, absolutely delighted and thrilled."

Outside the Palace, the Band of the Codstream Guards played the tune "Congratulations." In Highgrove, where the couple would establish their home, there was a red carpet placed in the only existing telephone box.

Perhaps one of the only misgivings anyone might have had about the relationship was the age difference. A twelve-year age difference could be a substantial one. When asked how he felt about the difference, the Prince reportedly said, "You are as old as you think you are—and Diana will help keep me young." He also joked about her exhausting him. As for Diana's opinion on the subject, she thought that age depends on the individual, and she had certainly proved herself to be mature.

News of the announcement brought "great pleasure" to the nation, in the words of Prime Minister Margaret Thatcher. The press was overjoyed, as were the masses of Britons, and those around the world, who would soon be caught up in Royal wedding fever. The people of the world greeted the news with great joy. Many, especially those in Great Britain, were happy to see the Prince finally find a bride, relieved at the fact she was English and obviously possessing a dignity and beauty befitting a prince's bride. They saw her as a perfect foil for Charles: he was an extrovert, she was shy; he was formal, dignified; she was fun-loving and warm. From day one, everyone made preparations for the wedding, from the Queen down to the vendors on the streets.

The upcoming event, and the couple themselves, created an actual industry with all of the merchandise and memorabilia that became available. The wedding provided ample opportunity for manufacturers of everything from pencils to china to display the images of Charles and Diana on some or other piece of their merchandise. The Royal mint manufactured a special crown-sized coin with profiles of the couple. Vendors in the streets sold everything imaginable from their carts: tea towels, flags, hats, photos, vases, mugs, innumerable books, pamphlets and souvenir guides, spoons, plates, postcards. If their image could be put on something, it was. More formally, more than seventy countries, including a number of the Commonwealth countries, issued stamps with varying shots of the couple. Whether they were in dress uniforms or t-shirts, the smiling couple was prominently displayed.

Another large market for Royal Wedding keepsakes was china. Aynsley China Ltd. quickly responded to the engagement by producing a number of limited edition sets and pieces, among them a wedding chalice featuring Caernarvon Castle and wall plaques featuring St. Paul's Cathedral, the site of the spectacular event. Other companies, such as the Royal Worcester Porcelain Company, were also proud of the pieces they produced, including commemorative cups and plates.

But not all of the merchandise met the royal standard of "good taste." T-shirts featuring the royal insignia and even matching bra and panty sets emblazoned with the same somehow made their way to the shops. It was estimated that somewhere in the neighborhood of ninety percent of the items submitted for approval to the Design Center's committee were turned away.

Brewers even got in on the game. Champagene, wine and beer— one named "Dianamite"—appeared on the streets and in the shops around the country.

Soon after the announcement, the Royal PR machine was put in top gear. The much-coveted invitations were sent out to friends, family, politicians and dignitaries around the world.

Holding the wedding at St. Paul's Cathedral came as a surprise to many in royal circles. It represented a real break with tradition, as all other Royal weddings had been held at Westminster Abbey. While many speculated as to the real reason behind the decision, it came to be thought that the rationale behind it was the fact that the Cathedral had the larger seating capacity.

Immediately after the announcement, Diana moved into Clarence House, the residence of the Queen Mother. Diana would there be protected from the media as well as be advised on behavior, dress and protocol. This was only the beginning of her new life, and she was to be prepared for it in traditional style. And she was prepared, if only briefly and in a superficial sense.

On her first night in Clarence House, Diana was shown to her room. On her bed was a note, from Camilla Parker-Bowles, inviting her to lunch. Apparently, Camilla had some questions concerning Charles and Diana's plans to move to Highgrove. Diana had little idea at the time why Camilla would show such interest.

Within two days Diana was moved into Buckingham Palace. To be moved into the Queen's residence, Diana had to be invited. It was not only surprising that the Queen gave her blessing, but it was also somewhat surprising that her room was not only on the same floor as Charles, but in a room (bedroom, sitting room and bathroom, to be precise) between his and Princess Anne's apartments. Diana was now very close, indeed, to her charming Prince.

It is still amazing that the media never discovered the whereabouts of the future Princess of Wales. To the best of anyone's knowledge—aside from a few members of the staff and family—Diana was at Clarence House. But after being secreted away to the Palace, she was able to prepare for her new duties, as well as make the occasional visit to her mother, who lived nearby. Diana was set up very comfortably and was able to spend time with Charles when he was not attending to his official duties. She spent much time reading and watching *Coronation Street*, a favorite soap opera of the Queen, and Diana often explored the palace and grounds.

Charles and Diana's first official function as an engaged couple was to attend a gala recital at the Goldsmiths' Hall in London in support of the Royal Opera House Development Appeal. The evening of music and poetry was a special one, and Princess Grace of Monaco appeared, along with other stars.

Diana was dressed in a stunning off the shoulder black taffeta dress designed by David and Elizabeth Emanuel. Some thought the dress shocking for a future member of the Royal Family, especially Charles, who reportedly had a "discussion" with Diana about it later. An adoring crowd that gathered in the pouring London rain greeted her. She received a single pink rose, which she put in Prince Charles's buttonhole. This was the first of many floral gifts she would receive throughout her public life.

The cheering crowds that waited patiently in the rain for Diana's return were not disappointed. As the couple left, they smiled and waved once again to their fans.

The following day, it was announced that Diana had chosen David and Elizabeth Emanuel to design her wedding gown.

Diana was being immersed in the public life with which she was to become all too familiar. She attended banquets given by the Queen the week following the recital and then spent a week at Balmoral, where she and Charles took walks about the estate.

Everything about Diana made news. As the first Princess of Wales in over sixty years, and only the ninth ever, her popularity was unmatched. At every function she attended, whether it was the races at Ascot with Charles or at other functions with an escort, crowds of cheering and adoring fans lined up to see her. Near the end of March, Charles and Diana flew in a helicopter piloted by Charles to Cheltenham for an official visit. Diana watched as Charles rode his horse, Good Prospect. Upon their departure, crowds of people lined up to greet the Prince and his fiancee. Diana was a stunning hit, and one bold young man, Nicholas Hardy, offered Diana a daffodil and asked if he could kiss the hand of the future Queen. The photograph of the kiss—and Diana receiving it—was a smashing success.

It was also near the end of March that the Queen held a meeting of the Privy Council at Buckingham Palace. The meeting was held so that the Council could give its official consent to the marriage, as required by the Royal Marriages Act of 1772.

Two days later, Charles embarked on a long-planned five-week tour of New Zealand, Australia, Venezuela and America. Diana's only contact with him would be via telephone and messages, or by watching the inevitable coverage on television.

In the meantime, the Palace released further details of the wedding. Dr. Robert Runcie, the Archbishop of Canterbury, would conduct the ceremony—his first Royal wedding—and the Lesson was to be read by the Speaker of the House of Commons, the Right Hon. George Thomas.

Diana would have five attendants at the ceremony including Lady Sarah Armstrong-Jones, daughter of Princess Margaret, and India Hicks, daughter of David and Lady Pamela Hicks and granddaughter of the late Lord Mountbatten. Also attending would be Sarah Jane Gaselee, the eleven-year-old daughter of Charles's horse trainer; Catherine Cameron, daughter of Donald Cameron of Lochiel and Lady Cecil Cameron; and Clementine Hambro, five-year-old great-granddaughter of Sir Winston Churchill and student at the Young England Kindergarten in Pimlico, where Diana had worked.

Prince Charles, in keeping with royal tradition, would have no best man, but rather his brothers, Andrew and Edward, would stand as supporters. Lord Nicholas Windsor, the eleven-year-old son of the Duke and Duchess of Kent, and Edward van Cutsem, nine-year-old son of Mr. and Mrs. Hugh Cutsem, would be pages.

Diana, meanwhile, prepared by visiting dressmakers and milliners and attending to the many details needing her care. She frequented Harrods and Harvey Nichols with her mother, shopping for trousseau items. It was also at Harrods that Diana bought the blue silk suit she wore in early photographs with Charles.

Near the end of March, Diana, having lived in the palace for a month, wished to meet the staff. She was introduced to everyone in the house so as to be more comfortable in the daunting surroundings. In the meantime Charles began making plans to move the couple to Kensington Palace, or KP, also known as "Coronet Street," a play on the popular soap.

In the coming months many more engagement activities and much more wedding preparation filled Diana's schedule. She was becoming accustomed to her public life and beginning to outgrow her "shy Di" image.

Charles returned from his tour in early May. A much relieved and delighted Lady Diana was waiting for him when he drove to Balmoral from RAF Lossiemouth, where he'd landed. The couple had a brief holiday in the highlands, and Diana learned a bit about fly fishing. They caught up on wedding preparations and other news, including the growing number of letters and presents being received daily. Naturally, the press was never far behind Diana and Charles, and the couple took some time out of their holiday to pose for some photographs.

Shortly thereafter they took a trip to the Broadlands, the Hampshire home of Lord Mountbatten. They were there to open the Mountbatten Exhibition, and Diana, it seemed, was quite at home at the tree-planting ceremony, laughing and joking. For Charles it was a nostalgic visit back to the place where he'd spent much time. The rest of the month was full of public engagements and appearances, and details of the wedding were slowly being worked out under the guidance of the Lord Chamberlain.

Rehearsals began in earnest and the music was chosen for the service. After Diana attended the order of the Garter Service of Thanksgiving at St. George's, Windsor, she and Charles launched Royal Ascot week. They also attended the Queen's official birthday celebrations.

Diana's birthday on July 1 was celebrated quietly with only Charles, a few close friends and her family. The focus of the couple's lives was on the wedding. Shortly thereafter, the first official portrait of the future Princess of Wales was hung in the National Portrait Gallery. Painted by Bryan Organ, it was immediately the center of attention to all who visited the gallery. She was portrayed in a very relaxed style, sitting sideways in a chair in Buckingham Palace. Sadly, the portrait was vandalized, and after its repair it was hung next to one of Prince Charles.

While Diana was becoming used to her role and preparing for the future, she was, to some close to her, also noticeably nervous at times. In the few months prior to the big event she had attacks of nerves on

several occasions. These were understandable, as the realization of the
pressures due to come hit home.

At a polo match shortly before the wedding, Diana was overcome
when photographers began closing in on her. Attention to the future Princess of Wales was high, and as she nervously played with some flowers
she'd received she began to weep. Immediately Charles went to her side
to comfort her and he escorted her through the dense crowd to his car.
Reportedly, she later told her sister Sarah that it was not only the pressure of the upcoming wedding—knowing that millions would be watching—but also that she was trying hard to lose weight. As it turned out,
she had lost almost fifteen pounds in the previous six months.

On the evening of July 23rd, the couple did an interview with the
BBC, which was broadcast the night before the wedding. Angela Rippon
and Andrew Gardner conducted the interview at Buckingham Palace for
the BBC and ITV. Diana was relaxed and happy as she talked of her
gratitude to everyone who'd sent letters and gifts, especially the children who worked so hard on their cards and letters. Charles also thanked
those who had been so kind and supportive and he was open in discussing his feelings about the engagement and marriage. The couple discussed the pressures on them since the wedding announcement, and they
revealed how uncomfortable the media had made them. In written answers to Britain's press, Diana said, "It has taken a bit of getting used to
the cameras. But it is wonderful to see people's enthusiastic reaction. It
is most rewarding and gives me a tremendous boost" (Leonard Downie,
Washington Post Foreign Service, July 29, 1981: B01).

Not long after the interview, the stress of the upcoming ceremony
was becoming a heavy load for Diana to bear. Only two days later, on
July 25th, she left a polo match in tears, upset by the constant attention
from the press and photographers. At a different polo match later that
day, in which Charles was playing, Diana still looked uneasy, spending
as much time as she could out of the main areas and retreating to the
back of the royal enclosure. By this time, everyone suspected that Diana
didn't really like horses or enjoy watching polo. Such was not the case,
of course, but the rumor had been spread to everyone via the press.

Although still clearly distressed at times, Diana was becoming much
more comfortable in her public role. Those close to her noted a sense of
calm about her, and they sensed that she was not nearly so overwhelmed
at parties and other functions. At Prince Andrew's twenty-first birthday
party at Windsor Castle she was in good spirits, joking with the young

Prince. What most people there didn't know was the agony she had endured in just the past few days.

Upon receipt of a package at the office in Buckingham palace that she shared with Michael Colbourne, Charles's assistant in charge of his finances, Diana insisted upon opening the parcel. To her shock it was a bracelet with the initials F and G, which stood for "Fred" and "Gladys," nicknames Charles and Camilla had for each other. Earlier Diana had reportedly been upset when she found out Charles had used those same nicknames when he sent Camilla flowers when she was ill.

July 29, 1981, declared a national holiday, began with the gray light of dawn. When the sun shone, it shone brightly, setting the streets ablaze with color. The whole city had prepared for the day's pageantry. The streets were filled with tens of thousands of people, most of whom had camped out for days ahead of time to get a good spot on the procession route. In fact, by dawn of that morning there was little room for the bystanders to move in the last few hundred yards near the cathedral. By 9:00 a.m. when the first invited guests began to arrive, more than a million people were crammed together on the sidewalks lining the bridal route.

Diana awoke early, not having slept much the night before. She had returned to Clarence House the night before and rose at 6:30 to take a long, relaxing bath. As she prepared for the day ahead, she occasionally peered out from behind the bedroom curtains to gaze with astonishment at the crowds in the streets. It was all for her. Today she was the center of attention for most of the world. She also watched some of the morning television broadcasts as she ate breakfast.

People began to arrive for the final preparations and to help Diana get ready for the day. Her makeup artist and hairdresser arrived and immediately went to work. She was not heavily made-up, as Charles apparently did not like too much makeup and Diana's natural beauty needed only slight enhancement. As she finished, her aides and attendants watched the crowds with her. Diana was happy, and she just wanted to get on with the dressing.

But when she did put on her magnificent dress and saw herself in the full-length mirror, she began to sob uncontrollably. She was suddenly overwhelmed at the prospect of facing the millions of people and she wasn't sure if she could do it. All she wanted was to marry Charles quietly and be his wife. The world and its interest in her was unnerving to the nervous young woman about to become a bride. Diana'sisters comforted her, and she managed to control her emotions and regain her composure.

When Diana was finally dressed, the designers sewed in a traditional final stitch and she nervously made her way downstairs. To all that saw her, she really was a fairy-tale princess brought to life. Inside she was still shaking like a leaf.

Charles had also risen early, awakening well before he was called at 7:00. He, too, listened to radio broadcasts while he got ready, and he ate calmly before getting dressed, contemplating the most grand occasion in all of his life thus far. He dressed in the full dress uniform of a commander of Her Majesty's Royal Navy, wearing a blue sash that designated him as a member of ancient order of the Knights of the Garter. Minutes later he appeared in the Palace's Grand Entrance in front of all the staff members not going to St. Paul's. He thanked them each briefly and made his way to the coach to join his brother Andrew for the trip to the cathedral.

The procession of the Royal Family to St. Paul's was watched enthusiastically by the throngs of Britons lining the Mall, filling Trafalgar Square and the sidewalks along the Strand, down Fleet Street and up Ludgate Hill to the cathedral. To keep order were 2 800 policemen and more than a thousand Servicemen from the Brigade of Guards, The Royal Navy and the RAF. Seven landaus carried the family, and upon arriving at the steps of the cathedral, the Queen and the Duke of Edinburgh waved graciously to the crowd. The last coach to arrive carried Prince Charles and Prince Andrew. Escorted by two admirals they made their way into St. Paul's to take their places and try to relax before the arrival of the bride.

Even before the procession made its way, the guests were arriving.

Crowned heads from all over the world, government officials and celebrities were among those in attendance. Notable among them were Mrs. Nancy Reagan, English entertainer Spike Milligan, members of royal families from Sweden, Norway, Japan and the Netherlands, as well as Mrs. Ghandi and Princess Grace and her son, Prince Albert. Sitting in a seat designed especially to support his large frame was the King of Tonga.

Diana began her journey to St. Paul's from Clarence House. She and her father made their way in a beautiful glass coach originally built in 1919 and purchased by King George V for his coronation. Drawn by a pair of bay horses and escorted by mounted police, the carriage traveled along the procession route to the gasps of the crowd. All strained to catch a glimpse of the veiled bride inside.

For the wedding of the century, Diana wore the dress of the century. From early on the details of the dress were closely guarded. The designers, David and Elizabeth Emanuel, had set up business just four years earlier and became very well known after Bianca Jagger wore one of their designs to her birthday party. Diana was first introduced to them when she picked one of their pink chiffon blouses in which to be photographed for Lord Snowdon.

At first, exact details of the dress were secret. It was to be made of silk and it had to shimmer under the bright lights. It would be full and allow the bride to move freely, as she would have need. When the dress was finally revealed as Diana exited the glass coach, the world was in awe. With the help of chief bridesmaid, Lady Sarah Armstrong-Jones, Diana alighted from the coach. She made her way up the steps, and the train—over 25 feet—spread gloriously out behind her. It covered the entirety of the steps and the lengthy but delicate veil billowed in the breeze as the train cascaded over the steps and down the aisle.

The Emanuels waited inside to make final alterations before the service. Diana's walk down the 650-foot aisle, accompanied by the "Trumpet Voluntary," would take her more than three full minutes. She remained veiled, a tradition dating back to Queen Victoria, previously abandoned in 1973 by Princess Anne.

The awesome dress itself was perfect for her. It combined elements of Tudor, Victorian and Edwardian styles and was nothing short of exquisite. Its ivory silk taffeta crinoline glistened in the sunlight as she entered the cathedral. The lace-trimmed sleeves were ruffled with bows, and ten thousand mother-of-pearl sequins and pearls covered the dress. A small diamond-encrusted horseshoe was sewn in for luck. The V-neck was deep, but ruffles were in place to temper the daring neckline, satisfying those who called for the demure look appropriate for one marrying the future King of England.

The Spencer tiara held her veil in place, and the diamond earrings she wore were her mother's. Lace panels on the dress were of antique Carrick-made lace, presented to Queen Mary by the Royal School of Needlework. Diana's shoes were ivory silk with fluted heels, pointed toes and a heart-shaped decoration at the front. The soles were made of a special suede to prevent her from slipping.

Diana's bouquet was made by Longmans and consisted of Mountbatten roses, lily-of-the-valley, stephanotis, white freesias, white orchids and trailing ivy leaves. Following tradition, the bouquet also included myrtle and veronica from bushes grown from cuttings of Queen Victoria's wedding bouquet. In keeping with another tradition, after the ceremony the bouquet was laid on the Tomb of the Unknown Warrior in Westminster Abbey. The Queen Mother began this tradition after her wedding in 1923.

The bridesmaids wore dresses styled to echo but not imitate that of Diana's. Hemlines varied, but they were similar in color and general appearance. They wore headdresses or crowns of fresh flowers, and the younger children carried baskets of meadow flowers while the older one held bunches of posies. To add the finishing touch were the pages dressed in naval cadet uniforms from 1863.

Every head in the cathedral turned when they saw the stunningly beautiful bride. As Diana reached the front of the cathedral, where her bridegroom waited anxiously, Charles gave her a reassuring smile. The congregation sang the opening hymn and then silence overtook as the ceremony began in earnest.

"Here is the stuff of which fairy-tales are made," announced Archbishop Runcie. He then pointed out that those who live happily ever after must first try to create a better world than this one. This expectation was particularly true of "this marriage in which were placed so many hopes."

The couple was naturally and understandably nervous. The world was watching: an expected 750 million viewers worldwide, many up at all hours of the day and night to witness this historic event. Their vows were barely audible, and each made their own faux pas: Charles forgot the mention of "worldly" goods, while Diana transposed Charles's first two Christian names, thus marrying Philip Charles Arthur George rather than Charles Philip Arthur George. Charles was later heard to comment that Diana had married his father. Nonetheless, the vows, transmitted to the crowd outside, were greeted with approving cheers. The couple was then blessed.

The ring, made from the same piece of 22-carat Welsh gold as those of the Queen and Queen Mother, apparently a concern for Prince Andrew since he was put in charge of it, was safely placed on the bride's finger. The couple then listened to the Lesson, a composed anthem and the address by the Archbishop, before moving to the altar for prayer.

All joined in the last hymn, and after the couple was once again blessed, the National Anthem was played. Archbishop Runcie then led the Prince and Princess, followed by the chief bridesmaid, through the sanctuary.

After the Queen and Prince Philip, along with other members of the families, signed the register, they resumed their seats and the State Trumpeters heralded the return of the bride and groom. It was exciting and wonderful for everyone to see at last Diana's radiant face as her veil was lifted.

After bowing to his mother, Charles led Diana down the aisle and to the doors to the sound of Elgar's "Pomp and Circumstance."

It was an unforgettable ceremony, and as the couple made their way down the red carpet to the landau, the cheers from the massive crowd were deafening. Their vehicle was specially decorated with a gold horseshoe on the back.

The church bells sounded as the new Prince and Princess of Wales slowly made their way through the streets of London. The Earl Spencer escorted the Queen to her carriage, while the Duke of Edinburgh accompanied Mrs. Shand Kydd to her vehicle. All eyes were invariably set on the newly married couple, who waved and smiled at the adoring masses.

After the parties reached the relative peace of Buckingham Palace, chants came from the crowd: "We want the Prince and Princess" and "We want Charles and Diana." The cheers became louder and louder, until the couple emerged through glass doors and out onto the balcony. Family members joined them, and at last the couple gave their public what it wanted. Charles gallantly kissed Diana's hand, and then came, for the first time, an unforgettable moment recorded by all the media: the kiss, the kiss for all the world to see. They waved and smiled and at last, to the chagrin of the public, retreated to the comfort of the palace.

Once back comfortably at the palace, the couple were able to entertain the 120 relatives, friends and guests at the wedding breakfast held in the Ball Supper Room.

The wedding cake was a grand five tiers. The Senior Service of the Royal Navy was chosen to make it, breaking with still more traditions. Chief Petty Officer David Avery RN oversaw the design and preparation. The cake was designed at the Naval Technical Drawing Department and made at the Royal Naval Cookery School HMS Pembroke at Chatham. This was a true honor, as the base was being threatened with closure at the time.

The cake was made in March in order to give the flavor time to improve. Four weeks were allowed for icing it, and great care was taken.

Raisins were hand picked, eggs were broken one at a time, and, though the recipe was kept secret, it is thought that traditional Navy rum was among the ingredients.

The five tiers were decorated with pastel-tinted plaques depicting places linked to the couple, and it was safely delivered to the palace in time. Charles cut the cake with his ceremonial sword, and the party toasted the day and relaxed with each other.

Word got out about four o'clock that the couple was about to embark on their honeymoon. The crowd outside the palace waited eagerly for the couple to appear once again, and when they did cheers of delight echoed through the streets. Their coach, complete with a "Just Married" sign prominently displayed on the back, made its way through the streets to Waterloo Station. There a red carpet was laid out for the royal couple's boarding of a three-carriage train that would take them to the first part of their honeymoon at Broadlands. The quick eighty-mile trip went smoothly, and the couple received a flag-waving, excited welcome at the station in Romsey. From there they took a royal car to the estate in Broadlands, but the trip was longer than usual because of the crowd of sightseers and well-wishers. They remained at the six-thousand-acre estate in seclusion for a couple of days, after which they left, once again to the cries of the crowd, for Gibraltar. It is reported, unfortunately that aboard the yacht, photos of Camilla fell out of Charles's diary, tainting the honeymoon for the new bride.

The people of the colony warmly greeted the Prince and Princess, and thousands of flags and onlookers lined the streets. It was only a short jaunt to the dock where the royal yacht *Britannia* waited. After a visit to the Rock of Gibraltar, the yacht set sail for the sunny Mediterranean. The final destination and the route were a closely-guarded secret, but many speculated that the couple picnicked on the African coast and spent time on the Greek islands. Once again an unfortunate incident is reported. Apparently the gold cufflinks Charles wore were in the shape of two C's.

When the yacht docked at Port Said, Anwar Sadat, the President of Egypt, greeted them. The suntanned couple, the Prince smiling and the Princess in a soft pink dress, chatted with the President and his wife after Charles inspected a Guard of Honor.

The next day, Charles and Diana sailed through the Suez Canal and docked on the Red Sea coast to swim before flying back to Scotland. After the scorching heat of Egypt, Scotland was a cold change.

Diana wore a long cashmere coat as she got off the plane at Lossiemouth. After a few weeks of rest and relaxation at Balmoral, it was back to official duties.

But there was also much post-wedding work to be done. The wedding presents, many of which began arriving upon announcement of the engagement, included personal gifts and letters from children, jewelry, sporting gifts and practical gifts. Larger items were also given to the couple, such as a mahogany table and fourteen chairs from the Lord Mayor, Aldermen and Commons of the City of London, and three pianos. As well, they received maps, books, musical instruments and toys and gifts hand-made by donors. In Spite of a few unfortunate incidents, the wedding had been beautiful and the honeymoon a success. The couple, suntanned, cheerful and relaxed, was ready to begin their new life together.

Chapter 6

Wife, Mother, and Superstar

As Britain and its people prepared for another wet and dreary winter, a beacon of light and joy was introduced to cheer their spirits. Diana, sitting beside her new groom and looking radiant in white chiffon with a satin bodice, made her Parliamentary debut on November 5, 1981. Even at this early time in her public life, the press and public alike keenly noted Diana's presence. The excitement of the opening of Parliament, graced with the presence of a shimmering new princess, was nothing compared to the thrill felt when Buckingham Palace announced what Britain, and the world, had been hoping to hear: Princess Diana was expecting her first child.

Diana's public life was already well under way. In October, as her first official tour, she spent three days visiting Wales. Considering that she had been named princess of that particular realm of the kingdom, this seemed a most fitting choice for her initial public function.

Diana was well-received in Wales, in fact the public's infatuation with her was, if anything, growing with every public appearance. For the most part of this tour, Charles was ignored, and when the crowd called for Diana, he joked, "I'm sorry, I've only got one wife and she's over there on the other side of the street. You'll have to make do with me instead" (Wade, 1987, 60). For a proud Prince this must have been a bitter pill, and it was only to become more bitter and difficult as the public grew more and more to love the lovely and loving Diana.

Although the public received the news of the Princess's pregnancy with joy, some criticism was leveled against her for becoming pregnant so soon in her marriage. Some killjoys thought that this might set a poor example for young women in the country who would, without having time to settle into married life, take on the role of motherhood in haste. This view was not widespread, and it certainly did not pertain to Diana, for she was more than ready and eager for her own children. To add to the state of anticipation, there was speculation that Diana was expecting twins, since there is a history of twins in her family. How would the heir to the throne be decided if the Princess has twins, people wondered. The public was informed that twins pose no problem to deciding the heir to the throne: the first-born child is the heir, unless the first-born is a female and the second a male. Neighbors stood in doorways, gossiping and wondering about the baby, or babies, the Princess was carrying, and what names the Prince and Princess were considering.

Pregnancy was not a simple state for Diana. She felt very ill in the early part of her pregnancy, and she canceled a number of engagements, including a visit to Bristol, because of morning sickness. In fact, for the whole of November she felt quite ill and an earlier visit to Dartmoor also had to be postponed. With her numerous social engagements awaiting her, expecting a baby was a difficult condition, and the changes in her body, like the changes in her life, were unsettling and challenging. Her happiness at expecting a child was undiminished, but she felt unhappiness at the loss of her figure and the sickness she endured in the pregnancy.

Diana's adjustments to her royal duties, the physical changes she was undergoing and the stresses every newly married person experiences, were bringing great pressure to bear on her. She was still young, only twenty years old, and her life had changed radically in the past year. Diana needed support and love, but her husband, coming from a different background and having the experience of years, had difficulty understanding and meeting her emotional needs. Wanting support and company in the midst of this difficult time, Diana felt, at times, abandoned by Charles.

One day, six months into their marriage, as Charles was leaving to join the Queen's shooting party in a picnic lunch, Diana raged at him as he drove away. She wanted, needed, Charles with her as she struggled to adjust to her new life, her new body, her new partner. But Charles was forever going off, especially at the beck-and-call of his mother the Queen.

So, too, on this day, as Diana shouted to him through a window, then followed him in her car and stopped him on the side of the road, she was denied the comfort of her husband's love and presence. Although Diana was not entirely unhappy at this time in her marriage, and she felt great hope for the future of her union with Charles, the royal marriage was not turning out to be the fairy tale of which Diana had dreamed.

Towards the end of February, Diana was granted a rest from her royal duties and all the stresses pressing on her, and she and Charles went for a well-deserved holiday in the Bahamas. Here was a chance to be alone with her husband, away from duty and royal protocol. Diana loved the sun, and an escape from wet and overcast England in the midst of winter made her even more grateful for clear blue skies and warm, golden light. The idea of spending time with her husband, away from the scrutiny of the public, delighting in the new life within her and gaining a healthy glow, was akin to paradise to Diana.

Unfortunately, this idyll for the still newlywed couple was not to be. Diana held a fascination for the public, and their desire to know more about her motivated photographers to follow and find the royal couple on their holiday and to take covert photographs with powerful telephoto lenses. Pictures of the six-month pregnant, bikini-clad Princess appeared in print, and the sight of these pictures in international papers infuriated both the Queen and the public. Diana felt her privacy had been terribly invaded.

In the same month, February, Buckingham Palace reported that Diana had fallen down some stairs at Sandringham House a month earlier. After the slight fall, Diana went and lay down, all her thoughts for the safety of the baby. Now Charles comforted her. This was a concrete problem, one that he could clearly recognize and to which he could respond. He held her; he reassured her. Diana took comfort and strength in his presence and his loving concern. The Prince summoned doctors, and reassurances were given to the worried Princess that all was well with her baby. The public waited with bated breath for a healthy child and a safe delivery.

As Diana's health improved and she felt more confident in herself and her new condition, so, too, did her engagement calendar again begin to fill. She made a visit to Newcastle upon Tyne, and while there her natural interest and affinity for children helped to avert disaster. Amidst a great crush of people, Diana saw in the milling crowd a young boy about to be crushed against a barrier. Rushing to the rescue, Diana and

Charles helped the young lad to safety. Diana's love for children gave her a sensitivity to them that never diminished, no matter how busy her schedule, no matter how difficult her own life.

It was natural, then, considering Diana's great love for children, and her anticipation of motherhood, that the choosing of a nanny would be a grave decision. Together, Diana and Charles carefully selected a woman of experience. Miss Barbara Barnes, a 39-year-old nanny with experience minding children in France and Switzerland as well as, for the previous fourteen years, in England. She was not a graduate of any sort of nanny school, but had acquired her knowledge of children simply by being with them and working with them. Diana, her own nanny experience not too far behind her, could appreciate this down-to-earth approach to children. Perhaps even more importantly, Miss Barnes was not at all intimidated by Diana's very obvious desire to be an active and involved mother. She actually seemed to welcome the idea, noting that the nanny was not a replacement for the actual mother. Diana had no intention of letting anyone replace her in her child's heart, and, as the world would eventually see, no one ever could.

Now that the nanny had been found, all that the couple required was one small prince or princess to make the royal couple a Royal Family. At 5:00 a.m. on June 21, 1982, Diana entered the Lindo wing of St. Mary's Hospital in London. This part of the hospital was built in 1939 and opened by the Queen Mother. The wing is a bit gloomy on the inside, with drab colors and dark wood. It overlooks a seamier side of London, yet it is excellently equipped, with the most up-to-date medical technology available in the case of an emergency. A plaque of the Madonna and child ornaments the hall.

Several physicians, led by Mr. George Pinker, who had attended at seven previous royal deliveries and was the Surgeon-Gynecologist to the Queen, attended Diana. Under these capable hands, and after a 16 hour confinement, with her husband at her side, a baby boy was born to the Prince and Princess of Wales at 9:03 p.m. The health of the baby confirmed Mr. Pinker in his belief that nature should not be tampered with, though Diana's labor was longer than is considered ideal. The newborn prince weighed 7 lb., 1 1/2 oz. and he gave a hearty cry upon his entrance to the world. Diana's baby boy had fair to blond hair, and his father, and the world, was very pleased to note that he looked very much like beautiful Diana.

Diana had known the child she was carrying was a boy, and she was enormously relieved about it. The child born had more British blood than any heir to the crown since King James I. Coming from a very English upbringing, she very much felt her duty both to her husband and his family, and to the public itself, to produce a prince for England. An heir to the throne was desired, and she felt the burden of delivering one. In fact, before marrying Prince Charles, Diana had to be examined by a gynecologist to ensure her fitness for childbearing. Although Diana resented this physical exam, she accepted it as part of her role as princess and future queen. There must have been some relief on Diana's part as well, for she knew she desperately wanted children and she was now reassured she could have them. As far as the birth of the baby was concerned, Diana felt honored to be a part of such an important and desired event, as well as excited at the idea of motherhood. And she felt the love and support of the British people. Later she was to reveal that she felt the whole of the nation laboring with her as she bowed her fair head to her heavy task.

Charles and Diana were both thrilled with their small son. The issue they still had to resolve, however, was what to name this pink-eared cherub they held so carefully in their arms. Diana favored names like Rupert and Oliver, while Charles was more inclined to steadier names like George (Wade, 1987, 85). Finally they reached a compromise, and their young son received the noble appellation William Arthur Philip Louis. He was to be known as Prince William of Wales, or, as his father affectionately dubbed him, the Wombat, and officially his name was not to be shortened in any way.

Diana now entered a very difficult period in her life. Thrust into the public limelight, married to a prince, changed residences, and taken up her public duties, this shy young woman was now also a mother. She loved her son terribly, but the strains and stresses of the last year caught up with her. Diana began to suffer from postpartum depression. This terrible state can strike any person after the birth of a baby, and it is irrelevant whether they've had children before, or whether they are mentally and emotionally strong or not. This type of depression is a physical response that sometimes occurs after a birth. Unhappily, Diana suffered through such an experience, finding it difficult even to rise from her bed in the morning, or perform the slightest task. Because she had never experienced depression before, Diana was baffled besides feeling low. She desperately loved her son. She was so happy to have him. Why was she feeling this way, she wondered. Charles, and the entire Royal Family, was unable to support Diana through this time. The Windsors were not an emotional family, and having had no experience with tearfulness or sadness, they were at a loss as to what to do for the young Diana. They did seek treatment for the Princess, but patience, understanding and space were what she felt she needed.

Diana felt now, more keenly than ever, that she was letting people down. The emotions raging inside of her needed an outlet, and, unfortunately, she turned these feelings on herself. She injured herself, her arms and legs, in an effort to communicate the terrible pain inside of her. Charles, understandably, was quite shaken by these actions. He was concerned, and overwhelmed with worry for her. The world of the Royals had never seen this sort of thing before. Diana was a woman of passionate feeling, and those feelings would not be shut away and ignored. To Charles and his family, Diana was unstable and mentally unbalanced. She was not to be taken seriously, for in their minds no normal person would behave in such a way. Diana, crying out to be understood, was being further silenced. Finding no real comfort or support at home, Diana turned outward to the public, immersing herself in her royal duties. In the public she found healing, and in the end she triumphed over her depression through the people's love of her.

In the midst of Diana's inner turmoil was a joyous event. Prince William was christened on August 4, 1982. On this warm and sunny day (chosen to honor the Queen Mother's 82nd birthday), the family, guests and choir gathered for the ceremony in the music room of Buckingham Palace. Six individuals were chosen as godparents: The King of the Hellenes, Lord Romsey, Sir Laurens van der Post, Princess Alexandra, the Duchess of Westminster, and Lady Susan Hussey.

Diana held the young William Arthur Philip Louis, comforting him with her finger in his delicate mouth. The little Prince gave several warbles when the Archbishop of Canterbury poured water on his head over the lily font. Diana's young son didn't seem to make any distinction between this ordinary palace water and the Jordan water, which the Royal Family had run out of some royal babies before. William's christening was not entirely traditional; it contained modern elements. Already Diana was showing her preference for taking on the new, not simply settling for the tried and true. Champagne and lunch followed the christening ceremony, and the christening cake was cut. This cake is, by tradition, the top layer of the parent's wedding cake. Pieces of the cake were given out to men of the Welsh guard and the Parachute Regiment wounded in the War of the Falklands. Diana, in spite of her inner pain, looked beautiful, and hope shone out of her clear, blue eyes as she rejoiced in the naming of her young son and his entrance into the Church of England.

Diana became frailer as her struggle to regain a sense of inward peace continued.The people, their love for her growing with her every sensitive gesture and graceful glance, soon began to notice that their attractive, blond and tall Princess was looking thin and worn. Rumors began to circulate that Diana was suffering from anorexia nervosa. Buckingham Palace formally denied these rumors, though there was an acknowledgment that one of Diana's sisters had suffered from "slimmers' disease," but that Diana herself was in the best of health. Nevertheless, Diana was looking thin. At the Remembrance Day ceremony at Albert Hall, Charles arrived alone, explaining that the Princess was unwell. Diana arrived later, looking wan and tired.

The public's love affair with the Princess grew with her every appearance. People were genuinely concerned for the Princess's health and well-being, and her every move and mood became the subject of news and conversation. A telling article appeared in the *Sunday Times* in January 1983. The article, entitled, "Diana the Hunted," spoke of the loss of freedom the lovely Diana now had to endure. Everywhere she went, photographers followed her. On skis, in helicopters, hiding behind bushes, Diana was now a constant target; Diana was now considered public property.

Of course, Diana initially enjoyed the attention. What woman on earth wouldn't enjoy being told she was beautiful? But the press never had enough, and this had an inevitable effect on the Princess. Suzanne Lowry, in the *Sunday Times* in January of 1983, noted, "You have only to look at how that rounded Sloane Ranger's face has changed so quickly. Into the elegant bony beauty, with eyes now so luminous they look almost haunted, to start wondering what we (press and people) have done to her." With her marriage, with beauty, with responsibility, came a certain loss of privacy, of self. Diana was starting to recognize this all too well, but that didn't make it any easier for the young, fun-loving Princess.

They arrived in Australia to flooding and torrential rain. The young Royal Family visited Canberra, Sydney, Tasmania, Adelaide, Perth, Melbourne and Brisbane. They also spent two weeks in New Zealand. The crowds were wild for the blonde, beautiful Diana. Even the normally overly sophisticated people of Sydney went wild for the tall and stately Princess. Kindness shone from her eyes, and her obvious devotion to her child made her even more popular. Diana, always sensitive to those around her, felt bad for Charles. He was, she knew, a good and kind person with many diverse interests and a true concern for the people. Yet, because of Charles's shyness, he was often unfairly considered aloof. Seeing Diana's immense popularity hurt Charles, not because he begrudged her the spotlight, but because he felt his own gifts and talents seemed so unfairly overlooked. Diana, by nature a fair and just person, felt his disappointment keenly, and she always maintained that such total concentration on herself was quite unfair to her husband. Eventually, the media's obsession with Diana, and the public's total devotion to her, carved a wedge between the couple that no amount of understanding and compassion, on Diana's part, could overcome.

Diana considered this trip to Australia a turning point in her life. The public role Diana now had to play was here made very clear to her. She realized the intense level of interest she held for people, and how demanding her life would be, from then on, as she sought, with a humble sense of duty and responsibility, to fulfill the role expected of her.

With this new awareness of her life and its duties came a change in style for the fashion conscious Diana. She had been criticized in the past for her extravagant clothes shopping bills, the press sometimes claiming that she was used to spending thousands of dollars a week on her wardrobe. Although Buckingham Palace denied such reports, the rumors persisted. While in Australia, reporters asked about her clothing purchases. The demure Diana only smiled and claimed that, since she had to change often during the course of a day filled with various engagements, she had need of many different outfits. Up until this time, her taste in clothing had been very much in line with the fairy-tale princess theme. She had favored full-skirted, girlish gowns, which echoed her lovely, virginal wedding dress of just two years before. Toward the end of the Australian tour, however, Diana emerged a new woman both in terms of her awareness of her public image and her personal sense of style. The tall and slender Princess matured into a self-assured woman who wore figure-hugging crepe de chine with style and grace and not a trace of awkward shyness. The world, dazzled by her beauty, could hardly catch its breath.

Taking her newfound glamour with her, the Princess returned to England ready to step out and show the world the new Diana: a woman in her own right, not a girl clinging to the arm of a prince. Back in England, Diana attended the premiere of *Octopussy* and rubbed shoulders with the superstars of showbusiness, amazed by the fact that she was now one of these people. Diana, blond, dazzling, kind and giving, was now a superstar in her own right.

The next official trip abroad for the Prince and Princess was to Canada. Diana was heart-broken because she had to leave William behind, and, sadly, she would have to miss his first birthday. While in Canada, she reflected on the fact that her life, her time, her schedule were no longer her own. She noted that before her wedding, she often didn't know what she would be doing the next day, now her schedule was laid out 18 months in advance. This sort of planning, over which the Princess only had marginal control, was the reason she had to miss her son's first birthday, and the reality of how much her life had changed really came home to her now. She left some small gifts for her fair-haired young son in the nursery of Kensington Palace, which he could open on his special day, but the big present would wait until she and Charles returned from Canada. Diana just couldn't bear to miss the whole of William's first birthday celebration, so she kept something in reserve for her return, when she could watch his face light up with joy at her gift.

Arriving in Halifax, Nova Scotia on the Royal yacht, the *Britannia*, the royal couple held a small reception. Diana, always straightforward and honest, made a reference to the journalists and photographers who had been hounding her in Britain. The Princess noted that when the press writes hurtful and horrible things about her, she actually gets a physical pain in her chest and she wants to hide away and not go out. As far as Diana was concerned, journalists of this sort were like a wolf pack, and she was their prey. When news of Diana's statements made headlines, there was a general furor. The press didn't appreciate Diana's remarks, her simple honesty seeming to them to carry too much criticism. The real upset, however, lay in the fact that Diana's remarks, which had very quickly appeared in the newspapers, had been made in private. Her comments, revealed publicly in the press, had been made in confidence.

Despite these problems with the media, which seemed to follow her everywhere, Diana was enthusiastically welcomed all over Canada. Seventy thousand people met Diana and her Prince in St. John, New Brunswick. In Shelburne, Nova Scotia, hundreds of people broke through barriers to race after the royal couple. In Edmonton, Alberta, more than a thousand people endured the rain to stand and wave to Diana and Charles as they found their way to a banquet where they would celebrate the Princess's 22nd birthday. When Diana stepped out onto a balcony later in the evening, 300 people, waiting for hours despite the poor weather, spontaneously burst into a rousing rendition of "Happy Birthday." While visiting the housing area of the World University Games, Diana confided to the Canadian swimming team that she always beats Charles when they have swimming competitions at home. Diana beamed as she relished the idea of trouncing her Prince at a sport she had enjoyed and excelled at for many years.

Diana and Charles entered into the spirit of their visit to Edmonton. The annual Klondike Days celebrations, a time for dressing in the style of the 1890s and celebrating the history of the Gold Rush, were an opportunity for the royal couple to dress up in costumes and mingle with the people in a less formal fashion. Diana looked lovely in her period dress, proving to everyone that she would have been considered a great beauty in any era, but there were comments on how thin the Princess looked. Composed as ever, the Princess put concerns about her health to rest by blaming the pressures of married life for her slender appearance.

Diana's new, sophisticated style and glamorous appearance did not change or diminish her genuine interest in people and her profound love of children. Always sensitive to others, Diana held a special place in her heart for the young, and she never forgot them or overlooked them, despite her busy schedule and the many demands on her and her time. Even though she was attending glitzy events like the Duran Duran and Dire Straits concerts when she was back in London, she always remained most at home with the young and those who needed nurturing and care. Diana always had room in her schedule for tasks she felt were important, like her visit to a charity event for the Royal National Institute for the Blind. There she thanked children who had helped to put together a book of bedtime stories for Prince William. Diana's considerate nature shone as she made every effort to tell these children how much she appreciated their contribution. The book, *Stories for a Prince*, was published to raise funds for the RNIB.

Another issue which caught Diana's attention and caused her to focus her energy, in order to do good work, was sparked by her own commitment to motherhood. In becoming a mother, a whole new part of Diana had emerged, and she could relate even more fully with the pain and anxiety people felt in their own lives for their loved ones, especially their children. A rubella (German measles) epidemic broke out in England, and the implications of this for pregnant women were horrible. An infected woman carrying a baby has a much greater chance of giving birth to a baby who is deaf, blind, brain-damaged, or who has heart-defects. Diana was appalled and upset that such a disease, with vaccination against it possible and available, was still rampantly threatening women in Britain. Diana herself asked what she could do to help eradicate this terrible disease. She wanted to be active in helping people become aware of rubella and its awful implications. Finally, she wrote a letter that the National Rubella Association could use in their attempt to educate the public about this needlessly tragic disease. Her letter, written in a way that communicates without talking down to the people, was sent all over the country in an effort to reach everyone.

While the Princess dedicated herself to working for the good of the people, speculation about a second pregnancy followed her everywhere, and the press was more than ready to spread rumors of pregnancy. Diana very much wanted another child. When she found she was expecting again, she was overjoyed, though she had to grit her teeth a bit at the thought of possibly being ill again, and at the inevitable loss of her hard-won and very much enjoyed slim figure. Speculation about her condition had reached a fever pitch when, during the summer of 1983, Diana flew from Balmoral, the traditional vacation place of the Royal Family, to visit the doctor who had delivered William, Mr. George Pinker. Whatever the Princess, and the public, suspected at that time, it was not to be. Happily, Diana and Charles did conceive, but not until late in that year. Buckingham Palace postponed the announcement of the happy news until the 13th of February, giving the newspapers a perfect story for their Valentine's Day editions. Diana was thrilled at the idea of another baby. Charles couldn't have been happier. The Royal Family was overjoyed, as was the Spencer family, and the British public was jubilant when news of the expected baby was received. It was estimated that the birth of the baby would follow Prince William's entrance into the world by two years and three months, a spacing that medical opinion generally holds to be an excellent interval. With such perfect timing, previous rumors that Diana had been having trouble conceiving were quickly put to rest.

Diana was in good health, despite being remarkably thin, and when news of her pregnancy came out, she was spending precious time with her husband. A fifteen-day visit to Italy was canceled, though, because it was thought prudent not to overly-extend the Princess early in her pregnancy. Diana didn't change any of her commitments at home in England, though, and she planned to stay active throughout the whole nine months. However, only two official functions were planned for after the end of May. Charles, on the other hand, made no changes at all to his own calendar, which included three trips abroad. This meant more lonely times for Diana, which must have been a difficulty at this time. Since Diana's baby was due in September, the last stage of the Princess's pregnancy would naturally not include a lot of public appearances anyway, since the Royal Family traditionally holidays at Balmoral in the last weeks of summer. Diana, then, would have some time away from the hustle and bustle of royal duties to enjoy the last days of expectation and prepare, in the quiet of the Scottish countryside, for her new child.

As with anyone living so public a life, strange reactions to events are inevitable. Despite the widespread rejoicing which news of Diana's pregnancy brought, there were some unusual suspicions. Rumors circulated amongst some members of the general public that after the birth of this second child, Diana would be forced to undergo sterilization in order to avert a copy cat baby-boom. There was speculation that young women, wanting to emulate the mesmerizing Princess seen so often in the news, would make rash decisions concerning their own families. Buckingham Palace quickly denied these rumors, but, in so doing it was clear how serious was the people's concern for Diana and her welfare. Anyone who knew Diana, however, knew that she would never allow anyone to restrict her decision to have as many children as she felt was right for her.

Toward the end of Diana's pregnancy, the Princess, vulnerable in her expectant state, received a shock. Her 45-year-old uncle, Lord Fermoy, committed suicide at his home, Eddington House, in Hungerford, Berkshire. He had been suffering depression for some time, and an estate worker found his body. He had taken his own life with a shotgun, and he left to mourn his passing his wife and a family of two sons and a daughter. The news of his death was terribly upsetting to Diana. The thought of her cousins having been deprived of their father was heartrending to the Princess, as she always felt deeply for children's hurts. Diana heard the news of her uncle's death while she was holidaying with the Royal Family at Balmoral. The Princess immediately left Scotland to attend the funeral, despite her very pregnant state. She had to plead with the press for privacy at this devastating time.

Family was very important to Diana. Her desire to be near her extended family at this sad time, no matter the late stage of her pregnancy or the interruption of a traditional Royal holiday, clearly showed that Diana would not let her own relatives take second place to her role as Princess. The Princess was equally firm about the role of the Spencers in her son's life, and in the life of her soon-to-be-born child. Despite a tendency for the Royal Family to take over people who became a part of their circle, Diana refused to allow her own family to be pushed out of her children's lives. Her own father once remarked that Diana was determined to have the Spencers as an active part of her children's lives. The Earl Spencer also said that Diana always gets her own way if she feels something is important. Nothing was more important to Diana than her children and her family, and she was committed to bringing up her children with pride in, and knowledge of, their Spencer family as well as the Royal Family.

Diana scarcely had time to regain her emotional balance when, on September 15, 1984, she left Windsor Castle for St. Mary's Hospital in London, arriving there at 7:30 in the morning. She was admitted to the very same room in which she had borne William, a Spartan but adequate private room on the fourth floor of the Lindo Wing. The Princess labored for nine hours, finally giving birth to a 6 lb., 14 oz boy at 4:20 in the afternoon. The baby had blue eyes and dark brown hair. The town crier of Mayfair stood outside of the hospital proclaiming the royal birth to the 300 people gathered and all who passed by. Charles phoned the Queen with the happy news of the new Prince's birth, then he called the Earl Spencer. The Earl was sure that William would find a fine playmate in this new little prince, but he expressed a hope that the boy would play more cricket than polo. The Earl Spencer, upon receiving the happy news, promptly raised the family flag over his home in Althorp and shouted from a balcony the joyful announcement of Diana's new son to amazed tourists.

The new baby was taken home by his parents within a day. A crowd, which had kept vigil outside of the hospital since news of the new Prince's birth, cheered him as he was driven away to Kensington Palace. He made his first journey in a blue Daimler, and the trip took a total of six minutes. Diana's new son was given the name Henry Charles Albert David, but Diana insisted that he be known as Harry. The Princess felt that this version of the name would be less stiff and formal, more accessible and friendly.

The country celebrated the news of Harry's birth and Diana's safe delivery. On Sunday, September 16th, St. Mary's Parish Church, Tetbury, near Charles and Diana's country home of Highgrove House, rang its bells for three hours to celebrate the Prince's arrival. The church of the parish where Diana was born, the royal estate of Sandringham, also pealed its bells in honor of the small Prince. The country was ringing with happiness and good will over the birth of Diana's new son.

Just after Christmas, young Prince Harry was officially christened and baptized into the Church of England. In spite of the dark skies and gloomy weather, Diana felt warm and happy holding her small son. To Diana, her children were a precious gift for whom she always felt thankful. The christening ceremony was held at Buckingham Palace, and the godparents were Lady Sarah Armstrong-Jones, Lady Vestey, Mrs. William Bartholomew, Bryan Organ, Gerald Ward and Prince Andrew.

Prince Harry was quite upstaged by his brother, Wild William. During the Queen's Christmas message of that year, William had stolen the audience's attention by running around during her speech. The Queen had tried to contain the young Prince, but her efforts were in vain. Charles was beginning to worry that his eldest son was growing up to be a spoiled and pampered prig of a prince. At Prince Harry's christening, William ran roughshod through the Palace, ignoring all efforts to calm him and ramming into elderly ladies. Diana never lost her patience. While Charles often suggested a more disciplined approach was needed, the Princess was a doting mother who always thought the best of her children and tried never to speak sharply to them. Her belief was that if you love them and expect the best of them, they won't let you down.

William, though, really was a parenting challenge. When he was two he almost destroyed the Queen Mother's dining room, and he set off a panic amongst the security people when he pressed a button in his nursery and sounded an alarm system, bringing police and special detectives from all over the neighboring county. His pranks weren't limited to staff and strangers. William once took Prince Charles's handmade Lobb shoes and, much to his father's anger, flushed them down the toilet. Even Diana had to admit that William behaved like a "mini-tornado."

The July 1986 wedding of Sarah Ferguson and Prince Andrew brought the family together for another happy occasion and gave William another chance to play the devil. William was given the role of page boy in this royal wedding, and he wore a nineteenth-century sailor's uniform, complete with hat. Diana was worried that William wouldn't behave well during the ceremony, and she felt nervous about the whole thing for days beforehand. Fortunately, William did little damage. Other than fidgeting, playing with his hat, and sticking his tongue out at a bridesmaid, the little Prince put his doting mother's fear to rest. William did, however, have to be stopped, by the Queen herself, from running after the newlyweds when they drove away in their bridal coach. Diana managed to pick him up and carry him back into the palace before he squirmed free of her loving arms.

Even Diana had her limits when it came to parenting the little fire ball of a prince. There was the time that Diana took William, without any nanny along as backup, to watch Prince Charles play polo. Sitting in the royal box, press cameras pointed and clicking, Diana was reduced to holding young Prince William by the seat of his pants as he struggled to climb out of their seating place and break for freedom. As Diana struggled to restrain her energetic son, he volleyed questions at her about where the horses were, when he could have ice cream and what other treats were awaiting him. Diana eventually admitted defeat for the day and took her young, headstrong Prince home.

No matter how much trouble Prince William caused, Diana remained firm in her child-rearing beliefs; wanted her children to have (as normal an upbringing as possible). As far as she was concerned, William's antics, no matter how trying, were natural for a young, intelligent little boy. She would far rather have a headstrong son than a child who was cut off from normal activity and normal life. Remembering her own childhood, with two older sisters and a younger brother, the Princess knew very well that impishness was part of the package. William, she knew, would soon enough pick up his princely burden. And Diana was openly affectionate with her children. There would be no formal shaking hands or stiff exchanges between mother and children. Diana hugged and kissed her sons, she threw over the reins of tradition and openly loved her children.

Diana's easygoing way with her children was obvious on many occasions. Once, when the family was practicing a fire drill at Sandringham House, Prince William started talking with the firefighters and climbing on the fire engine. One of the firefighters was kind enough to let the young Prince try on his helmet. When the time came, however, young William would not give the hat back to its owner. Diana pleaded with her son, but he refused to let go of the helmet, and eventually he ran off with it. The Princess giggled, watching him race away, then shrugged her shoulders. She assured the startled fire fighter that when William put the helmet down they would retrieve it and send it back to him. Although she was happy to eventually make the situation right, Diana was such a gentle mother that she wouldn't force her children and bend them to her own desires or expectations.

Diana's portrait with baby Harry and William, taken by Lord Snowdon, caused a sensation. The Princess was made up, and a hair-stylist consulted, to produce a sultry Diana. The press couldn't talk of anything but "Dynasty Di," with her beautiful face and fabulous clothes. Diana, however, was becoming fed up with all the attention her image and clothing were getting, along with the criticism of her spending. Early on she had decided to wear English designer clothing, to give the British fashion industry some support and exposure, but now she curbed her shopping and stepped out again and again in the same outfits. Diana had had enough of the "dumb beauty" label, and she was determined to change it. The world was being introduced to the real Diana: the hard-working young mother who truly cared about others and wanted to make a difference in the world. The press criticized her old outfits and her lack of cutting-edge designer wear, but Diana didn't care. The Princess knew she was more than a pretty girl in nice gowns, and she meant for everyone else to know it, too.

The media followed her everywhere, though, and this became a personal trial for Diana and caused a strain on the royal marriage. Not only did Charles feel slighted when the entire focus of the press was on the Princess, but their relationship itself was constantly analyzed and debated in the public eye. Often it seemed they never had a moment alone. Once, when visiting an art gallery, Charles commented on how nice it would be for them to someday come back and enjoy the gallery in privacy and at their leisure. Diana quickly reminded him that they were never alone. And there was little chance that that would ever change.

In August of the following summer, Diana left the family summer holiday at Balmoral to be with her sister who was due to have a baby. She visited with her sister and also went to the hospital the next day to lend support to the new mother. Diana was thrilled to be an aunt again, and happy for her sister, but she was frustrated at being followed everywhere by the press and that even a private family event like this would put her name in the news. It bothered Diana that her most ordinary actions were considered news when there were so many really important things happening in the world.

Diana's desire to start really making a difference in the world began coming true after the terrible plane tragedy in Manchester. After her return to Balmoral, the Royal Family learned that a fire had swept through an aircraft at Ringway Airport in Manchester, causing disaster. Upon hearing the dreadful news, Charles and Diana rushed from Balmoral to visit the seven survivors in Withington Hospital. One of the survivors, a 13-year-old girl named Lindsey Elliott, was badly injured and had lost her mother, aunt and uncle in the accident. After spending three days on a ventilator, the young girl, upon hearing of the loss of her relatives, shut her eyes and refused to open them or speak. Even the arrival of her father could not break through the girl's cage of grief. Charles and Diana took turns sitting by her bedside, and eventually, feeling the genuine love and concern near her, Lindsey found the strength to open her eyes and face her pain.

Having done as much as they could at Manchester, the royal couple turned to more personal concerns. As the summer turned to cooler days, Diana decided the time had come for three-year-old William to go out of the Palace and enter the everyday world. At her insistence, William attended a private kindergarten located five minutes from Kensington Palace and run by the daughter of an Anglican Bishop. The pupils of the kindergarten were placed in one of three groups: there were swans, little swans and cygnets. William was a cygnet. The children did crafts, singing and movement. When a child completed the program, at the swan level, they were expected to be able to paint and sing. The press was invited to the first day of William's kindergarten, but Charles and Diana wrote to Fleet Street asking that, after the first day, William please be left alone. The kindergarten was fitted with bullet-proof windows and, amongst other things, a bodyguard, to ensure the young Prince's safety. Diana was thrilled and proud to see her young son taking a step toward independence as he waved the little paper mouse he crafted on his first school day.

William, though, was still a handful. He started so many schoolyard fights that he was nicknamed "Billy the Basher" by the parents of other children in the school. Concerns over William's behavior caused Diana and Charles to reconsider the influence the nanny was having on their young son. There were also reports of Harry being left to cry while Miss Barbara Barnes lavished all her attention on William. She also indulged him, never reprimanding him at any time. Harry's unhappiness and William's uncontrollable behavior were becoming a real source of concern to Diana. At the same time, there were reports that the royal nanny was starting to act quite the royal herself, getting the footman to clean the children's shoes instead of doing it herself, and generally lording it over the other servants.

When it came time for Prince William to enter Weatherby School on January 15, 1987, Barbara Barnes conveniently announced that she would be leaving her position as nanny to the two princes. Diana hadn't wanted to be the one to dismiss Miss. Barnes from her position, but she couldn't hide her disappointment with the nanny over her son's care. When Miss. Barnes realized the depth of the Princess's unhappiness with her duties, she graciously stepped down as royal nanny.

Ruth Wallace was hired as the new nanny to William and Harry. She was a no-nonsense woman who had worked as a nurse caring for sick children. Her personality and way of dealing with children had an almost immediate effect on the two Princes. William's behavior improved, and Harry became much happier. Diana had known instinctively what her children had needed, and with patient perseverance she had provided it for them. This new nanny didn't put on airs, and she encouraged the boys to be normal children who treated others with respect. Both Charles and Diana were very pleased with her influence on their sons.

It was very important to Princess Diana that she always talk with her children, no matter where she was in the world. Eventually, Diana traveled without her sons, though she established a routine of speaking on the phone with them daily at 7:00 p.m. Greenwich Mean Time. Diana was sad to leave her children at home when she went away. She, however, very much wanted them to have a normal life. Taking the boys away on trips, she felt, would disrupt their routine and their schooling to such an extent that it would be harmful.

When Diana was at home, she rarely saw her sons before breakfast. They were awakened by their nanny, fed, groomed and dressed before they could see their mother, if she hadn't already left for an engagement. Diana, however, made a special effort to pick her children up from school in the family car and take them to swimming lessons at Buckingham Palace. She often had tea with them at 4:00 p.m. in her private sitting room, enjoying cucumber sandwiches and cream cakes together. They were allowed a minimum of television watching, and then Charles and Diana liked to play with the boys on the swings or do jigsaw puzzles with them.

On weekends the family tried to get away to Highgrove House, where they spent a lot of their time out-of-doors, learning the names of plants and flowers. Long walks and pony rides readied the boys for their 7:30 p.m. bedtime. The young Princes received many gifts of toys and stuffed animals, but they remained unaware of most of these gifts. Instead, these items were passed on to charities and hospitals. Both Diana and Charles did not want their children to be spoiled, so they limited the number of gifts and presents the Princes were allowed.

Diana's busy schedule wound itself around her children, and she found herself active in many different causes and at many different events. Her focus usually revolved around issues with children or the welfare of those suffering or somehow marginalized. In October of 1985, Diana visited a drug dependency unit in southeast London. During the visit Diana was very touched by the suffering of the people, and in fact the event left her upset for days afterward. The Princess extended her visit to more than an hour, most of which was spent talking to a 36-year-old heroin addict whose personal story clearly moved Diana deeply.

Diana was also concerned about the effects of the portrayal of drugs in the media on children, especially her two boys. She felt that the information they could pick up from television could be dangerous. The Princess was also clearly distressed and shocked to learn of children from broken homes who roamed the streets at night. Sensitive as always to those suffering, especially the young, the thought of children without loving homes or caring parents was painful to Diana. As a result of her educational visit to this clinic, Diana heartily endorsed BBC television's anti-drug campaign. Diana was now moving unhesitatingly forward in her goal to become a woman with substantial concerns and humanitarian causes.

As Diana's role as a woman of social awareness and compassion continued to grow, rumors of her lonely and empty marriage increased. There were reports that she and her husband had nothing in common, and that their royal marriage was a sham. Charles and Diana went public in a television interview to refute the wild rumors circulating about them. Diana complained that, with all the important things happening in the world, did she really have to be the source of news every day? Stories that she was domineering or control-crazy hurt her deeply, and after reading such reports she would have to force herself out into the public. Diana did laughingly reveal that she had banished some ties from her husband's closet, as well as some of his stodgier footwear. Charles had to refute notions that he was into the occult and partaking foolishly in

Family album picture of Lady Diana Spencer in her baby carriage at Park House, Sandringham, Norfolk in 1962.

Lady Diana Spencer at 7 years of age, with her brother Charles Edward, Viscount Althorp, a former Page of Honour to the Queen.

(ABOVE)- Another family album photo of Lady Diana Spencer taken at Itchenor, West Sussex, during the summer of 1970.

(RIGHT)- Lady Diana Spencer at 13 years old on the Isle of Uist in the Western Isles, Scotland, in 1974.

Prince Charles and the then Lady Diana Spencer on the grounds of
Buckingham Palace after announcing their engagement on February 24, 1981.

Prince Charles and Princess Diana on the balcony of Buckingham Palace on their wedding day, July 29, 1981. It is estimated that over 750,000,000 people around the world watched the Royal Wedding on television.

The coat of arms of the Prince and Princess of Wales, incorporating the shield of Prince Charles (left), with the shield of the House of Spencer.

(ABOVE)- Princess Diana and Prince Charles amuse their son Prince William during a photo session at Kensington Palace in London, in December 1982.

(LEFT)- A 1984 photo of Princess Diana with her sons. Prince William sits quietly while his mother cradles his new born brother, Prince Harry, in her arms.

(ABOVE)- Diana, Princess of Wales, enjoys a ride on the Maid of Mist at Niagara Falls, Ontario in October 1991, with her sons Prince Harry, then 7, and Prince William, then 9. Although her demanding schedule kept the princess busy meeting with foreign heads of state and campaining for the various charities that enjoyed her patronage, Diana always found time for her family.

(LOWER RIGHT)- South African President Nelson Mandela shakes hands with Princess Diana in Cape Town, Monday, March 17, 1997. Princess Diana met with Mandela to discuss the threat of AIDS in South Africa.

(UPPER RIGHT)- First Lady Hillary Rodham Clinton meets with Princess Diana at the White House on Wednesday, June 18, 1997. On Tuesday night the princess attended an American Red Cross fund-raiser in Washington to aid land mine victims around the world.

(ABOVE)- Princess Diana with the Duchess of York at an event honouring the 50th anniversary of the Battle of Britain held at Buckingham Palace. "Fergie" quickly became a close friend and confidante to the princess who admired her exuberant and independent spirit.

(RIGHT)- Princess Diana, one of the world's best dressed and most photographed women, auctioned 65 of her evening gowns to raise funds for charities. She also donated her wedding dress to London's Victoria and Albert Museum.

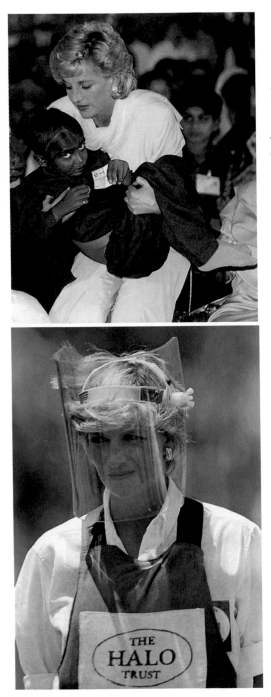

(UPPER LEFT)- Britain's Princess of Wales, Diana, cradles a sick child during her visit to the Shaukat Khanum Memorial Hospital, founded by Pakistani cricket star Imran Khan, in Lahore, Thursday February 22, 1996. The Princess was in Pakistan to help raise funds for the cancer hospital.

(LOWER LEFT)- Diana, Princess of Wales, wears protective equipment as she tours a minefield during her visit to Angola in January 1997. Diana had visited Angola and the former Yugoslavia in the previous year to lend her high profile to mine-clearance efforts.

(RIGHT)- Mother Teresa, left, says goodbye to Princess Diana after receiving a visit from her Wednesday, June 18, 1997, in New York. Princess Diana met privately for 40 minutes with Mother Teresa at The Missionaries of Charity in the South Bronx section of New York. The Roman Catholic nun died at 87 years of age—only 5 days after the princess' tragic accident.

(ABOVE)- Princess Diana sits beside British pop star Elton John, center, who is being comforted by an unidentified man, as they attend the memorial Mass for Gianni Versace, in Milan's gothic cathedral Tuesday, July 22, 1997. A celebrity pantheon mourned Versace a week after the fashion designer was slain in Miami Beach.

(UPPER RIGHT)- Map tracing the route of Princess Diana's limousine from the Ritz Hotel to the tunnel beneath the Place de l'Alma where her companion Emad (Dodi) Fayed and Henri Paul are killed instantly. Diana and bodyguard Trevor Rees-Jones are rushed to hospital in critical condition. After several hours of frantic efforts to revive her, doctors pronounce Princess Diana dead at approximately 4:00 am.

(LOWER RIGHT)- Police block access to the tunnel along the Seine River where Diana, Princess of Wales, died in a car crash that also killed her boyfriend Dodi Fayed and her chauffeur early Sunday August 31, 1997, in Paris. The car wreck is visible on the right side of the tunnel.

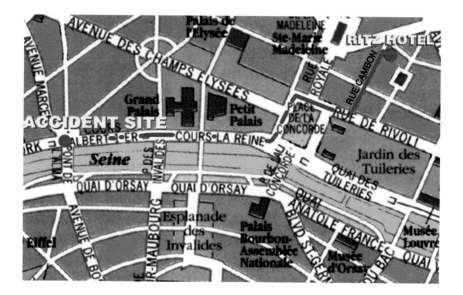

A TRAGIC ACCIDENT

(ABOVE)- Media reaction to the news of Diana's death was immediate and global in scale. Sunday editions of the New York City newspapers carried headlines of the tragedy which had occurred that same morning.

(ABOVE)- Princess Diana's casket is carried out of Westminster Abbey after the funeral service Saturday, September 6, 1997 in London.

(RIGHT)- The pain of loss is clearly visible on the face of the Prince of Wales as he looks towards his sons Prince William, left, and Prince Harry while they wait for the coffin of Princess Diana to be loaded into a hearse after their mother's funeral service in Westminster Abbey in London.

DIANA'S FINAL RESTING PLACE

Earl Spencer places flowers on the island in a lake at the grounds of the
Spencer family home at Althorp, Northamptonshire Monday,
September 8, 1997 where his sister Diana,
Princess of Wales was buried Saturday.

fringe medicine. The interview answered some questions, but the state of their marriage remained a mystery.

Diana and Charles did share many interests. Both devoted parents, they complemented each other in their parenting, Diana bringing warm affection and fun, Charles roughhousing with the boys while also insisting they learn discipline. They both loved to ski, and Diana polished her skills on their annual visit to Klosters. The image of Ditzy Diana who cared only for soap operas and clothes was a myth that grew out of self-deprecating remarks she made to nervous adults and children to put them at ease. In reality, Diana enjoyed evenings with Charles and his educated friends, often surprising people with her range of reading and interests. The royal couple also shared a love of music. Despite her portrayal as a pop-music addict, Diana was an accomplished pianist. In their rare moments of free time together, Charles sometimes accompanied her on the cello. When she flew, she often read biographies of the people she would be meeting, or she looked over books written by them. Diana was much more cultured and well-rounded than the press reported. Though the royal marriage was not without problems, and certainly living under the glare of the media must have added to the stress in their relationship, Charles and Diana did share areas of interest and moments of happiness.

The television interview Charles and Diana held couldn't stop the rumors surrounding the problems in their marriage, and Diana had to contend with lonely times and a sense of isolation. Although she and her husband were not the opposites the press made them out to be, her husband was often too busy for her, and he seemed incapable of understanding and meeting her needs. Her superstar media status further isolated her from normal relationships and the real world. Diana, beautiful and serene on the outside, was crying inside. She threw herself into her charity work to escape the pain of her personal life.

The Princess dedicated her time to helping the elderly, supporting different agencies and groups in their efforts to minister to these people. She reached out to babies in hospitals, touching them, holding them, comforting them and giving support and royal recognition to the people striving to make a difference in their young lives. Diana opened a pregnancy research center, the thought of her pregnancies, and her young sons' births, still very much in her mind. Most of her time now was focused on children and young mothers, and she was also becoming increasingly aware of, and involved with, people in desperate situations.

Later in her life, Diana spoke of this time. She noted that she slowly became more and more involved with people that society had, for one reason or another, cast out. Her own feelings of loneliness and rejection gave her a sensitivity and understanding that was genuinely heartfelt. Tall and blond, the darling of the media, the Princess knew that loneliness and suffering could strike everyone, no matter their beauty or wealth. As Diana waded into the midst of the suffering people in the world, she found strength in the honest vulnerability she found in them. These people were a far cry from the stuffy rules of the Palace and royal life, but to Diana this was much more genuine. She gave these suffering people a respect and dignity they rarely experienced, and in them she found herself renewed.

The glare of the camera followed Diana everywhere. Every hand she held, every child she comforted, was recorded by groups of photographers, their cameras clicking. Under this intense scrutiny, Diana's resolve to appear attractive had, over the years, become more and more a part of her life. She was strict about her weight, never wanting to add pounds to her frame and leave herself open to attacks like that which had hounded the Duchess of York. The press had had a field day with Sarah, calling her the Duchess of Pork and generally belittling her figure. But Diana, in her loneliness, so eager and able to comfort others, didn't know how to comfort herself. Turning to food as a source of consolation, the Princess became bulimic during this time, and this was very hard on her health. This disease became another physical and emotional strain that the vulnerable Diana had to struggle with alone.

In May of 1986, Diana and Charles went to visit Expo '86 in Vancouver, British Columbia, Canada. The tour was especially grueling, with much travel packed into a very short time. During their time in Vancouver, they began one day with a visit to Burnaby, a suburb of Vancouver, to dedicate a new park, and then they lunched with the 54 commissioners of Expo's pavilions. It was a very hot and sunny day in Vancouver, and the Expo site, with its concrete and asphalt, was stifling. The royal couple was due to visit five pavilions on the expansive grounds, and as they left the US site and were walking to the California pavilion, Diana put her hand to her forehead, swayed and fell. Her personal physician caught the Princess, and it took her almost ten minutes to recover and go on with the tour.

The stresses and strains of Princess Diana's personal and public life were now taking their inevitable toll on this young and beautiful woman.

She had been in the spotlight for over six years, and she had had to mature and find her own way in front of the world, with little support from her husband and his family. There had been little tolerance in the Royal Family for the mistakes of a young woman only learning about her role and duty, and even fewer moments of support and understanding. With her self-esteem tottering, her self-image entwined with the press reports of her, and her duties as a mother pressing on her, she also had to face the growing difficulties in her marriage. Her eating disorder was a sign of greater problems in the life of this lovely and lonely young woman whom had become a fairy-tale princess and now found that the fairy tale had never existed.

Chapter 7

Separate Ways

It is difficult to pinpoint the exact moment that Diana's marriage went irrevocably wrong, though cynics would say that it was a doomed venture from the start. The ten years between 1986 and 1996 certainly began with problems for the Princess, but no one could have predicted the increasingly horrible sequence of events that would take such an exacting toll on the Princess of Wales.

Though she would not seek help until a former flatmate threatened to go public in 1988, Diana's rumored eating disorder had a long history, and as the '80s wore on it became quite serious. Her sister Sarah had suffered from anorexia nervosa in her youth, a situation that had reportedly caused a bit of an embarrassment during Charles and Diana's courtship. Diana, in her youth, was described as a girl who enjoyed food and had a tendency to put on weight yet was active enough to keep any gain under control. Whatever self-confidence she had in her appearance was shattered by the publication of her engagement pictures, which Diana thought were, to say the least, very unflattering. Determined to be thin and beautiful for her wedding, Diana adopted some very unhealthy practices as her food intake became more and more erratic. The nervousness and emotionality caused by her purging was written off as pre-wedding jitters, and as the world fawned over the beautiful bride who glided into

St. Paul's Cathedral, her body image became fixed as one of thinness at all costs.

Though careless of her own health, Diana's outlook changed when she became pregnant soon after the wedding. It is perhaps fortuitous that the pregnancy occurred so quickly (though some said it was too quick), as her bulimia had not yet affected her fertility. She adopted an almost fanatically healthy lifestyle, including a sensible diet and plenty of exercise, and she and the world were rewarded with the birth of William, Prince of Wales and second in line to the throne. Unfortunately, Diana (who had a pregnancy full of morning sickness and other uncomfortable symptoms) was then overtaken by postpartum depression, something which, in the early '80s, was not openly discussed and certainly not recognized by the emotionally reserved Royal Family. A new label, "Diana the mentally unbalanced and emotionally unstable," was put upon her. Perhaps fortunately, she did not have much time to slip back into her bad old habits, as she was soon pregnant again. The birth in September 1984 of Prince Harry, while delighting the world and the Royals as fulfillment of some sort of maternal responsibility to produce a "heir and a spare," once again took its toll on Diana. It had been another queasy pregnancy, and more postpartum depression followed. Coping on her own, and refusing to admit that she had a problem, Diana not only lost the weight she had put on during the pregnancies, but began to thin down further. There would be no third pregnancy to give her body a respite from the abuse it was taking, and as the world watched, Diana began to grow thinner and more emotional, no longer the "Shy Di" of past years.

Though her increasing weight loss had been discussed in the press for several years, things came to a head in 1986 when Diana fainted in Vancouver. Fair in Vancouver, British Columbia, Diana fainted outside the California pavilion. Charles reportedly upbraided his wife for causing a scene and questioned why she couldn't wait until they were out of public view to falter. Despite this stinging criticism, later that night Diana delivered a speech at a dinner party, appearing rested and healthy. The *Times* noted that not only was the Princess in top form, but she had also eaten everything on her plate, which may have been intended to assure the public that it was only a passing fit of illness. It may also have shown that they confused Diana's bulimia with her sister's anorexia: like many bulimics, Diana appeared to be eating regularly, even heartily, but was then purging later, in secret.

Unfortunately, this was not the only source of stress in her life, for it was also during this time that Charles renewed his close ties with his old flame Camilla Parker-Bowles. There are many who doubt that the relationship was ever truly suspended, as Diana was reportedly devastated to unwrap what she thought was a wedding gift, instead finding a bracelet that was a present from Charles to Camilla. By the time of the Expo trip, Diana had realized that the more she tried to get her husband to spend time with her, the more he was pulling away, and Diana certainly had an idea about where he was pulling to.

During 1987 the Prince and Princess spent more and more time apart, a fact certainly not lost on the press. The length of time they spent in each others presence was the source of unending tallying, while a public appearance together was treated with the surprise of a UFO sighting. In April of that year, Charles spent a considerable amount of time in Africa on safari and almost immediately followed this up with a painting trip to Italy. As always, Diana was the one who was there for the young Princes, who the press reportedly speculated seemed more likely to adopt their bodyguards as surrogate fathers as to forge a bond with their real father. It was the company of her sons which filled up Diana's lonely days, and she was determined to provide William and Harry with a loving mother, something which the divorce of her own parents had deprived her of.

November had the press's tongues wagging again, as Diana was conspicuously absent from the wedding of a Mountbatten relative, Amanda Knatchbull, a young woman who had dated the Prince in his bachelor days. It was noted on more than one front that the couple had been apart for almost 40 days until they appeared together in Wales, visiting flood victims, and they parted company again immediately after.

During the next few months both the public and the press watched anxiously as the couple appeared together only infrequently, though this was explained away by the Palace as being merely the result of strenuous royal schedules. Charles and Diana, all were assured, were still very much in love.

Despite these protestations to the contrary, the royal rift began to publicly widen after a tragic incident during a skiing holiday in Klosters, Switzerland on March 10, 1988. Diana and Charles were joined by the Duchess of York, Major Hugh Lindsay, Charles and Patti Palmer-Tomkinson, and expert guide Bruno Sprecher, and a jolly time was being had by all, both on the slopes and off.While Diana and the Duchess of York elected to return to their chalet (the Duchess being three months pregnant), Charles and the rest of the group decided to continue their skiing. The decision was made to leave the marked runs (despite avalanche warnings) and opt for the deep powder of an off-limits area, the rationale being that the skiing would be more exciting, something that undoubtedly appealed to the daredevil Prince. The excitement soon turned to terror as an avalanche swiftly overtook the group, sweeping up Hugh and Patti and forcing the others to scramble out of the path of the angry torrent of snow. Rushing down the slope, Charles helped dig Patti out of the icy pile and revive her. Unfortunately, it was already too late for Major Lindsay, whose body lay a short distance away: he had been killed instantly by the sheer force of the snow. A rescue team took Patti to the hospital, as both her legs were badly crushed. Dozens of plates and screws would eventually be needed to afford her any mobility.

Charles held himself entirely responsible for the accident, as everyone (including guide Sprecher) had deferred to his judgment. The Prince had always been adventurous (being the first Royal ever to parachute during his Navy days), but never before had anyone been harmed by his actions. Diana rushed to comfort him as he returned to the lodge, but he reportedly brushed her aside. His grief and his anger at himself would be his own, or so Diana thought.

Puzzled and hurt by Charles's reaction, Diana instead comforted Patti's distraught husband Charles and helped make arrangements for the group's return home. Major Lindsay's body would accompany them on their flight. As her husband nursed his pain alone, Diana suddenly realized that his inability to lean on her in his time of grief was not due to her personally, but more a result of his upbringing. Raised in a royal atmosphere where the proverbial British stiff upper lip was a way of life, emotion was a sign of weakness for the Prince. Diana could only silently observe her husband's pain, feeling useless and unwanted.

At the time of his death, Major Lindsay's wife, Sarah, was pregnant with the couple's first child, which was the reason that she did not join her husband in Switzerland. She was shattered by Hugh's death, and Diana constantly visited her and helped out as much as she could. After the birth of Alice Rose Lindsay, Diana worked to lift Sarah out of her depressed state, knowing all too well the seriousness of postnatal depression. She urged the new mother to enjoy her baby but also urged her to return to work when she was able.

Charles' continued indifference toward his wife was a source of puzzlement to the public, prompting one insider to note in 1990 that Charles was probably the only man in London who was not in love with Diana. The public Wales were undoubtedly growing cooler toward, each other, but the public still had no real grasp of the seriousness of the problem.

In the spring of 1991, the Prince and Princess of Wales traveled to Czechoslovakia for an official visit, and the press immediately pounced on the fact that the couple had separate bedrooms in Prague Castle. Though appearing together at some official events, Diana had a separate schedule from her husband's, and this seemed to the press as being certain evidence of a subtle power struggle emerging between the Wales. The same day that Charles was giving an important speech on education, Diana was at a different venue speaking on AIDS. Of course the press coverage had to be split to accommodate both events, and Diana's appearance reportedly brought in more journalists than her husband's. Fueling more speculation about the Prince's jealousy of his wife's popularity, it was reported that Diana was purposely going out of her way to upstage her husband.

In June of that year, the bad luck that had plagued Diana's marriage reached out to include her beloved children. During a game of golf with some school chums, Prince William was accidentally struck on the head with a golf club, opening up a large gash that bled profusely. Diana raced over from Kensington, reportedly weeping as she drove.Charles hurried in from Highgrove. Convening at the local hospital, Diana quickly took charge of the situation, overriding Charles's wish to have William transferred to the hospital which had treated his broken arm after a polo accident some time ago. Instead, and with the approval of the doctor, the young Prince was transferred to the Great Ormond Street Hospital for Children in London, his mother at his side during the ambulance trip. Charles followed close behind, and it seemed possible that the Wales might put aside their differences and make their son their priority.

The setting aside of differences, even for the their son, was not to be. Charles left the hospital barely halfway through his son's operation for an evening at the opera. He then proceeded with an overnight trip to Yorkshire for a speaking engagement. He would not return to William's bedside for over 24 hours, to his wife's (and country's) lasting anger.

Diana, consumed with worry for her eldest, stayed at the hospital for 72 straight hours, leaving only once to briefly shower and change and once for a brief appearance at a hospital housing mentally handicapped patients who would not understand why the visit was being postponed. For the rest of the time, she was with Wills, even sleeping in the room adjacent to his.

All the world knew of Diana's enormous love for her sons, but even so her maternal solicitude was heartening. As if to allow her to concentrate solely on William's recovery, the public and the press took it upon themselves to call the Prince of Wales to task, and they were not shy in voicing their opinions.

"What Kind of Dad Are You?" screamed one headline as editors and readers alike put pen to paper in a withering dissection of Charles's priorities. Though his devotion to duty was legendary, and usually appreciated by his country, this was clearly a time when family should have come first, and no one was reticent about articulating that opinion. For weeks, letters would pour in to the Palace chastising the Prince for his hard-hearted behavior. If Charles was conscious of his blunder, he didn't let on, seemingly secure in his performance of duty, something that had been drilled into him from earliest infancy.

To Diana, perhaps, her husband's indifference wasn't quite as surprising as it was to the rest of the world. Three years previously, Prince Harry had undergone hernia surgery for a twisted testicle. Though promptly informed, Charles did not bother to cut his Italian painting holiday short, leaving Diana to cope on her own and leaving her to explain a father's absence to a sick three-year-old.

The beginning of July saw press reports of Diana spending her 30th birthday alone. The press condemned Charles for ignoring his wife, and "furious unnamed friends" of the Prince reported to the media that Charles had offered to throw Diana a party but was refused. These sources went on to state that Charles was sick of always being portrayed as the villain. Both Charles and Diana were hurt by the uproar, but as the press concentrated on gathering more tidbits from "friends" of both sides, by midweek the couple had seemingly reached a sort of truce. They were seen together at several public appearances, and both seemed to be calmly making an effort. It was also reported at this time that the royal 10th anniversary would not be marked by any special celebration, by mutual consent.

Unfortunately for Diana, the press seemed to be of the opinion that the 10th anniversary of the Prince and Princess of Wales certainly deserved some celebration aside from the usual color supplements. More harsh words for Charles and more speculation on the seriousness of the couple's marriage problems ensued. Reportedly at the urging of the Queen, Charles and Diana began appearing together in public in what appeared to be a contrived attempt on the part of the Palace to make everything seem all right. Though some papers (perhaps wistfully) spoke of the couple as a strong team who could benefit from a rest from the pursuing media, the tabloids kept up a relentless pursuit. For the rest of the year there was a frenzy of articles about the rocky state of the marriage (which was constantly on the verge of collapse), and pictures, any pictures, of Charles and Diana, preferably with a member of the opposite sex.

On February 11, 1992, during an official visit to India with her husband, Diana visited the Taj Mahal alone while Charles stayed in Delhi to deliver a speech. Photographs of the Princess in front of this great monument to lost love seemed to speak volumes about the state of her marriage. Despite the rumors these photos generated in the press, the first few months of 1992 were comparatively bearable for Diana.

The pressure of the press had eased off Diana and her husband somewhat, as other royal crises of what would become "Annus Horribilis" unfolded. Though they still lived essentially separate lives, Charles and Diana seemed to have reached a detente, at least for the sake of their sons. A skiing holiday in Lech, Austria saw Diana and her family enjoying the slopes (skiing was one activity all four of them enthusiastically engaged in), though this peaceful interlude was soon to be shattered in a way that would change Diana forever.

It was March 28, and after a day of romping in the snow with her sons, Diana was preparing for a swim when the phone rang. The caller was her brother-in-law, Sir Robert Fellowes, the Queen's private secretary. With sadness, and as gently as he could, he informed Diana that her father, Earl Spencer, had passed away suddenly from a heart attack. Diana was devastated. She had visited her father only a few days ago as he recovered in hospital from a bout of pneumonia. Both the Earl and his doctors assured Diana that he was on the mend and soon to return home, so Diana left for her holiday as planned. The Earl's sudden decline caught everyone off-guard, the result of which was, as Diana's brother, Viscount Althorp, grimly noted, "no one was with him at the end."

Diana and her father had drifted apart after his remarriage to Raine Cartland, whom Diana disliked intensely, but the Earl was always very special in Diana's heart, and he was enormously proud of his daughter. Diana remembered the man who had worked so hard to recover from a stroke in order to walk her down the aisle. He even arranged with St. Paul's to take "practice runs" to be sure he could manage the distance. Despite reservations on the part of the Palace, he had been there for her. With a huge rush of guilt, Diana realized that this time she had not been there for him, and she would never have an opportunity to make amends.

Nearing tears, she went to the balcony to call to her husband and tell him the sad news. Charles rushed in to comfort his wife and made arrangements for them to return home immediately, with the boys and their bodyguards following soon after. Terrible though the situation was, it seemed that Charles was going to be there for his family in this time of grief. Unfortunately, it was not to be as, instead of staying with his grieving wife, Charles left early to have tea with the Sultan of Brunei. Diana comforted and received comfort instead from her brother and sisters, and of course from her sons, whom she had always encouraged to call Earl Spencer "grandpa".

On an official trip to Egypt in May, Diana was again photographed alone, this time in front of the Pyramids, symbols of permanence and eternity. Like the Taj Mahal pictures, they were Diana's mute confession of her sense of isolation and abandonment. Diana's enemies began spreading rumors that she had staged both events in order to humiliate Charles and claim public sympathy, allegations that upset Diana greatly.

To some, these rumors were strengthened when The *Sunday Times* began a five-week serialization of Andrew Morton's upcoming biography of Diana, on June 7, 1992, focusing on the more sensational parts of the book such as Diana's bulimia, her alleged suicide attempts and the outright misery of her marriage. Considerable criticism in the book was directed at members of the Royal Family, including the Queen, for their lack of support for the marriage. The public was astounded by these forthright revelations, most of which came from named sources who, when questioned, stood by the veracity of their reports. Unlike the sensational reports of times past, this book had a definite air of authority about it. There was more than one suggestion that Diana had a direct hand in the writing, which was completely incorrect but continued on in the press as a tantalizing possibility for speculation on the depths of Diana's perfidy.

It was on this same day that Camilla Parker-Bowles was personally welcomed into the Royal Enclosure at Windsor by the Queen, a further example of the disdain of the Royal Family for Diana, and perhaps tacit approval of Camilla's relationship with Charles. Due to her husband's position in the Palace, there was certainly nothing improper with the Parker-Bowles being there, but the way that the Queen singled Camilla out showed that she was making a point. Either way, it was a stinging and very public rebuke for the Princess, and Diana soon began to feel the full disapproval of the Royal Family.

Questioning her involvement with the Morton biography (which she had no direct hand in, though she had given her friends permission to speak with him), Diana reportedly wondered if perhaps her well-meaning friends had been a little too candid, or if Morton himself had seen fit to exaggerate things. She found herself in the position of having to answer very private questions on a constant basis. Had she really tried to kill herself by throwing herself down a staircase, despite the fact that she was several months pregnant with William? The pressure was intense. Even Diana's public composure had its limits, and the overwhelming support of a crowd at a speaking engagement finally tipped the balance. On July 12 she attended a function at a Southport hospice, and the Chairman delivered a heartfelt welcome to Diana, closing with the words, "may you stay exactly as you are." This most unlooked-for show of support, loudly echoed by the roaring approval of the crowd, was overwhelming for the Princess, and she wept openly as her car pulled away.

Fate had more cruel surprises in store for Diana. On August 24, transcripts of a conversation allegedly between the Princess and her close friend James Gilbey were published in the *Sun*, and the press had a field day. The 23-minute conversation, illegally taped, consisted mostly of idle chatter about clothes, mutual friends and astrology, interspersed with declarations of love by Gilbey, who referred to Diana as Squidge or Squidgy. The tapes had reportedly first been offered to the press in 1990 (the conversation having taken place in 1989), yet apparently the press still had enough scruples to question the ethics of publishing the transcripts. The fact that the publication occurred during a press war was, the *Sun* stated, a complete coincidence.

The public, being for the most part sensible creatures, saw the tape for what it was, and Diana's popularity was little affected by the incident. The tapes were more embarrassing than damaging, for the passion seemed to be entirely one-sided. In response to Gilbey's fevered declaration "Oh Squidgy, I love you, love you, love you", Diana diplomatically replied, "You are the nicest person in the world." Nice people were in short supply for Diana at this stage, and the public seemed more amused than offended by the giggly schoolgirl talk, which only reinforced her image as a real, normal person instead of another Windsor automaton.

The only potentially damaging parts of the conversation consisted of scattered remarks about her marriage and her in-laws. Telling Gilbey about her day, Diana confessed that she had not been in good spirits, and had ended up thinking "Bloody hell, after all I've done for this f***ing family." Aside from the shock of the Princess using an expletive, there was no denying (in the public's eye) that the statement rang true. From day one, Diana had consistently improved the public image of the Royal Family, not to mention the fact that she was the mother of the children who would ensure the continuation of the House of Windsor.

Her comment about Charles's grandmother rankled some, as the Queen Mother was a perennial favorite with everyone, no matter what crisis her family was undergoing. Once again, though, it was hard to argue with Diana's observation that the Queen Mum was "always looking at me with a strange look in her eyes. It's not hatred, it's sort of interest and pity mixed up in one." By 1992, most of the world was looking at Diana in that way.

Though the conversation was three years old, it was clear that the marriage had been on the rocks for some time, and Diana did not mince words with Gilbey, stating "I'll go out and do my bit in the way I know how and I'll leave him behind. That's what I see happening." Charles, she revealed, "makes my life real, real torture."

As the Palace damage control team once again swung into action, officials at Buckingham reportedly met with officials of several London papers at the end of October, and soon articles proclaiming the marriage to be on the mend began to pop up. Sources alleged that the Queen herself issued the royal couple a direct order to shape up, at least in public. An upcoming tour of Korea was suggested pointedly as the perfect launch-pad for the new, improved marriage. Reportedly originally against the idea of Diana coming along, Charles bowed to his mother's authority and off they went.

Primed by the imminent release of the updated version of Andrew Morton's sensational biography, the press dogged every step of the royal visit to South Korea. No mercy was shown to the couple, who were supposedly on the verge of working out their relationship, as they engaged in what Buckingham Palace had touted as the "togetherness tour." The only togetherness the couple managed was to occasionally be in the same vague geographic location: Diana was visibly unhappy, while

Charles was trying to ignore his wife, a situation which led the press to nickname them "The Glums." the *Daily Mirror* scathingly asked "if they could not be bothered to put on a better show in public, they might as well give it up." Again reporting their separate itineraries as sure signs of imminent royal separation, the press gave only minimal coverage to the success of these individual endeavors which were so well suited to each party. Charles promoted British exports and strengthened the British-Korean trade links (which had become increasingly important for his country), while Diana was in her element promoting social causes, visiting the Salvation Army and charming the public with her own special brand of captivating charm.

Though perhaps not in a state of wedded bliss, Charles and Diana seemed to have come to an arrangement that seemed to combine their strengths. As a public relations team for Britain, they each did their own thing, which both guaranteed that they would not be forced to spend much time together, as well as allowing both of them to do what they enjoyed. Charles had always been a tireless promoter of all things British and was at ease in front of a room of businessmen. Diana, of course, was more at home with meeting the public at large and with promoting humanitarian causes. They both agreed to this arrangement not only because it would make things easier for themselves, but would also be putting on a show of solidarity for the monarchy, in which not only the Prince and Princess, but their beloved sons had a vested interest.

The press, however, focused on the fact that the Royals seemed much happier apart than together. Why, they demanded to know, should the couple continue with what was obviously a loveless marriage? This was the same press that ran fear-mongering articles about the peril to the monarchy and the British people if the split did occur.

Three days later, after Diana returned home alone (while Charles continued on to Hong Kong), the *Sunday Times* reported comments by Diana herself that her marriage was in trouble. Armed with this, plus a similar private remark by Charles's deputy private secretary, the press shouted from their mastheads about the elaborate hoax that Buckingham Palace was trying to foist on an unsuspecting British public. "Truce" had turned to "Charade," and things were only going to get worse.

The next week saw the *Sun* publish extracts from the updated Morton biography, which outlined the "second honeymoon" cruise and Diana's discovery of Charles conversations with Camilla. The book also reported an angry exchange of letters between Prince Philip and Diana, in which he allegedly upbraided her for the first Morton book and essentially stated that the Royal Family could do quite nicely without her.

The press and the public began to turn their resentment toward Buckingham Palace for reportedly forcing the couple to stay together for so long. Even some of the more respectable members of the fourth estate begin to voice an opinion that the Royal Family should face up to reality and see the need for a sensible separation.

Finally, to no one's surprise but to many people's sorrow, the separation of the Prince and Princess of Wales was officially announced in a statement released simultaneously by Buckingham Palace and Prime Minister John Major in the House of Commons on December 9, 1992. It was a remarkably brief document to sum up the agony of eleven years, but it spoke volumes about the torture that Diana's life had become:

"It is announced from Buckingham Palace that, with regret, the Prince and Princess of Wales have decided to separate. Their Royal Highnesses have no plans to divorce and their constitutional positions are unaffected. This decision has been reached amicably, and they will both continue to participate fully in the upbringing of their children.

"Their Royal Highnesses will continue to carry out full and separate programmes of public engagements and will, from time to time, attend family occasions and national events together.

"The Queen and the Duke of Edinburgh, though saddened, understand and sympathise with the difficulties that have led to this decision. Her Majesty and His Royal Highness particularly hope that the intrusions into the privacy of the Prince and Princess may now cease. They believe that a degree of privacy and understanding is essential if their Royal Highnesses are to provide a happy and secure upbringing for their children, while continuing to give a wholehearted commitment to their public duties." (*Times*, Dec. 10, 1992: 1)

The House was remarkably silent after the announcement, and one Member of Parliament rose to say that he had nothing to say on the topic, then sat back down. Even the Archbishop of Canterbury, in a message read by the Archbishop of York, endorsed the announcement, stating "separation is the lesser of two evils."

Prime Minister Major's speech on the separation raised eyebrows when he boldly stated that the separation raised no constitutional issues and that it was no barrier to Diana becoming (one day, perhaps) the Queen. Though technically correct, this stance was not a certainty, as politicians of every stripe rushed to assure their constituents that the will of the people, through their elected officials, would have a large say in the decision.

The tabloids outdid themselves with anti-Diana stories during the next few months, calling her "Devious Di", the gold-digger who had walked away from Charles with everything she wanted, at the expense of the monarchy and the British public. Even the timing of the announcement was blamed on her. The date had been agreed upon by all the involved parties in order to have the news broken to William and Harry before the end of their school term, but certain elements of the press saw it as Diana's last kick at the Royals, as the announcement overshadowed the wedding of Princess Anne on the upcoming weekend.

Diana bore these stories with considerable stoicism, though reportedly articles that questioned her fitness as a mother reduced her to impotent tears of rage and frustration. To make matters worse, Charles was practically in seclusion at Highgrove, which had been his primary residence for some time (Diana would continue at Kensington). Puttering away behind the walls of his garden, he neatly removed himself from much of the media storm.

As if to outdo the horror of 1992, Diana's new year began with the most humiliating occurrence, a happening which shocked not only her, but the whole world. On January 12, 1993, the *Sun* published the transcript of an alleged phone call between Prince Charles and his old friend Camilla Parker-Bowles, recorded in December 1989.

Unlike the ultimately harmless "Squidgygate" tapes of the previous year, this conversation was raunchy to the extreme and left no doubt that the speakers were on very intimate terms. Britain was scandalized by such filthy talk by the royal heir, who joked about being reincarnated as his lover's underwear, or perhaps even a tampon, in order to always be with her. The entire conversation was one long chain of sexual innuendo that seemed so completely out of character for the Prince that some immediately assumed the tape to be faked. Unfortunately, there was no evidence to indicate that this tape was a forgery.

Though incredibly hurtful to Diana just on general principle, as they confirmed what she had known all along, the tone of the tapes was especially upsetting. Why had Charles never been so uninhibited with her? She had tried for years to get him to open up to her and had ultimately decided that he was incapable of such a relationship. Yet now here was graphic proof that she had been completely wrong.

The "Camillagate" tapes set the tabloids on fire, especially since Charles and Camilla had been seen together more and more frequently since his separation. Camilla was still married to Andrew, who was by now promoted to Silver Stick in Waiting at Buckingham Palace and promoted to Brigadier. The lack of his concern for the relationship was summed up by one Palace informant who quipped that when a man was cuckolded by another man, he reached for a gun, but when he was cuckolded by royalty, he reached for the champagne. Certainly the former Major's career had not suffered because of the affair.

Because of security concerns, Diana had continued on living at Kensington, though she longed for a place of her own. The separation couldn't really begin until she was physically removed from royalty, but it seemed impossible to find a suitable place which also met with the approval of the security team which still protected Diana and her sons. "Camillagate" gave her further incentive to move out of the house which had been intended as the home of a happy Prince and Princess. The perfect solution came about it April, when Diana's brother came to her rescue by offering her Garden House, a smallish house on his estate at Althorp. Diana was thrilled at the prospect and immediately took her sons and an interior designer to have a look at the place, which was exactly the sort of refuge the Princess had been looking for.

Her wonderful new life, unfortunately, was not to be. Three weeks later the Earl withdrew his offer, explaining that the required level of security for their residence would interfere with the running of Althorp (which was open to the public as a stately home). As a consequence, her residence there would not allow Diana the freedom she was seeking. Her brother would not be swayed in his decision, and, though Diana understood his reservations, she remained quite hurt at the sudden collapse of her dreams. For the foreseeable future, Diana would remain a prisoner of the Windsors at Kensington. The stress of these living arrangements was beginning to take its toll on Diana, who did not feel comfortable at Kensington. Yet, due to the constant presence of the press, Diana could not freely leave her residence without a confrontation.

The first week of November was a misery for Diana. The tabloids reported that her bulimia had resurfaced (which it hadn't, despite all the stress she was undergoing). Diana chose to face the issue head-on, and she made light of the constant reports of her fragile physical and emotional states at a charity relaunch on November 4. "Ladies and gentlemen, I think you are very fortunate to have your patron here today.

I was supposed to have my head down the loo for most of the day. I'm supposed to be dragged off the minute I leave here by men in white coats. (But) if it's all right with you, I thought I might postpone my nervous breakdown." ("The Outsider" *People,* Dec 6, 1993). Diana had not been scheduled to speak at this engagement, and the impromptu speech surprised many. The audience, who empathized with her problems and appreciated her ability to make light of it, was clearly sympathetic. Others, however, saw this as yet another example of how fragile Diana was becoming. It was only a matter of time, the tabloids speculated, until she snapped. Her postpartum depression was once again brought up as the press tried to establish a pattern of emotional irrationality for the woman they once labeled mentally unstable.

If anyone had good reason to be emotional that day, it was the Princess. Unknown to most, that day had also seen the resignation of Simon Solari, her chauffeur. The fact that she would be losing another friend was enough of a blow, but Simon had decided to go to work for Charles, since, as he delicately put it, Diana's situation was unstable, while the Prince's was secure. Though she understood his need to think of his family's future, Simon's departure was deeply wounding.

Nor was Simon the only member of her staff to leave her employ. Only the previous day her favorite bodyguard, Ken Wharfe, was reassigned to look after some visiting dignitaries. This departure was hard not only on Diana, but it was also hard on her sons, as Ken was reportedly very popular with the young Princes as well. Rumors circulated that the reassignment had occurred because it was felt that the bodyguard was becoming too involved with his charges, and one particularly malicious rumor insinuated that Diana herself had ordered the change because the Princes had occasionally preferred Ken's company to hers.

Following hard on the heels of these domestic upheavals was the publication on November 7 of the infamous "workout" photos, taken secretly at L.A. Fitness, a London gym where Diana occasionally exercised. If this betrayal and humiliation were not enough, reports soon began to circulate that Diana must have known about and even participated in the taking of these less-than-flattering photos. The reasons for this were incredibly flimsy: the pictures were too clear and appeared "posed," and (the ultimate proof), Diana did not appear to be sweating. What this proved to Diana was that nowhere was safe, and no one could be trusted except for her sons, who were rapidly becoming her only lifeline. They, she knew, would never betray her.

During this year, while Diana was being mauled by the press, Charles was actually enjoying some favorable coverage. Though his forte was business and architecture, he stole a page from Diana's book and was seen several times at engagements where the theme was more social than economic. Imitating Diana's secret visits to hospitals and shelters, he casually dropped in to chat to an astonished former paratrooper who had lost his legs in an IRA bomb attack. While some of the press viewed this as an attempt to repair the damage of the "Camillagate" tapes, favorable reports of the Prince began to appear. With the full force of the Palace's PR machine behind him, Charles's image in the last half of 1993 was improving.

Whatever sympathy Charles had garnered was soon dispensed with after Jonathan Dimbleby's new book (which he cooperated with) hit the bookstores. The book combined with the Prince's subsequent television appearance. The British public listened dumbstruck as the heir to the British throne admitted that he had been unfaithful to his wife. Though he seemed to have been expecting his candor to be applauded by the public, Charles received instead loud suggestions that perhaps it would be better for everyone if he stepped aside and let William take the throne when the time came. At the same time, the public began to reassess their opinions of Charles's parents, who, in the book had been portrayed as aloof and cold, resulting in a rather lonely childhood for their son.

Diana felt understandably vindicated by her husband's admission, though she reportedly was upset that he stated that the adultery happened only after their marriage broke down. Like many people, Diana knew that Charles's "friendship" with Camilla had been going on since before the wedding. The criticism of the Queen and Prince Philip was surprising, as it was the first time Diana had heard firsthand of his childhood. Why, she reportedly wondered bitterly, couldn't he confide this to me?

The summer of 1994 saw Charles and Diana spending little time together, and the tabloids became more aggressive in their pursuit of them both. Pictures of Charles and Camilla were everywhere, much to Diana's dismay. Unfortunately for the Princess, her husband's affair would soon be old news, as a treacherous skeleton came rattling out of her own closet.

Diana had known for some time that her long-speculated at affair with Life Guardsman James Hewitt was in danger of being exposed, but she had no idea as to the cruelty with which this would be revealed. Rumors indicated that Hewitt himself was the source of the leaks, but the man himself phoned Diana to inform her that he had written a book, and to reassure her as to its contents. Naively (or stupidly, as she later recalled the situation), Diana believed him. Ten days later, on October 3, *Princess in Love* was released to an unsuspecting nation.

Written by Anna Pasternak (grandniece of *Dr. Zhivago* author Boris Pasternak) from interviews with Hewitt, and presented in the style of a romance novel, the book was condemned by Buckingham Palace (and most papers) as "tawdry, grubby, and worthless." Even in a country over-burdened with royal scandal, the book proved to be a sensation, despite (or perhaps because of) its obvious literary failings. Even the *Financial Times* made mention of it. The book that Hewitt had assured Diana was harmless was provoking a genuine crisis for the monarchy. Confronted with Hewitt's book and Charles's own admission, the public could only conclude one thing: both the Prince and Princess were adulterers. This state of affairs shocked the nation. The press viewed Diana's fall from grace in a much darker light than Charles, the reason being that at least Charles had the dignity to tell the public himself, while Diana had waited for her paramour to sell his story to the highest bidder.

The book was kiss-and-tell at its worst, chronicling in torrid detail a five-year relationship, and Diana was once more held up for public ridicule. Headlines portrayed the entire Royal Family as ridiculous. Observing that cuckolding the Prince of Wales was an act of treason, one witness to the events suggested that Hewitt deserved execution. For her part, Diana might have been first in line for the axe to execute Hewitt, but she had other concerns on her mind. While Hewitt was universally censured as a scoundrel for his actions, and rejected by his fellow officers (the tabloids dubbed him "the love slug"), Diana's immediate concern was for her sons.

Rushing to them at school, Diana explained the situation as best she could and tried to answer questions of her sons honestly. In a much-needed and much-appreciated show of support, William reportedly gave his distraught mother some chocolates, saying, "Mummy, I think you've been hurt. These are to make you smile again," showing the same sensitivity to his mother's emotions that had him stuffing tissues to Diana under the bathroom door after she'd had a row with Charles years ago.

Satisfied that her sons would be all right, but exacting a promise from the headmaster that they would not be reading any newspapers, Diana returned to London to face the controversy. As she feared, many articles attacked her fitness as a mother, particularly as the mother of the future King of England. Rumors of Charles and Camilla paled in comparison with Hewitt's boasts, and for several months Diana had the glare of the spotlight all to herself. The Royal Family, in its stony silence, was not amused.

The new year allowed Diana no respite, as the tabloids stalked her mercilessly. Every man she was seen with was hounded by the press and became the subject of very unflattering public debate. Every sign of irritation at the press was proof of an unbalanced mental state, and every gracious smile was examined for any signs of sarcasm or fakery. The cameras descended on her the moment she set foot outside her door and did not relent until she returned, worn out and anxious.

On March 3, 1995, Camilla Parker-Bowles and her husband were divorced. The media immediately began speculating about the possibility of Charles marrying her, and the hunt for the Royal Divorce was on. Matters were not helped by the revelation that Camilla was settled into a mansion that was only miles from Highgrove. The pros and cons of a remarried monarch versus a separated one were hotly debated. Strangely, the issue of William and Harry's upbringing was all but ignored. The possibility of Camilla assuming the role of a stepmother to the boys apparently wasn't an issue for the press, yet the possibility of Diana remarrying caused the press to recoil in horror. Camilla proved a tolerable choice for the press, but the prospects that another man, any man, could raise the future monarch was unthinkable.

This paranoia of the press was highlighted in August, when they linked Diana with the married captain of the English National Rugby Team, Will Carling. The relationship was completely fictitious, but the fact that Carling and his wife separated by the end of September lent the fiction an element of substance in the eyes of the tabloids. They eagerly reported on the ex-wife's allegations that the Princess of Wales ruined her marriage. Diana the homewrecker was the newest press fiction, and like all the others it hung around for far too long, considering its lack of substance.

As 1995 was coming to an end, so was Diana's patience. The separation was supposed to have allowed her some breathing room, but instead public scrutiny had increased tremendously, and there were no longer any moral guidelines holding the baser elements of the press in check. As a separated member of the Royal Family, her police protection was not as formidable as it once was, and photojournalists thrust their lenses right in her face. Not only frustrated by her own situation, but also worried about the effect the pressure was having on her sons, Diana decided that the time had come to take matters into her own hands. On November 20, 1995, an interview with the Princess of Wales appeared on the BBC news program "*Panorama*."

Appearing poised and self-confident, Diana outlined her naive first years of marriage and how the intrusion of the press turned partners into rivals. With no hint of embarrassment she answered questions about her bulimia and battles with postpartum depression. She professed admiration for the courage it took her husband to publicly admit his adultery, but though she stopped short of blaming her husband's mistress, Camilla, for the separation, she wryly noted "there were three of us in this marriage so it was a bit crowded."

Accepting half the blame for the separation, Diana then confirmed her own adulterous affair with James Hewitt and spoke of the pain caused by his betrayal when he knew how much she had adored him. Recognizing that she still had a role to play in royal life, she expressed hope of becoming an ambassador for Britain, something that she had been unofficially for years. She had long ago given up the notion of ever becoming Queen of England, and instead hoped to be a "queen of people's hearts." Any ambition for the throne would be limited to William's prospects, and Charles, she suggested, needed to sort himself out so the pressures of Kingship wouldn't overwhelm him. She also came out strongly against those who had accused her of deliberately sabotaging the monarchy. Such a suggestion was ridiculous, as it was her children's future and destiny, and Diana would sooner hurt herself than deliberately allow her children to be harmed.

The interview had been done without the knowledge of the Palace, or indeed of her own staff, and her press secretary resigned the next day, as the aftermath of what one reporter described as the biggest crisis since the Abdication began. Crisis it may have been in some quarters, but right after the interview ended the BBC switchboard lit up with calls, most of which expressed support for Diana, praising her courage and control. Many pointed out that her affair began only after years of loveless marriage, while Charles had been with Camilla practically since Diana was a child (Charles and Camilla reportedly first met at a polo match in 1970), and had possibly married Diana while maintaining a relationship with Camilla.

Either oblivious to the interview or perhaps exercising some damage control, Buckingham Palace announced on November 24 that Diana would be spending Christmas at Sandringham with the Royal Family. They were forced to retract this on December 18, as Diana decided to spend the holidays elsewhere, though William and Harry would make the journey. Despite everything, Diana readily acknowledged the fact that her boys were part of "the Firm,"and she had no desire to keep them from their relatives because of her marital problems. Only Buckingham Palace stood to gain from Diana's inclusion in the Christmas party, and Diana had no intention of helping their cause. The television interview was her Declaration of Independence, and she knew that there was no going back.

On December 20, finally bowing to the inevitable, and perhaps with the welfare of her grandsons in mind, Queen Elizabeth urged Charles and Diana to divorce. Despite her own personal vow to keep her family intact and not repeat her family history, Diana realized that to stay with Charles would cause more harm to herself and her sons than a divorce. The negotiations began quietly, but the press soon caught wind, and not only was the fate of the monarchy again up for debate, but wild speculation about the possible divorce settlement began to appear. More than one report indicated that Diana was allegedly threatening to take her sons and move to another country, which was completely ridiculous. The sums of money hinted at were equally fictitious.

More serious discussions began to take place in higher circles. No one had ever been faced with a divorced Princess of Wales, and debate raged over what her status in the royal scheme of things would be. Once again, certain anti-monarchists saw this as the perfect time to bring an end to the monarchy, which to their minds was admirably demonstrating its own redundancy. It was speculated that Queen Elizabeth II might very well be the last British monarch. The eyes of the world focused on Britain, and Diana, as this painful spasm carried on for weeks.

Finally, on February 28, 1996, the press announced that Diana, Princess of Wales, had agreed to a divorce. A whole new chapter in British legal history was about to begin. And with it, hopefully, a happier chapter for the latest casualty of Windsor matrimony.

Chapter 8

Stepping Out

While news of Charles and Diana's separation in December, 1992, created worldwide disillusionment with the story that had begun as a fairy-tale—a bride and groom gloriously dressed in their finery lighting up millions of television screens with a kiss. Diana soon proved herself an independent woman of the '90s and impressed the world with her sense of duty, charity and tenderhearted concern for the outcast and downtrodden. Diana demonstrated a caring for others which ignored his or her station or physical condition. She became an icon not only to the most unfortunate but also to an entire generation of women struggling to gain control of their lives. Diana appeared to a feminist generation to be a woman who knew what she wanted and how to get it, while simultaneously appearing to be the perfect mother. In the public perception, Diana was growing stronger, a survivor of incredible circumstances—including a very publicly failed marriage.

An impending separation first became evident in the late '80s when Diana began to strike out on her own in fulfilling official duties, leaving the public to wonder why Charles and Diana spent so much time apart. Diana initially tried to excuse the obvious, suggesting that with literally thousands of invitations to visit places around the world, the couple could not possibly get through so many if they did them all together. She explained that she and Charles had decided to accept as many invitations as they could by appearing separately.

While the public face of Diana valiantly covered up her struggles with Charles, privately she could take no more. Some believe that the turning point for Diana came in March of 1988 during a skiing holiday in Klosters. Her strength of character returned when Prince Charles's press secretary, Philip Mackie, entered the chalet where Diana and Sarah Ferguson were visiting. Diana overheard Mackie talking about an accident and though he tried to put her off, Diana, for perhaps the first time, would not be dissuaded by court staff. Insisting that he tell her what was happening, Diana learned that a man had been killed on the slopes during an avalanche. According to biographer Andrew Morton's account of the incident, Charles later wanted to return to the slopes. Diana, however, took command of the situation and persuaded her husband to accompany the body of Major Hugh Lindsay (former equerry to the Queen) to Britain, where Diana would play a role in comforting Hugh's widow Sarah, then six months pregnant. It was this situation, according to Morton, that proved to Diana her ability to take on even the most difficult situation and make decisions despite opposition from her husband.

Shortly thereafter, after much urging from her friend, Carolyn Bartholomew, Diana sought treatment for her depression and bulimia. As if determined to rid herself of all the demons that had been terrorizing her, Diana confronted Camilla Parker-Bowles at a birthday party in May of 1989. Interrupting a chat between Camilla and Charles, and dismissing others in the room, Diana informed Camilla that she suspected something was going on between her and Prince Charles. It was during that confrontation that she poured out her anger, jealousy and frustration about the intervention of Charles's mistress in her marriage. Her venting brought about an observable change in Diana's attitude that set off a string of events that would forever change the face of the British Monarchy.

It was also during this time that Diana's interest in spiritual matters began to peak. While seeking the predictions of astrologers, Diana began a journey of self-discovery that would ultimately lead to her becoming more self-assured. She developed regular habits that included daily workouts, swimming and training in Tai Chi Chuan, and experimentation with such techniques as aromatherapy and hypnotherapy, reportedly spending as much as £12 000 a year on colonic irrigation and other forms of therapy and massage.

The Princess put on a brave face in her isolated position and worked to develop an image of a strong person. When depression, boredom or loneliness crept in, however, Diana reportedly treated her symptoms by going shopping. According to Royal watchers, Diana loved to shop, preferring trendy stores such as the Gap, where she would buy jeans. Her finer apparel was often purchased from well-known designers such as Catherine Walker, Victor Edelstein, Thomasz Starzewski and later, Versace. Diana did not just spend money on herself, however, but was said to enjoy buying gifts for her inner circle and their children and for the men in her life.

During her shopping excursions Diana frequently included dinner at her favorite restaurants: San Lorenzo (where she ate with her sons William and Harry), Mimmo D'Ischia (where she dined with Oliver Hoare) and Daphne's (where she had a special corner table). With her friends she enjoyed west-end restaurants: Mortons, the Caviar Kaspia, and Le Caprice (where she had been seen with British television personality Clive James). Most of the time, however, Diana ate alone at Kensington Palace, where she attended to her duties: preparing for official visits or for the receiving of visitors who worked with the charities she patronized. Her evenings were a time when the Princess liked to make private visits, away from prying eyes.

Queen Elizabeth described 1992 as her "annus horribilis," and it was in June of that year that *Diana, Her True Story*, written by tabloid reporter Andrew Morton, was published. Although Diana had not met with Morton personally, she cooperated in the writing of his book by allowing her friends to speak with Morton. Diana was at the end of her tether and desperate that the public understand that she was neither stupid nor crazy. She had been described during earlier times as mentally unstable, suffering from bulimia and depression. In Morton's book, Diana is depicted as having been trapped inside a loveless marriage in which she resorted to suicide attempts in order to attract the attention of her unconcerned husband, Charles. Diana later discussed her reasons for approving of the book, saying she hoped "people would have a better understanding." Diana reasoned that her own experiences might shed light for other women dealing with suffering on the same level but in different circumstances.

Morton's book resulted in a push for Charles and Diana to mend their fences or separate. Though Diana clearly did not relish the idea of a divorce, having been raised in that environment, their relationship seemed headed in that direction, with the couple unable to find healing once the problems had been admitted openly. While Charles and Diana continued their public engagements together, their private lives remained in tatters. Powerless to repair the damaged marriage, Charles and Diana sought the advice of lawyers, and discussions began about a formal separation. Diana described her feeling during this time as a "deep, deep, profound sadness," though she also admitted that her feelings were mixed with a sense of relief, knowing that she and her soon-to-be ex-husband had finally made up their minds.

Then on August 25, 1992, fuel was added to the fire when newspapers published excerpts of a telephone conversation taped in 1989 between Diana and her friend James Gilbey, a distillery heir, who called her Squidgy and told her that he loved her. Though their conversation seemed to imply that their friendship had deepened and become adulterous, Diana denied that it had. Some tabloids conflicted with her claim, however, saying that Diana had been seen leaving Gilbey's London apartment late at night. Diana expressed her worry that Gilbey's life would be messed up because of his connection with her. She believed that the tape had deliberately been given to the press for the express purpose of harming her reputation. It was then that Diana knew what it was like to be an outsider rather than part of the Royal Family.

In October of that year officials attempted to persuade the public to believe that the royal marriage had taken a turn for the better. A headline appearing in the *Daily Mail* asked the question "Was the magic returning to Diana's marriage?" The paper reported that Diana had a fresh look in her eye and proposed that she and Charles were starting over. But any hope that had been put forward fell dead in November, 1992, when Charles and Diana attended their last engagement together, a disastrous tour of South Korea where their downcast faces were broadcast all over the world. The couple's sour expressions were interpreted to be defeating their pursuits as goodwill ambassadors for Britain. All was not necessarily as it seemed, however, as the tabloids construed their expressions to be something other than what they were. One photograph of the couple staring stony-faced, apparently miserable in each other's company, was in fact taken during a wreath laying ceremony at a monument for soldiers killed in the Korean War. While doleful looks were completely appropriate for the occasion, newspapers claimed the marriage was over.

In contrast to her sadness standing alongside Charles in Korea, Diana brightened on a solo trip to Paris while Charles stayed home and celebrated his 44th birthday. The Princess arrived in Paris, where she met with President Mitterrand. Alone with the French president and his family, Diana confidently discussed social and humanitarian issues without her husband by her side. Her confidence had grown in recent years and was such that she was unafraid of being herself, a good sign that she would be able to survive the blow when their separation was finally official. According to a biographer of Diana, Penny Junor, she did not hesitate to use her limited French on that trip to Paris, remaining unintimidated by fluent speakers of the language. It was this relaxed demeanor, along with her direct approach to life and people of all classes and ranks, that endeared her to the world. Diana had blossomed from the shy teenager who had wed the future king of England into a confident spokesperson, holding court with presidents and royalty as if she'd been born to do it. Yet while she was clearly adept at being very much a princess, Diana had an extraordinary ability to remain just as much a vulnerable, open and loving human being.

Shortly thereafter, on December 9th, the official announcement of their separation was made. Diana was on an engagement at the time and heard the announcement on the radio. A week prior, Diana had traveled to see her sons, still in school, to tell them about their parents decision to separate. Almost immediately people's perceptions changed. Diana was now the separated wife of the future king of England. She was considered by the Royal Family to be a liability and she soon found herself at odds with those on her husband's side.

Immediately following the news of the separation at the end of 1992, it was unclear whether Diana would remain legally a part of the Royal Family, although Diana made it clear that she valued the prospect of going her own way. By the time their separation was announced, Diana had already adopted charity work as her royal duty, having carved it out for herself rather than having had it thrust upon her when she married.

Royal watchers suggest that Diana began her walk down the humanitarian road when Prince Charles broke his arm in 1990. While visiting Charles at the hospital, she also spent time with other patients. Andrew Morton described a more memorable visit to the hospital, where Diana saw housewife Freda Hickling in the intensive care unit. She was on life support, having fallen into a coma, and was flanked by her husband, whom Diana had noticed holding his wife's hand. According to Morton's description of the visit, Diana entered the room with Mr. Hickling's permission and spent two hours holding both his and his wife's hands before Mrs. Hickling was pronounced dead. Her compassion for a complete stranger did not go unnoticed.

Over the course of time Diana became an ardent supporter and spokesperson for numerous charitable organizations and humanitarian causes. She had a particular soft spot for underprivileged children, especially for those suffering with AIDS, cancer and other forms of illness and deprivation, though her heart reached out to children and adults alike. Diana, in fact, had first taken on AIDS charities against the advice of Palace officials, though Diana's desires had prevailed, and she had ignored them. As a result, Diana helped to remove the fear surrounding a disease that was perceived at the time as creating untouchables.

By the end of 1993 Diana was feeling the pressure her separation had caused. While she desired to remain active in her charitable efforts, Diana needed a rest. She described herself as having been constantly tired and unable to give her full attention to her duty. Consequently, Diana made a speech effectively withdrawing herself from public pursuits. She remained out of view for a period of about four months in an effort to avoid the continued negative publicity that had focused on her separation from Prince Charles.

Having ensured her public that she was not going away for good, Diana indicated in a later interview with the BBC that she never really stopped working but simply avoided the limelight. During this time she had continued to support many charities for homeless children and those dealing with the treatment of drug abuse and AIDS. But her retreat surprised the enemy, as she came to call her detractors, and her move to confuse them was a success in relieving some of the pressure.

Guided by her brother-in-law Sir Robert Fellowes, the Queen's private secretary, Diana eventually began taking on more public engagements. In February, 1994 she toured Japan for four days, where she was mobbed by fans chanting "Diana-san, Diana-san." Clearly Dianamania had not yet run its course. It was in Japan that Diana made a particularly good impression, winning the hearts of her hosts by beginning her tour with a short speech in Japanese. With just 34 words, according to reports, Diana proved her confidence was back.

June took her to Venice and Moscow, followed by a visit to Paris in September. Diana was to visit Argentina that November and then appear at a Manhattan charity gala. To Royal watchers the change in Diana was dramatic. Just a short time before, Diana had seemed less sure of where she was headed. Her numerous visits to the United States had suggested an aimlessness and created a belief that she was considering leaving Britain for good.

Her new sense of direction was not to be established without more shattering revelations along the way. In July of 1994 Charles publicly admitted having committed adultery with his long time paramour, Camilla Parker-Bowles. The royal soap opera was wholly on the table then, with no more denials about what had caused the end to their storybook marriage. Though Diana was devastated by his public confession, she was admittedly somewhat in awe of his confirmation of the ongoing affair that the world had always suspected. In November of that year, during her interview with the BBC, Diana described Charles as being rather brave, saying that "it takes a lot to do that...to be honest about a relationship with someone else, in his position—that's quite something."

Following Charles's confession, the attacks on Diana continued. She was accused of having made a series of harassing phone calls to friend and art dealer Oliver Hoare. Though she denied making the rumored 300 prank telephone calls, the press hounded her and she believed a campaign was being waged against her out of fear that she would retain the upper hand. Diana was well aware that her every movement was always highlighted by the press while Charles was often ignored by the media—and that situation didn't change even after their separation.

Diana continued to focus on the future. Amid rumors of an impending divorce, she met with the Queen's private secretary, reportedly hoping to carve out a role for herself as an official goodwill ambassador. Then in October of 1994 a final blow struck the royal marriage. *A Princess in Love* was published, in which James Hewitt claimed to have had a very close relationship with the Princess beginning in 1989. Hewitt, an army captain, was the man in whom the lonely, bulimic and self-pitying Diana had taken solace. Their affair ended in 1991, and in 1994 his book proclaimed that he was the man who had succeeded in cuckolding Prince Charles—technically an act of treason.

Diana supported his claim during her televised interview with the BBC, remarking that he had been a great friend to her during a very difficult time in her life. But she was understandably shattered when he broke her trust and told all. While Diana admitted that Hewitt's book contained some fact, it was greatly mixed with his own fantasy. Ultimately Diana was let down by this man, someone she had trusted, that later turned on her for a cash prize.

As a result of his admitted affair, Hewitt became a virtual outcast among his peers. Reportedly he had been blackballed at the private Cavalry and Guards Club in London, and the South Devon Hunt had refused to accept his payment of dues. One Hunt member reportedly indicated that if Hewitt showed up at one of their meetings he would likely be the one being chased while the fox was left alone. Hewitt lost face with the women in his life as well: his fiancee breaking off their engagement when he plainly boasted about his relationship with Diana.

Having left the army in 1993, Hewitt reportedly used book proceeds to buy an estate outside the village of Bratton Clovelly in 1994. According to Anna Pasternak, co-author of *Princess in Love*, Hewitt believed that his only crime was in giving Diana the love she so desperately wanted. It was widely speculated, however, that Hewitt (who had a reputation for living beyond his means) would continue his betrayal and consider publishing the reported 46 letters Diana had written him while he was in the Persian Gulf in 1991. Although snippets described as coming from that collection found their way into the press, Royal watchers believed that the real letters were still hidden. Though newspapers are said to have offered Hewitt up to $500,000 for the letters, he hadn't accepted. It was speculated that if he had, he would have been severely castigated by his fellow officers for the ultimate breach of faith.

Another book, also published in October of 1994, entitled *The Prince of Wales* by Jonathan Dimbleby, portrayed Diana as a troubled wife and Charles as a long-suffering victim.

When the question of divorce surfaced, Diana dumped the pressure for an answer on her husband, saying she didn't want one but was waiting to hear his wishes. In the meantime, Diana made it abundantly clear that if there were to be a divorce, it would not be an easy one. She indicated that she wouldn't go quietly and that she would fight to the end because she had a role to fill with two children to bring up.

The Palace response to Diana's determination to retain a public role was at first conciliatory, suggesting continued support to her as a member of the Royal Family. But later she was to be stripped of her title, HRH, effectively removing her as a member of the family. Either way, with or without the support of the monarchy, Diana knew that she held the hearts of the people. Her desire to maintain a role as a goodwill ambassador was strong. Diana made it clear she expected to keep a firm grip on her status as an important princess. She was still the mother of a future King. But beyond that Diana's future would be difficult to determine. There was no historical precedent to suggest what role the former depressed bulimic wife of Prince Charles should play. But whatever her role was to be, Diana's chance to be her own woman was finally hers.

Diana had decided that work, rather than a husband, was her best chance for emotional fulfillment. She was particularly eager to continue working with the charities that mattered to her most: organizations for the homeless and those for AIDS patients. Without her full status as a member of the monarchy, Diana would no longer need to spend time in strictly ceremonial events and would be free to pursue her humanitarian efforts in the way she wished.

Diana's critics agreed that her effectiveness as a force in changing world views would greatly depend on the maintenance of her public image. While Diana is said to have wanted to be seen as a cross between Mother Teresa and Margaret Thatcher, her persona as a compassionate stateswoman would require careful consideration of both her public and private activities. Her critics seemed to agree that Diana would do best to stick to noncontroversial causes such as her work with children's hospitals and AIDS charities. It was also widely felt that her working with the less fortunate in her own country would serve to improve the growing idea that she had become self-indulgent. Continued public attacks on the Royal Family, it was thought, might well destroy her.

Yet it was during a very public attack on Charles during a televised interview with the BBC in 1995 that Diana seemed to garner the sympathy of the people. While her account of her battle with bulimia and depression that led to episodes where she attempted to injure herself may have endeared her to other women facing the same unhealthy affliction, her comments about the ongoing affair between her husband and Camilla Parker-Bowles seemed to secure for her the sympathies of the world at large. Effectively living separate lives, Diana had explained the cause: overcrowding, being only one in a marriage of three.

Even Camilla's ex-brother-in-law, Richard Parker-Bowles, later attacked Camilla saying that she had urged Charles to wed Diana because she believed Diana to be no threat and that she could be easily manipulated. Parker-Bowles described Camilla as a home-wrecker.

Sir Ivan Lawrence, a Conservative lawmaker, said Diana's interview with the BBC was self-indulgent. Though he admitted it was great television and attracted a lot of sympathetic attention, it was unfortunate for her children that she should have made such public confessions. Journalists believed that if Diana continued to tell all about her romantic life, her good standing as a mother would be threatened and irreparable damage could be rendered in the lives of her two children. In contrast, a gallup survey suggested that Diana had every right to bare her soul on

TV, perhaps an indication of the general acceptance of wearing of one's heart on one's sleeve so prevalent in '90s culture.

Ironically, while Diana unveiled her soul on television, she claimed to find the interest the press had in her still intimidating. She went so far as to say that she really didn't like being the center of attention while she literally spoke to millions at that moment. Although Diana had at one time experienced a workable relationship with the press, it had devolved into a fox-and-hound chase, leaving Diana often frustrated and not a little afraid. In a rare move, Diana had once expressed her disdain for the British press, saying she would have left Britain long ago but for her sons. She described the press as ferocious, pardoning nothing and hunting only for mistakes. Indeed, the press had hounded her mercilessly since her marriage to Charles.

Perhaps the most vicious attempt to defame the Princess came in 1996, when a video tape supposedly showing Princess Diana stripping and playing around with former lover and riding instructor James Hewitt appeared all over the news. Although the woman in the video resembled Diana, the woman and the man purported to be Hewitt were hired actors.

According to reports of the incident, the original color video had initially been obtained by the *Mirror*, the *Sun's* closest competitor, but they had decided that it was a hoax. The story goes that the tape was subsequently offered to the *Sun* during a meeting in west London by a man described by the *Sun* as an American lawyer claiming to be acting on behalf of a group of soldiers or bodyguards led by another man known as the Sergeant. The paper relayed that the unidentified American had told them that the images on the video were going to be used against her if the Princess made things difficult during her divorce negotiations.

Running with this information, the paper devoted numerous pages to the video that showed a frolicking "Diana." Independent Television broadcast the original color close-up video that had then, goes the account, been edited for the *Sun* into a blurry black-and-white version made to look as though it had been shot from a distance. Throughout the day, *Sun* editor Stuart Higgins claimed to have had a reasonable purpose for printing the images. He justified his actions by suggesting that the video proved the rampant invasion of privacy that Diana had been complaining about all along.

According to a Palace statement, the Princess recognized the video as a hoax, leaving only the media red-faced. Although the paper's editors had spent the day arguing that publishing these sensational images of a supposed Diana flashing a bra at the fake Hewitt was in the public interest because it highlighted the issue of the right to privacy, by the end of the day it was backpedaling and claiming it was a victim of the hoax of the decade.

Embarrassed, the *Sun* complained that it had been conned into believing that a poor-quality film had portrayed the Princess of Wales and her former lover James Hewitt. However, when they had earlier been reporting "the news," the quality of the video was not called into question. Instead, the paper had used it to create a counterpoint to Diana's claims that Charles's friends were determined to ruin her.

According to some reports, the *Mirror* was pleased. Its editor, Piers Morgan, was reportedly relieved that his paper had recognized the hoax, and for good reason. It has been reported that the year before, while working for another newsgroup, he had been duped by Diana's brother Charles, the Earl of Spencer, when he had gotten a friend to "leak" to the paper that he was about to leave his wife. Morgan published the story only to have Spencer quickly reveal that the story was a hoax. Apparently it was Spencer's way of condemning Morgan for his continual unflattering reporting. Within a few weeks, Morgan had announced that he would move to the *Mirror*.

Some of Diana's experiences with the press had deteriorated past the point of comfort. At one point Diana became involved in a physical scuffle with a photographer outside a gymnasium where she had been working out. When she asked a passerby to grab the film away from the photographer, the scuffle that ensued made for even better pictures. Clearly the line between photography and the duties of the press had become blurred with harassment.

Despite the continuous criticisms and controversies that continued to plague Diana, she remained steadfast in her dedication to her public responsibility as the queen of people's hearts. Over the course of her years as a public figure she had to learn how to overlook these attacks. She once declared that she believed the censures she endured had ironically been useful in giving her a strength she didn't know she had.

Not all her contacts with media people were detrimental, however. Clive James, associated with British television, claims that he had played a role in keeping at least one of Diana's comments out of the press. According to James, he lunched with Diana often during the time of her separation from Charles and knew her to some degree. He described himself in a self-authored article appearing in the *New Yorker* in 1997 as having been in a sort of "cahoots" with the Princess, keeping her secrets while he shared his own with her.

Clive stated in his article that he first met what he called the "living human being" Diana at the Cannes Film Festival. After complimenting James's television show, she suddenly expressed her feelings about another member of the media she spied in the room. James reported that Diana made a face like she'd just sucked a lemon and said: "There's that odious man Maxwell (of *Maxwell's Mirror*) over there. Don't want to meet him again. Yuck."

Clive James suggested that after having known him for not much longer than a minute, she had just given him a story that would have caused her and the Royal Family a great deal of embarrassment at her— having uttered the word "yuck."

Though he claims that he could have created this embarrassment with one quick phone call to the press, he chose rather to keep the Princess's confidence—and enter into cahoots with Diana.

In the months following the BBC interview, Diana expressed that she had no regrets about speaking out. Though the Queen was said to have been disgusted with her, Palace aides indicated that a position as a minister of good works would be established for Diana. Her duties would be marginal, to avoid seeming to set her up as a rival of the court, but her charity work would continue.

Later that year, on December 20, 1995 it was confirmed by the Palace that the Queen had written to Charles and Diana urging them to divorce. Ten days later, Prime Minister Major assured Diana that her role in public life would be maintained despite a divorce. Following this assurance, in February, 1996, Diana announced her agreement to divorce her husband, calling it the saddest day of her life. However, the battle between the Royal Family and Diana was not over. Along with her announced agreement to a divorce she also indicated that a settlement had been agreed upon. The Palace had clearly not been informed of this "settlement," and a new battle began between the camps.

During the lonely years between her separation from Charles and their divorce, Diana's relationships with other key members of her family were said to have changed as well. Over those years it had been rumored that Diana had grown estranged from her own family, including her sisters Jane and Sarah and her brother Charles. Patrick Jephson, her longtime private secretary, quit, and her chauffeur left, too.

At the time of Diana's divorce statement in 1996, she was reportedly represented by a PR firm.

While reports on Diana's relationship with Sarah Ferguson wavered, they seemed to remain close although their relationship had become complex. It was believed that the two women would use each other as sounding boards, discussing their respective woes.

Her trickiest role remained that of mother. Even if the marriage had remained intact, Diana's boys were quickly growing toward their teenage years and she would have had to face their natural separation from herself as they matured.

Despite the intensity of the divorce negotiations that created havoc for months, Diana continued to fortify her image as a great humanitarian. Despite all her hardships, this is the image that will remain of Diana. Her sense of personal style and commitment became evident as she continued to head numerous charities, winning the public's respect, as had her sister-in-law, Princess Anne, for her campaigning. Diana became known to some as "Saint Di" for her work in promoting AIDS awareness and for her services to other charities involved with the homeless, sick and dying. Diana saw in herself the answer to what she believed the people of Britain wanted: someone in public life who could give them affection, a sense of importance, support and hope.

Diana seemed a natural for the work she loved. She felt close to people, whoever they might be, and was obviously at ease with any member of society, from kings and presidents to AIDS and leprosy victims. And that was perhaps why she irritated certain circles. She seemed to relate much more readily to the people at the bottom than to the people at the top. She had once expressed her disappointment over those very people at the top for being unforgiving of her genuine feeling of closeness with the humblest of people. Diana's father had taught her to treat everyone as an equal, and her greatest hope was that her sons, William and Harry, would follow this example as well. Diana understood the heavy responsibility that being in the public eye placed on her, and she fulfilled those expectations admirably.

Realistically, though, Diana wasn't a saint and she didn't appear to possess any special talent. What set her apart was that she cared about others and was ready to listen, qualities not easily found in a self-centered era. Diana believed her role was that of a messenger and that her job was to speak and to demonstrate a message that would sensitize the world to a worthy cause. Not unlike Mother Teresa in her humanitarian concerns,

Diana was never happier than when she was trying to help society's most vulnerable. It was not unusual for Diana to hasten to the side of someone who needed a compassionate ear to comfort them during an illness or while they lay dying.

June Callwood, a writer and founder of Casey House, an AIDS hospice in Toronto, recalled a visit Diana made to Casey House in 1991. While the media were to be excluded from the visit because the hospice was very protective of its residents, one man suffering the latter stages of AIDS volunteered to meet Diana publicly inside the front door. While a chair for Diana had been placed at a discreet distance, Callwood explained in an article to *Maclean's* magazine in 1997, Diana sat down and pulled the chair closer to the man, putting her hand on his. This simple demonstration of concern for the man and understanding of AIDS transmission removed any mixed feelings Callwood had had about Diana's appearance.

Furthermore, Diana astonished observers of her visit to Casey House when she was approached by a woman whose son had died there earlier . The woman spoke to Diana in sign language, but before a nurse could translate, Diana signed back. According to Callwood, the woman and Diana enjoyed a few moments conversation, including a laugh about something, without the help of an interpreter.

Not all of Diana's good intentions came to successful fruition, however. In fact, Diana made several serious mistakes during her solo ventures into the international scene. She did not always seek the advice of the Foreign Office, which occasionally meant the creation of uncomfortable situations. The week before her divorce statement was issued in February of 1996, Diana visited Pakistan, where she spent two days at the invitation of cricket player Imran Khan and his wife Jemima Goldsmith, a British heiress. This particular trip reportedly angered Pakistan's Prime Minister Benazir Bhutto, who did not approve of Kahn's political ambitions.

In another example of Diana's ability to incite international anger, Caribbean island residents of Barbuda were said to have complained about the closing of a public beach when Barbuda's Defense Force offered to protect Diana's privacy. The island citizens were angry about not being allowed on what was normally a beach open to all, and this seemed particularl insulting because Diana had turned down an invitation to present awards to people who had helped in the recovery from the aftermath of Hurricane Luis.

Though Diana had not endeared herself to every last member of the public, she certainly had succeeded in gaining the love and support of the majority of the people. It was the widely accepted image of a magnanimous Diana that opened the pockets of the world's rich and famous in support of the charities she endorsed. On October 31, 1996, for example, the elite of Sydney, Australia spent $790 each to dine with the Princess of Wales at the Sydney Entertainment Center. The black-tie dinner-and-dance fundraiser was to benefit the late Victor Chang's Cardiac Research Institute. The pioneering heart surgeon had been murdered in 1991. Wearing a blue Versace gown, Diana described Chang as a visionary as she paid tribute to him, raising a reported $790,000 initially for the institute, which was then reported to have been increased by $2.4 million more from one of the guests, Kerry Packer, an Australian media tycoon.

The ever-present press, meanwhile, paid more attention to the personal side of the Princess, suggesting as a possible suitor for her the very married pop star Sting, who performed at the above-mentioned charity event. It was during this same time that the 35-year-old London-based Pakistani cardiologist Hasnat Khan was also reported to be one of her admirers.

In a much-publicized event, Diana, a privileged woman with an enviable wardrobe, offered a selection of her worn and made famous clothing for auction in 1997. On June 25, 1997, 79 cocktail and evening dresses belonging to Princess Diana were sold at an evening auction held at Christie's in Manhattan, raising an estimated $3.26 million for cancer and AIDS charities. The charities that benefited from the sale of Diana's gowns were reported as having been: in Britain, the Royal Marsden Hospital Cancer Fund and the AIDS Crisis Trust; in the US, the Evelyn H. Lauder Breast Center of Memorial Sloan Kettering, the Harvard AIDS Institute, and the AIDS Care Center of the New York Hospital Cornell Medical Center.

At the auction, *Harper's Bazaar* purchased a silk chiffon gown of Princess Diana's for a reported winning bid of $25,300. The dress had been worn by the Princess on an official visit to Nigeria. Liz Tilberis, who had been editor-in-chief for *Harper's Bazaar* and who was said to have shared a friendship with Diana for many years, was described as being very excited about the purchase. *Harper's Bazaar* planned to feature the dress in a future issue of the magazine.

In 1991 the Princess had posed for Tilberis, who at the time was the editor-in-chief of British *Vogue*, appearing on her first fashion magazine cover. It was the first time Diana had actually sat for a fashion magazine photo shoot, but this photograph was to be followed in 1995 by an exclusive cover story and fashion spread for *Harper's Bazaar* appearing in that year's December issue.

The Princess's sense of style had been much admired as she began finding her own way. Even her hairstyles spoke of her newfound independence and free spirit. She had evolved from a shy girl with a conservative appearance into a renowned Princess whose glamour and sophistication were imitated by women around the world. Her clothing choices spoke of her self-assuredness, with plunging necklines and shorter skirts. A much shorter, modern haircut reflected her practical, sporty, down-to-earth woman of the people image. It took her from elegant affairs to the dusty roads along which she walked to raise awareness about the unnecessary pain brought on innocent civilian victims of landmines buried around the globe. Perhaps her most talked about style was the slicked down wet look she sported at an awards ceremony in New York, possibly a perfect picture of her sometimes reputation as the rebel of Royals. It was possibly the perfect event at which to display her new look as she presented an award to Tilberis at the fourteenth annual Council of the American Fashion Designers Award gala. But no matter how Diana dressed, or how she wore her hair, she was always a perfect picture of a woman of the '90s—with sophistication and femininity combined. It is this image and her ability to gain publicity for good causes that will be missed by those who appreciated her.

The drama that was the Princess's life unfolded the way it did, it seems, primarily because of her search for love. Diana wanted to be loved for what she was, not for who she was or for what she had. But many rightfully wondered if such a love was truly possible for someone so consistently in the public view. Who could she trust?

As her efforts to inspire human compassion in others continued, so did the reports of her suitors. Appearing cautious, especially in matters of the heart following the "Squidgy" tapes and Hewitt's book, Diana was linked, accurately or inaccurately, with many men. Among the most remembered suitors reported in the media were James Hewitt, followed by James Gilbey, Will Carling, Christopher Whalley, Hasnat Khan and, finally, Dodi Al Fayed.

While James Hewitt had succeeded in winning her heart for a time, his publication of *The Princess In Love* destroyed the affections she had once had for him.

James Gilbey, a distillery heir, will forever be remembered for his now famous pet name for the Princess: Squidgy. Though Diana had admitted her affair with Hewitt, she had insisted that nothing adulterous had occurred between herself and Gilbey.

In September of 1995, Diana was accused by the tabloids of having played a role in the break-up of British rugby captain Will Carling's 14-month marriage. Diana denied she had caused the dissolution of their union.

Diana's image as a woman devoted to good causes was tarnished after this string of flirtations with other women's men. Some of these allegations may have cast Diana as a manipulator and home-wrecker as much as Charles was seen as deserving the blame for the failure of his own marriage because of his ongoing affair with Camilla.

Dr. Hasnat Khan, a 35-year-old Pakistani-born London cardiologist who allegedly wooed her by letting her watch open-heart surgery, was in the limelight next. About the same time Diana was said to have been smitten with London property developer Christopher Whalley, 40, whom she reportedly brought into her Kensington Palace apartments in the middle of the night. However, other reports that surfaced suggested that it was Dr. Khan whom Diana hoped to marry...until the intense public scrutiny turned out to be too much for him.

Most Royal watchers thought Diana should be wary. She didn't need a rich husband, and linking herself with the wrong man could risk the loss of public sympathy. Remarriage might certainly have diminished her role, but it seemed obvious that the only thing Diana truly wanted was love.

According to Andrew Morton's reports, Diana saw herself marrying a foreigner or at least someone whose background was foreign. He described Diana as seeking prophetical guidance from astrologers who, he reported, had indicated that they repeatedly named France as the birthplace of a future love interest as well as her new home. As a result of these predictions Diana spent time learning French and making frequent visits to Paris.

Diana appeared willing to risk her station in life, testing public opinion once more when she began her romance with Dodi Al Fayed in July of 1997. Al Fayed, son of Egyptian Mohamed Al Fayed, owner of Harrods department store in London, had a sordid history and was depicted by the media as a playboy who didn't pay his bills. But by all appearances, the Princess was in love.

Though she had previously gone to great lengths to keep her male acquaintances out of public view, she seemed at ease with Al Fayed in full view of the public, even through the paparazzi's lens. Recent newspapers before her death showed the couple on holiday aboard Al Fayed's yacht at the Italian resort of Portofino.

The most recent reports of the budding romance between Diana and Al Fayed included his gift to her of a ring, rumored to be an indication of an impending engagement. While Diana appeared keenly interested in Al Fayed's affection, it was reported in the *London Telegraph*, by writer Rose Moncton, that Dodi Fayed's generosity made the Princess of Wales uneasy. In her report she suggested that Diana had been angered by Dodi's showering of gifts, claiming that that was not what she wanted. According to Moncton, Diana had stated that she didn't want to be bought and that she had everything she wanted; she just wanted someone to be there for her and to make her feel safe and secure.

Surely all Diana ever really wanted was love. Perhaps it was her romantic involvements and her struggle to discover who she was and what she was supposed to do that especially endeared her to a generation of women. Even if the majority of women around the globe could not relate to her privileged position, they could understand her struggles in the midst of hurt, betrayal and humiliations. Like many other women, even the Princess was cruelly awakened by a cold, hard reality that followed her wedding day. While not everyone experiences marital breakdown, the stuff of all little girl fairytales is all too fleeting. Women were able to relate to Diana's disappointment and then to her ability to weather the storm, to face it courageously and to reinvent herself when life threw her an unexpected turn. It was this stronger, survivalist Diana that was perhaps even more appealing than the fairy-tale princess to whom the world had been first introduced.

Appropriately, Diana's memory will remain particularly cherished by those who actually knew her. Diana remained a presence in the lives of her friends and a demonstration of her friendship was never more evident than when she was seen comforting a saddened Elton John during the funeral of Gianni Versace in 1997. On July 15, Gianni Versace, a world-class designer whose clothing had been worn by Diana, was killed outside his home in Miami. Diana attended Versace's funeral, which was to be the last time she would see her friend Elton John, an enthusiastic admirer of the man who had designed his stage costumes. Like Diana and Elton John, Versace had also been a supporter of AIDS activism around the world. Diana had comforted John when he broke down in tears at Versace's service, unaware of the tragedy that lay just ahead that would bring Elton John to sing for her one last time, reciprocating her demonstration of friendship for him.

Elton John's rework of his famous "Candle in the Wind" that he sang in an emotional tribute to "England's rose" will carry on Diana's legacy, with all profits from the sale of his recording reportedly being directed to the Diana, Princess of Wales Memorial Fund for her favorite charities, ever remembered both by those who desperately needed her and those who admired her.

Diana will remain an icon not only for the most forsaken of society, however, but for women of the '90s generally. She appeared to have it all: beauty, worthy pursuits, two fine sons and the admiration of millions. But while it had been intended that she become the storybook version of a princess, Diana had had other ideas. She demonstrated to a world of women that it was possible to make the world a better, safer place when compassion reached out to cover hatred, prejudice and fear. If a delicate princess could take on the world and win, what could stop any woman from making her mark on the world around her?

Diana's brother, the Earl of Spencer, suggested in his eulogy that, though there was a temptation to canonize his sister, there was no need to do so because she stood out well enough on her own as a unique human being. To declare Diana a saint would in effect deter from the memory of who she believed herself to be: just another human being, though privileged beyond most people's dreams, trying to make her way in the world the best she could. According to her brother, what set Diana apart was that she had an instinctiveness for what was ultimately important in people's lives. This instinct, he suggested, was a result of her feeling connected through her own suffering to those he called her "constituency of the rejected."

In his eulogy, Charles confirmed what the world had suspected: that the beautiful Princess of Wales had desired to leave her country and escape to a more accepting place. Baffled at the treatment the papers gave her genuine attempts at creating good will, Charles sniped at the press, suggesting that perhaps the only explanation for the media's determination to bring her down was that they wanted her off her pedestal and down on their own level. He then added what may be a frequently quoted line throughout the coming years: that "a girl given the name of the ancient goddess of hunting was, in the end, the most hunted person of the modern age."

Although Diana was probably the most talked about woman in the world for 16 years, there is scarcely a word she said that is memorable. Diana will not be remembered as having made any remarkable statement, nor as having been a saint, for she clearly could serve it up as good as she got when it came to such things as marital infidelities and divorce strategies. She was not perfect. Even the youngest of children would have been able to remind her that she should have been wearing her seatbelt during the last moments of her life, whether or not it may have saved her, and that riding in a speeding car was a risky and foolish thing to do.

But Diana will always have the sympathy of the people of the world who remember a beautiful woman who entered a loveless marriage as a kind of sacrificial offering. She was a princess for the new age who took a hold of trendy philosophies and opportunities for public confession, who danced with the likes of John Travolta and who touched the leper's hand. She will remain an example to those who struggle, not having glossed over her problems but having faced them, conquering some while losing the battle to others. Throughout it all Diana remained forever human.

Diana was a woman of strength with her own agenda and, as a result, the monarchy will never be the same. She believed she had rights, but she exercised them while fulfilling her responsibilities. She was determined to raise her children to be compassionate and to have an understanding of the "real" world. While Diana maintained that Charles was unsuited to become King, believing that the monarchy was claustrophobic and outdated, she emphasized her determination to bring up her sons to be different than their predecessors. While the monarchy seemed to her to have no relevance to today's life, she wanted her sons to experience what the common man knew: that there existed people different than themselves, who were not necessarily rich or privileged, who needed a helping, compassionate hand. Diana's desire was that her sons develop the same tenderheartedness she had for those who suffered. Should the monarchy survive, a compassionate King William and his brother Harry, having been schooled in homeless shelters and cancer wards, may well be her enduring legacy.

Chapter 9

The Divorce...and Life After

On February 28, 1996, following years of unhappiness and shattered dreams, Princess Diana finally agreed to divorce Charles. This shocking revelation came from Diana herself, through her press secretary, without the knowledge or approval of the Queen or Prince Charles. Following a private meeting with Charles at St. James's Palace, Diana had reportedly negotiated with him and then went public with her shocking statements. The Royals were not amused.

Diana's surprise announcement stated that "The Princess will continue to be involved in all decisions relating to the children and will remain at Kensington Palace with offices in St. James's Palace. They will share equal access to the children." Diana would retain the title of Princess.

On December 19, 1995, the Queen wrote letters to Diana and Charles, which expressed her "anger and frustration" over the public squabbles. Diana had just returned from taking her children to a movie and was watching the evening news when she discovered the letters had been leaked to the press, some say with the full cooperation of the Queen herself.

Aside from reprimanding them for their public airing of Royal dirty laundry, the Queen's letters advised the couple to attempt an early divorce. This, of course, followed Diana's shocking and unprecedented television interview in which she detailed the breakdown of her marriage, admitted to adultery and revealed her knowledge of Charles's continuing unfaithfulness. At that time, she said she absolutely did not wish to divorce, admittedly because she was a child of divorce. She did not want that for her own sons.

The Associated Press reported that the Kensington Palace spokesperson for Diana confirmed that Charles had agreed immediately to the Queen's December request, but Diana first consulted her lawyers before making the decision final. Other sources claimed that the settlement was reached after testy negotiations.

On July 12, 1996 it became official. Buckingham Palace announced on behalf of the Prince and Princess that the "decree nisi" would be pronounced on July 15 and the decree become absolute on August 28, 1996.

The official announcement from Buckingham Palace reads, in part:

"TRH The Prince and Princess of Wales have concluded settlement terms for their divorce. The negotiations, which were amicable, were greatly assisted both by the fairness of HRH The Prince of Wales's proposals and by HRH The Princess of Wales's ready acceptance of them.

"TRH will continue to share equal responsibility in the upbringing of their children.

"While the financial terms of the settlement remain confidential to the parties, they recognize that the nature of HRH The Princess of Wales's future role is of legitimate public interest, and an agreed statement on that role is being released by Buckingham Palace....."

The status and role of the Princess of Wales included in the official statement reads:

"The Princess of Wales, as the mother of Prince William, will be regarded by The Queen and The Prince of Wales as being a member of the Royal Family.

"It has been agreed that her style and title will be Diana, Princess of Wales. She may retain any orders, insignia and other titles, consistent with her being known as Diana, Princess of Wales.

"As she will be regarded as a member of the Royal Family, the Princess will from time to time receive invitations to State and national public occasions, as for any other member of the Royal Family, at the invitation of the Sovereign or the Government. On these occasions, the Princess will be accorded the precedence she enjoys at present.

"Being regarded as a member of the Royal Family, the Princess will continue to live at Kensington Palace with The Queen's agreement. Kensington Palace will in this way continue to provide a central and secure home for the Princess and the children.

"The Princess's public role will essentially be for her to decide. However, as for any other member of the Royal Family, any representational duty, whether Royal or national, at home or abroad, will only be undertaken at the request of the Sovereign, acting where necessary on the advice of Ministers. As for any other member of the Royal Family, any visits by the Princess overseas (other than private holidays) will be undertaken in consultation with the foreign and Commonwealth Office and with the permission of the Sovereign.

"The Princess has asked the Queen if she may relinquish all her service appointments and the Queen has agreed.

"The Princess will continue to have access to 32 (The Royal) Squadron and to the State Apartments at St. James's Palace for entertaining on the same basis as all other members of the Royal Family, namely with the permission of the Sovereign.

"The Princess will maintain a private office in Kensington Palace, the size of which will depend on the nature and extent of the public role she undertakes.

"As for any other member of the Royal Family, any activity of the Princess which involves the use of public funds will be undertaken only with the permission of the Sovereign acting where necessary on the advice of Ministers."

Diana's nightmare had come true; the fairy tale in which she had once believed had become a farce. Stripped of her title "Her Royal Highness," the dark days following the divorce announcement began. For this she got approximately £12 million and almost £280 000 per year to maintain her private office.

Charles had moved out of Kensington the day following the separation announcement, and he would continue to officially reside at St. James's Palace. The day before the announcement, it was business as usual for Prince Charles, as he presented the first Duchy of Cornwall Education Awards at St. James's Palace. On July 14th, he was off to Brunei to celebrate the Sultan's birthday and carry out a number of public engagements.

Diana had no official engagements, and her last official engagement was to attend a meeting in London with the National AIDS Trust, visiting Mortimer Market Centre on June 27th.

In a comment about her children during the divorce, Diana said "I will fight for my children on any level in order for them to be happy and have peace of mind and carry out their duties."

In the case of overseas representation outlined in the Buckingham Palace press release, Diana must consult the Foreign and Commonwealth Office, again with the permission of the Sovereign. This point would soon prove to be a barrier to Diana's activities, and, in her opinion, was used to "isolate" her further from the family following the divorce.

The British people's fairy-tale dream also shattered when the announcement came. When Diana entered the Royal Family, she breathed into it a life and a romance that had been missing since the days of Queen Alexandria. She had held so much promise for the future of the monarchy, and the people seemed full of sorrow and disappointment. The dark days of the monarchy, following Sarah and Andrew's marital breakdown, seemed to be far from over.

Diana's revelations during that pivotal TV interview that Charles may not be fit to be King were being supported by the British public, and sympathy for Diana as the betrayed wife and devoted mother was also being established. Her publicly stated insecurities and difficulty coping with a destructive relationship created a kinship with Diana that women all over the world understood and acknowledged.

Charles's acknowledgment of his unfaithfulness to Diana, and his public declarations of love for Camilla, further developed public support for Diana. Revelations that he never used the "L" word with Diana, and that Camilla was the only woman he ever loved, evoked feelings of protectiveness from the public for the woman who would have been their queen. Diana's obvious human frailty was more easily understandable than Charles's stoic, seemingly cold, unfeeling acts of duty. He needed an heir to the throne, a woman with an unblemished past, someone who could be molded into the perfect future queen. The only problem was that Diana had a mind of her own and eventually overcame her fear of rocking the Royal boat.

Some unsympathetic to the Royal divorce declared that the Charles and Diana show had evolved into a "grotesque public spitting match." Writer Bruce Wallace gave a historical perspective to the breakdown by declaring that had this happened centuries ago, they would have "retired to their country castles, raised armies and returned to settle scores on a battlefield." Instead, they used the media to wage their war. Wallace credits Diana with being much better suited for "marital guerrilla warfare" than Charles. Some speculated that in the good old days they would have just beheaded her.

Diana was to embark on yet another lonely path, relentlessly dodging the persistent press. Her family's demise was being touted on the front of every legitimate newspaper, and the tabloids were stepping up the pressure.

Predictably, the public's unending thirst for juicy details was constantly quenched by the paparazzi, who regularly reduced the Princess to tears, publicly and privately. It seemed that her only support came from her children and a few close friends who remained loyal. The somewhat protective umbrella of the Monarchy had been officially collapsed.

August 28, 1996, a British court granted a decree absolute: the fifteen-year marriage was officially over. The year that would be the last in Diana's life had begun.

With her life lying in bits about her feet, Diana's inner strength and obvious determination were paramount to overcoming the hellish nightmare in which she was embroiled. She began to rise from the ashes of her former self to transform into a confident, loving and strong-willed spokeswoman for the poor, the homeless, the sick and dying, and all those who felt unloved and rejected by society.

A new Diana was in the works, and her struggle to be out from under the Royal's iron fist was just beginning.

In early January, *People* magazine outlined Diana's most immediate supporters. In Diana's camp were: Anthony Julius, Susie Orbach, Patrick Jephson, Sarah Ferguson and Lord Palumbo. Julius was Diana's divorce lawyer who had earned Diana's trust when he secured an injunction to halt the *Daily Telegraph's* publication of the now-famous gym/workout photos.

Susie Orbach healed an emotional wound in Diana by first counseling her for bulimia in 1994. She then grew to be one of Diana's most trustworthy friends. Orbach continued counseling Diana following her divorce when she was constantly being harassed by photographers.

Diana's private secretary, Patrick Jephson, had been a stoic supporter for Diana, especially during the troubled and tearful times of her separation from Charles. A former lieutenant commander in the Royal Navy, it was Jephson who publicly stood by Diana the day after Camilla and Charles made their first public appearance together following the divorce. *People Magazine* reported in January that a Royal insider stated, "Nothing happens without his knowledge and approval."

Diana's "foxhole" friendship with Fergie was once again strengthened by Diana's divorce. Both women were feeling isolated and ostracized by the Royal Family, and they found solace in each other's company, encouraging each other to find their own new paths away from the House of Windsor. Diana was introduced to Rita Rogers, Fergie's psychic, and the pair continued exploring alternative spiritual practices. London's the *Daily Mirror* reported that "the two women, outlawed from the Royal Family, laughed and giggled as they discussed Diana's plot to tell all." Sarah's own tell-all books *My Story* and *Sarah: The Life of a Duchess* reportedly cooled their friendship somewhat.

"They were extremely close," says Diana's long-time press confidant Richard Kay. "Fergie's book definitely put a distance between them. When she went on tour and was criticized for undermining the monarchy, she'd say, 'What about Charles and Diana?'"

Lord Palumbo had been friends with Prince Charles and played polo with him, but following their own falling-out, it was Palumbo who directed Diana to her present legal team. One Royal insider stated that their friendship stems from their mutual dislike of Charles.

Though Charles has a camp of his own, the most distressing betrayals that Diana experienced came from those whose confidences she sought, offering her own personal, tragic experiences in order to better relate to them.

In May of 1997, Diana told *Press Associate* that she was deeply saddened when a private conversation with a bulimic woman was leaked to the media.

The Princess's spokesman stated, "Diana, Princess of Wales, was deeply disappointed to learn that one of the group of patients who she visited last week at the Priory (a private hospital in London) has disclosed to the *Daily Mirror* details of private conversations." Diana had been trying to help a patient overcome her eating disorder, but the woman turned coat and fled to the nearest newspaper instead of taking Diana's private offerings of support.

Diana's personal experiences and success at overcoming bulimia make her easier to relate to, and those who suffer from eating disorders have gained strength from the Princess's admissions.

But once again, while opening her heart, someone slipped in another dagger.

"Her frankness about her own eating disorders, which are long in the past, gives her a unique understanding for those with similar problems. She is able to encourage people by drawing on her own experiences, which gives her a deep appreciation of their needs," said the statement.

"The benefits to patients depend enormously on privacy being respected and it is particularly sad that on this occasion the visit has been sensationalized." The statement concluded by saying "The Princess hopes that the repercussions do not undermine the positive aspects of this visit or jeopardize any that she may make in the future."

Aside from her friends and enemies, paid and otherwise, Diana continued her quest for an expanded spirituality. This aspect of Diana also had to be rebuilt. When dreams and lives are shattered, everything needs to be put back together again, and Diana's spiritual quests were a part of that recovery process. Diana was searching for answers and guidance.

Consultations with psychics and other alternative spiritual advisors may have opened doors that Diana never dreamed possible. Could she really open her heart, use her intuitive feelings and trust them to be true, rather than constantly being told what to think, how to act, what to believe? While being partially fulfilled with her charity work, as many women are following traumatic events in their lives, she realized that her own fragile spirit also needed care. She began believing in herself and trusting her own feelings, regardless of what people may say of this "fringe" or "New Age" spirituality. Obviously, Diana's yearnings in this direction did not steer her wrong.

With the official divorce behind her, Diana was now able to test her wings. Selectivity of public events increased along with her ability to decide how much of herself she was able to give. Determined to do some good with her status, popularity and charm, she continued working with her core charities at home and abroad.

While some in the Royal establishment still seemed more interested in themselves than others, Diana's cause-minded identity won accolades from the public. It was reported that a London opinion poll released in early 1997 showed that only twenty-one percent of those surveyed believed the Royal Family was "concerned about people in real need."

Her first official visit to the United States following the divorce was to attend a September fundraiser for breast cancer and to meet with Hillary Clinton. Next came a December conference on leprosy in London, then she travelled to New York for the Metropolitan Museum of Art's Costume Institute Ball.

Her January trip to Angola to combat the landmine issue was one of international interest. In her first one-on-one interview since her startling tell-all BBC appearance in November 1995, Diana expressed her ambition to help wipe out the use of landmines across the world. "I didn't have any set agenda. I didn't know what to expect. I was open-minded about it. But I'm surprised by the level of injuries I've seen. I've never been to anywhere like this before. I think it struck us all. I found it very humbling," Diana told Peter Archer, *Press Associate's* correspondent in Luanda, Angola's capital.

"There was a little girl we met in hospital who had her intestines blown out. She's very, very poorly, and I think just looking at her and thinking what was going on inside her head and her heart was very disturbing. But she's just one statistic."

Diana had initially been invited to visit some other countries, but it wasn't politically appropriate. Her wishes to visit Cambodia, Bosnia and Afghanistan were made very clear in that interview. "They are the ones most affected...I hope very much to be able to go in there as a British Red Cross volunteer—if they'll have me," Diana said. Rocking the Royal boat, Diana's visit to Africa's war-ravaged Angola was seen at home as being intrusive and inappropriate. Some politicians reportedly believed her to be on a "collision course with the Tory Government."

The announcement that Diana would contribute seventy-nine gowns to a Christie's auction sparked yet another round of controversy. Some reports that Diana would pocket half of the sales receipts were vehemently denied. In defense, a libel suit was filed against the London Newspaper *Express on Sunday* for its inaccuracies. This was the first time Diana had ever taken libel action against a newspaper. She won and the amount in damages, £75 000, was awarded to charity. She determined that every cent of the money raised from the gowns would go directly to AIDS and cancer charities, and was equally determined that everyone know it. Diana attributed the fundraising idea to her son, William, who proposed that Diana auction off her designer dresses for charity.

Metaphorically, it was a highly public severing of her former self, Diana's emergence from the Royal cast in which she had been molded for fifteen years.

"These dresses really don't fit into the life she leads now," said Meredith Etherington-Smith, the Christie's marketing director who worked closely on plans for the auction. "She's left the past where it should be— in the past."

The incredible sum of £2 million pounds was raised through the auction that benefited the British AIDS Crisis Trust and London's Royal Marsden Hospital Cancer fund, with some of the proceeds going to the host country's AIDS Care Centre at New York Hospital and Cornell Medical Center, Harvard AIDS Institute, and the Evelyn H. Lauder Breast Center of Memorial Sloan-Kettering Cancer Center.

Diana's unforgettable midnight-blue silk velvet gown that she wore to the White House in 1985 garnered the highest price: a whopping £120 301. This was the Victor Edelstein creation she wore while dancing with John Travolta.

Through her search for a new public role, Diana was still mindful of the institution which her sons would one day lead. In deference to possible offense to the Royal Family, Diana decided to withdraw her previously offered support of a book by one of her favorite fashion designers, Gianni Versace.

"Last year I was approached by Mr. Versace to contribute a foreword to a book entitled *Rock and Royalty* which he was to produce to raise funds for Elton John's AIDS Foundation.

"I had an interest in this foundation and was pleased to support Mr. Versace's book. I was assured that the book would not contain material which would cause offense and I therefore signed the foreword."

Once Diana actually saw the book, she became "extremely concerned that the book may cause offense to members of the Royal Family."

Diana's concerns are understandable, since one photograph in the book of the late Duke and Duchess of Windsor is placed facing a picture of a British football star wearing a crown while his genitals are apparently visible.

Diana withdrew her permission to use her foreword and canceled her anticipated attendance at the gala book launch benefit on February 18, 1997. To protect Diana's interests, Versace announced that he would cancel his gala benefit, and said "The money that I would have spent on this party will be donated directly to the Elton John AIDS Foundation."

Diana's stormy relationship with the establishment continued, and she had received flack in April for not visiting Wales for two years. After all, she was *their* Princess, and she hadn't been there in an official capacity since June 1995.

Diana thought it best to stay out of Charles's turf, wishing to give Charles the spotlight without competition. "Obviously as heir to the throne it is important that he takes precedence in every way in terms of official engagements, and for that reason she thinks it inappropriate to visit Wales in an official capacity at present," said her private secretary Michael Gibbins. "Obviously after the Princess's divorce last year things are a little bit sensitive, and the thing the princess is particularly anxious to avoid in connection with Wales is upstaging the Prince of Wales."

The papers were full of difficulties Diana experienced over the following months. The Princess lost a half-dozen of her staff in just one year, fired or leaving of their own accord, and one of Diana's aides, Victoria Mendham, quit following Diana's demand that Mendham pay for her own travel expenses for a trip overseas. Mendham maintained that she was invited to go on the trip free of charge, but Diana thought otherwise. They settled out of court. Brian Hoey, who has written twelve books on the Royal Family, said that Diana's inner circle was quickly crumbling, mostly due to her demanding and difficult ways. "She's running out of friends, and there are no romances—none whatsoever," he said.

Meanwhile, Lord Runcie, the former Archbishop of Canterbury, denounced Diana publicly in his biography, describing her as a schemer and a sad figure. In October 1996, Diana's name was dropped from the parliamentary daily prayers. Though these personal attacks, private mistakes and public rebuffs from the church and government officials continued, Diana refused to be dragged back into the depths of depression and solitude. Her time to shine once again had come, and it was a blazing shooting star, indeed.

Diana's battles with the media continued, and in April 1997, what would have been a private victory over a harassing photographer turned into a front-page tabloid extravaganza.

While leaving a London gym, Diana confronted an intrusive photographer, demanding that he turn over the film to her. A passerby intervened on Diana's behalf, backing up her demands. They successfully got the film away from the photographer, but not before yet another paparazzo snapped pictures of the entire altercation. The photographs showed 28-year-old Kevin Duggan pinning the photographer to a wall, with Diana watching while her champion grabbed the film. Duggan reportedly took the camera off the photographer while holding him in an arm lock. Diana's reaction to the incident was obviously outrage and disgust, and she wanted the world to know. A statement released from her office read, "Once again the Princess of Wales has been harassed by a photographer. Once again this has become the subject of inaccurate press comment.

"The Princess hopes that the recently passed Protection from Harassment Act will give greater protection to people such as herself who are the victims of this kind of distressing intrusion into their private lives."

The *Sun* newspaper quoted Diana as having encouraged the violent altercation, and the object of Diana's distress, photographer Brendan Beirne, reportedly said, "I am stunned she did not step in and stop it. It was outrageous. She knows I'm not a stalker or a threat. I have taken photographs of her for ten years."

Maybe ten years had been enough for Diana, because she was growing increasingly tired and angry at being constantly dogged through her everyday life. Maybe his very presence was a threat to her personal well-being, her privacy. The media had been a threat to her since she stepped onto the Royal stage fifteen years ago. Though she had tried to leave the official limelight, there were those who refused to let her go. Diana has been chased down streets on foot, tailed at high speeds and has even reportedly bumped the bumper of an intrusive photographer who trailed her through the streets of London. Of the constant media attention, Diana had been quoted as saying, "I still to this day find the interest daunting and phenomenal because I actually don't like being the center of attention. I never know where a lens is going to be."

Her dislike of the media has been passed on to her children, especially William. Their close relationship has seen William comforting his mother through many troubled times, and he's seen enough of his mother's tears, as a result of the rampant press, to harbor a dislike that could easily grow into hatred. Regardless of the fact that her children have grown up in a fishbowl, Diana has made sure that they maintain their privacy at school and, with the Queen's help, they are largely left alone by the press, unless on official rounds with their parents. Secluded from the public glare in their boarding schools, the children are treated in a mostly hands-off manner, but it has been reported that some photogra-

phers are following William when he's in London. The newspapers, remarkably, are the ones that are keeping the lid on these pictures, refusing to buy them from William's part-time stalkers.

It has been said that both William and Harry blame the media for the
breakup of their parents. Through the difficult times, William supported
his younger brother, shielding him from the media circus that surrounded
his family. Through it all, Diana has managed to carve out many special
outings with her children, but always under scrutiny, Diana received
public criticism in June 1997 for taking the boys to see *The Devil's Own*,
a film described as being pro-IRA. Harry had been let into the cinema,
even though he was underage for the film's rating due to the movie's
violent scenes. William barely met the age requirement, having celebrated
his birthday just the day before.

Kensington Palace issued a statement that formally apologized for
taking the boys to the film, and said "Diana, Princess of Wales, was
unaware of the subject matter of the film...she apologizes for any distress which may have been caused by her taking her sons to see this
film." Even the stars of the film, Harrison Ford and Brad Pitt, described
the film as being irresponsible, glamorizing an IRA-supporting mur-
derer. Harrison Ford being one of Prince William's favorite actors, Diana
and the children picked the film out of the paper and sent someone to
pre-buy the tickets. She didn't want to leave Harry behind or disappoint
William, so the cinema let them in anyway. In comment on the film's
violence or pro-IRA vision, maybe it wasn't so bad that the kids got to
see the film. After all, the violence in Ireland is in direct cause of the
British occupation, and it is a reality of a violent world that the boys will
one day be instrumental in governing.

Regardless of the rare criticisms of Diana's parenting, she was raising her children to be a new breed of Royalty: aware of their privileged
status, thankful for their position, and willing to use that position to ease
the suffering of others. Diana secretly took her children out very late at
night to visit the many homeless shelters around London, giving them a
first-hand look at their "subjects": the real people of England and the
world over. They were aware of their privileged status, and William has
already counseled his mother on fundraising ideas, including the afore-
mentioned donation of her clothes to be sold for charity.

Diana managed to expose her children to the pure joys of just being
alive, whether it was cavorting at a theme park or standing in line for
movies. While being schooled for their Royal role, they were made aware

of their own humanity, being aware of their mother's emotional frailty and the possibility of unhappiness in the lives of others. Though constantly urged by her sons to move away from England, Princess Diana has held on, knowing full well that any such move would effectively remove her as an integral, reliable source of love and affection for her children. In July 1997, the Princess told reporters that William and Harry realize that by continuing her life in London, the paparazzi's constant hounding takes its toll. They "are always urging me to live abroad...maybe that is what I should do," Diana candidly told reporters. But then the rumor mill started again and she had to instruct her Kensington press office to quell rumors that she would soon make a surprise announcement. Though her desire for more privacy led her to dream of a quiet life away from the media, Diana knew that her sons would never be able to live with her. Fully supportive of her children's role in the monarchy, Diana continued to live in London while sharing parenting duties with Charles.

The Queen herself is also instrumental in the children's lives, instructing them in Royal behavior and conduct. William is reported to frequent the palace under the Queen's close tutelage. Most Sundays, William comes by car to Windsor Palace to spend time alone with his grandmother. "The Queen feels responsible and has great concern for him," says the Queen's biographer Sarah Bradford. As for Prince Harry, Diana is teaching him how to play a supportive role in relation to his older brother. The Princess's closest friends and even her rivals agree that Diana's demonstrative mothering, including lots of hugs, kisses and playful fun, was admirable; she was shaping her sons to be part of a growing and changing monarchy.

Diana was painfully aware that Charles's stoic, stiff upbringing had created a man far removed from his people, who was reluctant or unable to demonstrate any emotion that might be regarded as human, and *who sometimes* considered people, including herself, as part of Royal duty. Charles's obvious commitment to conservation, environmental awareness (one of his passions is organic gardening) and global awareness are a few of his interests outside the Royal role, and he is said to be a lot more demonstrative of affection to the boys when the cameras are not around. After all, his own upbringing was emotionally distant and removed from his parents. He obviously agreed with Diana that for his sons, it would be different. Their children are the hopes for the future of England, and they will be the ones to take the monarchy into the next century. Diana, aware of the enormous pressure being placed on her children, has given them the tools necessary to be strong leaders who could be capable of ruling with their heads and their hearts.

In many eyes, Princess Diana could do no wrong. Her energy for other people's grief and hardship seemed endless while she was struggling to cope with living under a microscope with her laundry flying in the wind. Aside from all the public good, there are inevitably those who are unwilling to see the good side of anything, and there are those who go to any length to interject their own inherent nastiness.

The Royal Family itself seemed to offer Diana little support in many arenas of her life, from mothering her sons to criticism of her public displays of "unseemly" emotional responses. The stiff upper lip that seems genetically inherent to the blue bloods just couldn't rub off on someone as human as Diana. Many on Charles's side of the battle for public opinion had little good to say of the Princess, it seems, whenever anyone would listen to them. Following Diana's 1995 *Panorama* interview when she described Charles's supporters as "the enemy," some cruel and unnecessary comments were made regarding her mental state. These comments only reinforced the fact that Diana did, indeed, have enemies. Armed Forces Minister Nicholas Soames stated on BBC's post-interview special that Diana's admitted unhappiness and depression had grown into "mental illness." He stated she was "in the advanced stages of paranoia." If anyone in the world had good reason to be paranoid, it was the Princess of Wales. But in immediate response to those comments, then Prime Minister John Major was reportedly irate at Soames's comments and warned him not to repeat them in public.

Soames was not the only one to wield a dagger in Diana's direction. There were those in the media that refused to buy Diana's pleas for understanding, purporting her to be manipulative and spoiled, and using the media to raise her public image as a woman scorned. The irony was, of course, that she *was* the woman scorned, and millions identified with her without any conniving necessary on her part.

London reporter Bruce Wallace had written a review of Prince Charles's biography *The Prince of Wales*, by Jonathan Dimbleby. Wallace used that opportunity as a platform from which he lambastes the Princess, and the Prince, as being self-obsessed, privileged and selfish. In his review, Wallace also points out that Andrew Morton, author of Diana's two biographies *Diana: Her True Story* and *Diana: Her New Life*, tried to paint a sympathetic portrait of her, but "could not hide the cranky woman within." Wallace describes Diana as being brittle, vindictive and "more than a bit flighty."

"This is a woman who cried when Demi Moore and Woody Harrelson were reunited at the end of the silly Hollywood movie *Indecent Proposal* (as if she was the only one who did), and who believes that in a previous incarnation she was a nun. Her life is governed by a battery of tarot-card readers, clairvoyants, psychics, astrologers, osteopaths and masseurs." Wallace goes on to make condescending comment on aspects of Diana's regular treatments to flush toxins from her body (a practice not as uncommon or medically unfounded as Wallace seems to portray).

"And the Princess shows signs of paranoia, believing the Royal Family is conspiring against her," states Wallace.

Her own biographer, Morton, said that "she was conscious that for every point she goes down in the opinion polls, thousands of pounds (sterling) could be shaved off the eventual (divorce) settlement." To almost anyone, this awareness could be seen as being intelligent and thoughtful about her future, aware of the Royal eye and determined not to give them any reasons to further denounce her or harm her future. To Wallace, this only proved his own belief that "her behavior vibrates with manipulation: there is not a hospice visited, not a condolence letter sent, without an eye for how it affects her public standing vis-à-vis the Prince."

When Diana declined the Queen's invitation to spend Christmas 1995 with her in-laws at Sandringham, some saw it as a plea for public sympathy. William and Harry were with their father at Sandringham and Diana spent Christmas alone at Kensington Palace. Not willing to subject herself to the Royal glare just one month after the *Panorama* interview, Diana wisely removed herself from a potentially upsetting and embarrassing situation, not only for herself but for her children as well.

The Queen's letters to Diana and Charles in December had been leaked to the press just weeks before Christmas, swatting them both publicly for their un-royal behavior. This velvet-gloved smack in Diana's direction was in direct response to Diana's *Panorama* interview.

Yet, who could blame Diana for choosing to spend Christmas away from Sandringham? After all, who wants to spend the holidays with people who obviously don't like them?

This wasn't the first nor the last time the Queen stepped in to express her disapproval of Diana's actions. The Queen reportedly warned Diana that it would be possible that the Princes be removed from her custody and placed in the Queen's own care. The awesome head of the

Queen's powers having been raised, it was made clear to Diana that she tread very carefully over the next months.

Meanwhile, the press, as usual, were reporting anything they could get their hands and lenses on. Victoria Mendham's resignation hit the newspapers in December, 1996. In March, Diana settled out of court with a former maid, Sylvia McDermott, who sued Diana for wrongful dismissal. Diana reportedly complained about the work standard of McDermott, but eventually all parties agreed that McDermott's duties ended when her "position as a housemaid became redundant," said David Pannick QC, the Princess's attorney.

March also brought warnings from the Foreign Office that Diana's plans to visit southeast Asia would be too dangerous. Diana had wanted to continue her campaigning against landmines following her visit to Angola. She would receive more criticism in June from Conservative MPs for stepping on their political toes. Diana wanted to address the House of Commons concerning the landmine issue and their refusal to support the complete banning of the anti-personnel weapons but changed her mind when she received a round of harsh criticism for stepping into their political territory.

Her public apology over her son's attendance of the film *The Devil's Own* was well-documented in the newspapers, as was her alleged criticism of the children's nanny Tiggy Legge-Bourke following Prince William's invitation to her to attend his school's parents' day. The tabloids reported that Diana called Tiggy "thoughtless, foolish and idiotic," for attending the Eton function. Diana countered the tabloid reports by stating that she was "more than pleased" that Tiggy was invited by William and attended the family picnic. William had not consulted his parents before making the invitation. Diana and Charles decided against attending the annual outing in deference to other parents and students. Neither wanted to bring undue disruption to the event and so both decided to stay away.

Though there were many who believed, or wanted to believe, the worst of Princess Diana, she continued to profess that she derived pleasure and a sense of being needed from her charity work and unannounced visits to hospitals and hospices. "I'm not a political animal," she said, "but I think the biggest disease this world suffers from in this day and age is the disease of people feeling unloved, and I know that I can give love for a minute, for half an hour, for a day, for a month. I'm very happy to do that and I want to do that."

In Andrew Morton's second book, *Diana: Her New Life*, Diana's closest advisors explained that there would always be critics of Diana's behavior. "Diana is on a voyage of discovery at the moment. What we are seeing is her real personality coming through because she is no longer bound so much by the royal system. People in authority, be it journalists, politicians or courtiers, find it hard to handle her spontaneity, her vitality and energy as well as her genuine affection for people. They will always try and interpret her behavior as manipulative and unsuitable. Certainly her timing will be off occasionally but you have to remember that she married young and has conformed to an image for the last decade that is not her. She will make mistakes, but ultimately we will se a genuine manifestation of the real person." As usual, those people closest to her were correct.

Regardless of Princess Diana's personal motivations for her charity work, it is obvious that she had become a beacon of hope and a pillar of strength for women worldwide who related to Diana's public divorce, her challenges with bulimia, bouts of depression and her human response to personal crisis. Diana gleaned the love she craved from those she helped, the people who were willing and able to show their love and appreciation for her, and it gave her strength to continue, even after she stepped away from most of her favorite charities.

It was also obvious that her health regime continued to be an outlet for frustration and turmoil, and benefits from her regular visits to the gym showed visibly in her increased self-confidence, poise and demeanor, as well as the robust, physical sleekness she now posessed from her physical training.

While Prince Charles was losing public support and confidence of his people, especially among the Church of England's faithful, Diana was emerging into her new life with confidence. Having overcome bulimia some years before and no longer battling depression, Diana focused on her future, listening to her heart, and began living the dreams that she had stifled for fifteen years. Diana had once believed that she and Charles would have made "the best team in the world," according to Tina Brown, editor of *New Yorker* Magazine. During Brown's interview with Diana in June 1997, Diana said she had no plans to remarry, saying "Who would take me on?...I have so much baggage. Anyone who takes me out to dinner has to accept the fact that their business will be raked over in the papers. Photographers will go though their dustbins. I think I am safer alone."

Though this seemed sad and lonely for Diana, she continued to turn with enthusiasm to another, more important suitor: peace initiatives and using her profile to focus world attention on human suffering. She told Brown that the new Labour Prime Minister Tony Blair was willing to include her in upcoming peace initiatives. "I think at last I will have someone who will know how to use me," Diana said. "He's told me he wants me to go on some missions," Diana told Brown. Diana's desire to visit Bosnia, China and other war-torn countries made many politicians uncomfortable, but Diana's concern was not with the comfort of privileged politicians. She wanted to bring her limelight to focus on the horrifying conditions that real humans endure in the real world.

After her January visit to Angola and the political outcry that followed, Diana made a two-day trip to Pakistan in February that raised political eyebrows once again. The visit was not an official one, and Diana visited hospitals in Pakistan and met socially with Jemima Goldsmith Khan, a socialite who had just married Imran Khan. As Imran, who is seen as "politically ambitious" and "at odds with Prime Minister Benazir Bhutto," some felt Diana's actions were another political blunder. Diana's supporters, though, were thankful and always ready to show their public appreciation for lending herself to their interests. British Red Cross public affairs director John Gray said of her trip to Angola, "The aim of the Red Cross is not only to help victims of landmines but also to raise public awareness of the carnage that landmines cause amongst innocent civilians.

"The Princess of Wales has given an invaluable boost to our campaign. Thousands of people fall prey to mines every year. Above all, her commitment has highlighted the appalling human costs and unnecessary suffering inflicted by these pernicious weapons."

When Diana visited South Africa to visit her brother Earl Spencer, she managed to dodge the cameras almost entirely, except when President Nelson Mandela learned that Diana was in town and invited her for tea and a chat. During that informal visit, President Mandela and Princess Diana discussed some common concerns regarding her work with AIDS and landmine issues. South Africa is facing both of these disastrous issues, and Diana, "thrilled" to have met Mandela, reportedly offered her full support to AIDS prevention and treatment campaigns in South Africa. Mandela was obviously quite taken with Diana, and their obvious ease with each other was evident when the pair posed together for photographs.

High from her earlier successes, Diana continued to submerge herself in her campaigns. In June she traveled to the US to combine a meeting with Hillary Clinton and a visit to Mother Teresa. Again, it was an unofficial visit, but she was in Washington on another Red Cross mission to raise funds and awareness for landmine victims. Worried about the health of Mother Teresa, Diana bumped up her visit a week early to visit Mother Teresa, who was seriously ill from repeated heart surgery, kidney and lung disorders. Mother Teresa was wheelchair-bound following her surgery and was recovering at a New York hospital run by the Sisters of Mercy at St. Anthony of Padua Church in the Bronx. Peter Archer, Court Correspondent for Press Associate News, reported that the Princess's visit seemed to radically alter Mother Theresa's ailing condition. When Diana arrived at the Sisters of Mercy hospital, the 86-year-old nun summoned the strength to rise from her wheelchair. The pair walked the streets near the hospital, arm in arm, hugged, kissed and prayed together. Archer reported that during the forty-minute visit, Diana was blessed by Mother Teresa. It seems that Diana inspired strength and offered comfort to anyone who would receive it, even to the Nobel Peace Prize winning Catholic nun, revered for her life's devotion to the dying masses of Calcutta.

Shortly after visiting Mother Teresa, Diana attended the Christie's auction that earned millions of dollars for AIDS and cancer charities. Over 1000 people attended the auction, all of whom were chosen by lottery because the interest in the event was so high.

In July, devastation struck close to home, as Diana grieved the murder of Gianni Versace, one of her favorite fashion designers. Diana was in the south of France on holiday when she received the phone call from her staff at Kensington Palace informing her of the terrible news. "I am devastated by the loss of a great and talented man," was Diana's response. Again, she slipped into the role of supporter and loyal friend as she comforted a visibly grieving Elton John at Versace's funeral. She held his hand, patted him and spoke quietly to the weeping man during the funeral proceedings.

Traditionally committed to supporting the British fashion industry, Versace had been the first non-British designer Diana supported. Versace honored the Princess in 1995 by designing and naming an evening bag after the Princess. It was called the "Lady Di" and sold for £815, according to Shenai Raif of *Press Associate News* (July 16, 1997).

By July, Diana's spirits seemed to be lifting once again. Diana spent her 36th birthday attending a fundraiser for the Tate Gallery in London amidst many celebrities, including actor Steve Martin and Lord and Lady Attenborough. Her high, bubbly spirits were reportedly obvious from the moment she entered the gallery.

Princess Diana's August 1997 trip to Bosnia was a landmark occasion. After dreaming of visiting the war-torn country earlier this year, Diana was finally able to bring the international spotlight to bear upon the plight of yet another devastated country. Tom Walker, a reporter for the *Times* in Sarajevo, reported that Diana's original plans to visit Bosnia with the Red Cross had to be canceled to avoid having to meet with the Bosnian Serb Red Cross president, Liljana Karadzic, who is the "wife of the world's most-wanted war crimes suspect."

The Landmine Survivors' Network arranged a small dinner at the Vezir's Elephant hotel in Travnik in central Bosnia, and Walker reported that Diana seemed tired but in very high spirits. Diana spoke of her desire to return to the Serb territories of Bosnia, and her dreams to visit Afghanistan and Georgia. To Walker, Diana revealed her wish to become involved in work both for the mentally handicapped and for depressed people.

In an interview with Annick Cojean of the French publication *Le Monde*, Diana spoke openly about the controversy that she sparked with her newfound role as an ambassador of goodwill. "Over the years, I have to learn to ignore criticism. But the irony is that it gave me strength that I was far from thinking I had. That doesn't mean it didn't hurt me. To the contrary. But that gave me the strength I needed to continue along the path I had chosen," said Diana.

In that interview, Diana described the paparazzi as being ruthless. "The press is ferocious," she said. "It pardons nothing. It looks only for mistakes. Every intention is twisted, every gesture criticized. I think things are different abroad. I'm greeted with kindness. I'm accepted as I am, without prejudices, without watching for every faux pas. In Britain, it's the other way round. And I think that in my place, any sane person would have left long ago. But I can't. I have my sons to think about," she told Cojean (*Le Monde*, Aug 27, 1997).

Diana had the ability and will to change people's lives for the better, and she could even do this for those who had no idea of her identity. While in Bosnia, Diana made a very special birthday gift to a landmine victim named Mohammed Soljankic. For his 38th birthday, Diana first handed him a birthday cake and then told him that he would be given something that he thought he would never own—a new pair of feet. The Bosnian Ministry of Health had long denied Mr. Soljankic's request for a "real" pair of artificial feet, stating that they could not afford them, but the Landmine Survivors' Network, who arranged Diana's Bosnia trip, agreed to pay the £700 for the special birthday gift.

In the war-ravaged streets of Bosnia, few people knew or cared about who Diana was until it was explained to them. The lack of recognition didn't, however, stop Diana from forging a friendship with Soljankic's family. The barriers of language were quickly overcome by Diana's genuine interest in the family's children. Diana was "swinging hands with one young daughter and patting the heads of the others as they walked beneath trees in the garden," reported Roger Williams, Court Correspondent for *PA News* in Bosnia (August 9, 1997).

Ramiza, Soljankic's wife, spoke with Diana through an interpreter. The Princess, her own honesty inviting an openness in the woman, was told, "I am very happy, but I didn't know who Princess Diana was until I was told." Ramiza's obvious lack of recognition was evident when she saw the group of journalists waiting outside the Soljankic's home. "I don't really understand why they are here," Ramiza said.

Just when Diana had found a country where no one recognized her, the press was lying in wait. As usual, the paparazzi weren't interested in Diana's charity work; they were there to dig once again into her personal life, which had recently taken a surprisingly happy turn. "Isn't it wonderful news about your relationship with Mr. Al Fayed?" yelled one reporter, according to Williams. As Diana gave him a stony glare, she walked past him, then smiled and ignored him again as he called "What's it like being in love?"

After a remarkably long time alone, afraid to bring anyone into the world spotlight for fear they'd be ripped apart in the media's jaws, Diana's personal life had once again hit the tabloids' front pages. Speculative reports in July had said that Diana was about to make an announcement that would tip the world, at least the Royal one, on its ear. Although she denied those rumors, her newfound love life was certainly just the thing to do it.

Diana's love life had long been on hold. With her past relationships and affairs boldly splashed over every TV screen and newspaper in the land, she had retreated, taking comfort and fulfillment in her children and the causes she had taken to heart. Although she had earlier believed that no one would be willing to take her on, it was inevitable that this newly self-created dazzling woman that had rebuilt her life from the ashes would find love somewhere.

Early on, there was some fuss and a lot of paparazzi interest when Diana, William and Harry joined long-time family friend Mohammed Al Fayed and his family for a holiday aboard his yacht, the *Jonikal,* and, at his villa in Saint Tropez in July. The colorful and flamboyant character of Mohammed Al Fayed, whom the British establishment considered to be a huge troublemaker, was part of the reason for heated interest in Diana's latest holiday companions.

Mohammed Al Fayed, the Egyptian billionaire owner of Harrods and the Paris Ritz hotel, was at the center of controversy during the last British elections, when he allegedly paid off a number of Conservative Members of Parliament to ask questions for him in Parliament. He has done just about anything anyone can think of to be granted a British passport, but his requests have been consistently refused. Some reported that he chuckled while the Tory ship was sinking; some credited Britain's top merchant in having played a pivotal role in the Tory's crash in popularity that led to Tony Blair and the Labour party's victory.

Mohammed's long-time friendship with Diana's father, the late Earl Spencer, was so close that on his deathbed, he made Mohammed promise to "keep an eye" on Diana when he was gone.

Diana and Mohammed had a lot in common. They had both suffered at the hands of the establishment, and they both donated a lot of time to charity work, attending functions together over the years. Diana's first London engagement following the divorce was to join Mohammed at Harrods for a fundraising dinner. Mohammed made Diana laugh and was a strong supporter, offering his shoulder to cry on during the difficult times.

Then there was Mohammed's son: some say "playboy," some say "film producer," but all agree that Dodi was fun-loving, charming and as down to Earth as a jet-setting son of a billionaire could be. Dodi Al Fayed, the handsome, 42 year-old film producer, was also with the family on their July cruise around Saint Tropez. In character with his no-expense-is-too-great-for-my-friends generosity, Diana's children were spared nothing, and it was reported that both William and Harry got on well with the jovial Dodi. It was also reported that Dodi rented a disco in Saint Tropez so the kids, and the rest of their entourage, could dance and

have fun away from the imposing eye of the cameras, which dogged
their every move on land and sea. Diana later described the trip to friends
as being the best holiday in her life.

When Diana and her children returned home after their family holiday, the rumors of romance between Diana and Dodi were in full swing.
Some were outraged that Diana would link up with Dodi, the nephew of
Saudi arms dealer Adnan Khashoggi. Could this shameless playboy set
his eye on England's jewel, and could he really become stepfather to the
future king of England, they gasped. When Diana joined Dodi for a private holiday just a few days after returning the boys to England, more
than a few eyebrows were raised, along with the blood pressure of many
Royal watchers. Far from the weekend fling that some believed it to be,
the blossoming romance of Dodi and Diana had its founding in a solid
friendship. Diana met Dodi over ten years ago when his polo team beat
Prince Charles's team in a match.

The tabloids had their first sniff that something was up when Diana
was seen being driven to Dodi's Park Lane home in London, presumably for an intimate dinner, just before she flew to Bosnia in early July.
Following their romantic weekend in the South of France, Diana joined
Dodi again less than a week later to cruise the shores of Sardinia and
Corsica on August 1st. When the first blurry photographs splashed the
front pages of the tabloids, the official feeding frenzy had begun. Diana
and Dodi were being served up on the dinner tables of the world as the
main course. The *Sunday Mirror* won the bidding war for the pictures
which portrayed Dodi and Diana in an affectionate embrace. Though it
didn't actually show the pair kissing, the *Mirror* paid a whopping
£250,000 for those pictures. Other pictures also surfaced, this time taken
by children, when Diana and Dodi flew in the Harrods's helicopter to
meet with Diana's confidant and psychic, Rita Rogers, in Derbyshire.
Diana was reportedly upset by the photos. When the press tried to speak
to Rita, they were turned away at the door by an elderly man who was
quoted as saying, "Rita will not be talking to you at all. It is no business
of yours who comes here."

Though Dodi had been romantically linked to many beautiful and
famous women, some of whom had little good to say about him, his ex-
wife Suzanne Gregard quickly came to his public defense. "He was so
romantic and thoughtful," Gregard was quoted in *People* Magazine. In
an interview with the *News of the World*, Gregard said Dodi had told her
of his relationship with Diana, saying "It's not a fling, I promise.

It's serious. One minute it was private, the next we were overwhelmed with the publicity. I've never known anything like the interest in this," Dodi told her.

"He sounded quite somber, promised me that it wasn't a fling, then said, 'Diana and I are having a romance, a true romance.'"

Gregard's response was "Wow, so it is serious."

Dodi replied, "Yes, it is."

"I didn't ask him any personal details, but I know Dodi well enough to realize that he must be in love with Di— and I'm sure she's in love with him," Gregard said. Her 1986 marriage with Dodi ended amicably in less than a year because of their immensely different backgrounds. "We were always surrounded by bodyguards," she said.

Also in Diana's corner was her beloved step-grandmother, the world's most famous and widely read romance novelist Dame Barbara Cartland. She poo-pooed public comment that gruffed about "that foreigner" dating Diana. Some said that because Dodi is not English, he would be unfit as stepfather to the next king of England.

"Yes, Dodi ought to be an Englishman, but we know perfectly well that she's been with an Englishman and it was terrible. They've ignored Diana. I don't think it should be any of their business," said Dame Cartland. "It can just hit you, and you suddenly realize you are desperately in love," Dame Cartland told *People* Magazine. "I only hope she has found someone who will look after her—and see how wonderful she is."

Also in Dodi and Diana's corner was Mohammad Al Fayed. "They are both adults. She is a lovely girl and he is my son and I love him very much. They seem to enjoy each other's company a lot and it makes me so happy to see them both so happy," said the elder Al Fayed when asked for comment on the blurry photographs. Some speculated that because the British had denied him citizenship, something he coveted passionately, he would be most pleased to see his son end up with the biggest jewel in the monarchy's crown.

Like any father, he was more than pleased that his son was happy, and if that happiness was found with the Princess of Wales, then so be it. He was quoted as saying "We must wait and see what happens," but also alluded to a "serious and proper relationship that is developing." The Al Fayed family was embracing Diana with open arms, and, ready to come in from the frosty cold of the monarchy's grip, the Princess went willingly and happily toward her future. Her dreams were coming true.

Prince Charles was reported by several tabloids as saying "I'm happy if she's happy," but his alleged reaction probably stemmed more from personal motivations than genuine happiness that his ex-wife had at last found love. His relationship with Camilla Parker-Bowles had plummeted his popularity since the distasteful audio tapes in which he had expressed his desire to be extremely close to his long-time lover.

The jet-setting Dodi, with an Oscar under his belt for his production partnership in *Chariots of Fire*, had the ways and means to sweep the Princess off her feet and into happy, romantic oblivion. Even reports that Dodi's ex-fiancee Kelly Fisher, an American model, claimed that she and Dodi were trying to have a baby together didn't seem to phase Diana. Fisher decided to seek damages against Dodi for breaking their engagement after seeing the telltale pictures. Fisher was quoted as saying, "I knew he was seeing another woman but I never knew it was Diana. When I saw the pair of them pictured on TV I was horrified." With Fisher's knowledge that Dodi was not restricting himself to a monogamous relationship, it could be said that their "plans for marriage" were more than one-sided.

Diana's long-time confidant Richard Kay of the *Daily Mail* confirmed reports that the relationship between Diana and Dodi was the real thing, and it was going to take the world by storm. The intimate vacation, as intimate as you can get under a microscope, was obviously opening new horizons to Diana, probably some that she had never really imagined possible for herself.

When recently speaking to his father's advisor Michael Cole, Dodi was warned against developing a relationship with Diana because of her popularity and the chances that she could be labeled as a new girlfriend. Dodi turned to Cole and said, "Michael, I will never have another girlfriend."

"He said it in such a determined way that I knew he was sincere," said the spokesman in response to questions about the seriousness of their involvement. Meanwhile, dabbling on the shores of rugged and breathtaking Sardinia, Diana and Dodi swam together in secluded inlets and sunbathed on the luxurious deck of the *Jonikal*. They held hands, embraced and laughed...the beginning of a new fairy-tale uncovering itself in the brilliant Mediterranean sun.

Not that the press really cared whether or not it was a true romance. Their only concern was money, and that meant pictures. Italian paparazzo

Mario Brenna had made his £3 million...now it was time to spread the wealth around. It was reported that Diana was justifiably angry once again at the paparazzi's rude and mean-spirited intrusions.

The photographers' lust to get *the* picture even came to blows after the *Jonikal*'s crew prevented the paparazzi from intruding on Diana and Dodi's privacy as they swam peacefully in a secluded inlet nearby. Furious at the interruption of the hunt, two photographers came up to the *Jonikal* and began screaming at the crew, hurling insults and profanities. When the skipper approached the shouting group on shore, he was reportedly pushed by a camera man. The camera man then turned on his own side, punching another photographer twice.

Though this was just another day in the life of Princess Diana, others had begun to realize that the paparazzi's actions were proving more and more dangerous. A British MP had written an article in the *Spectator* in August regarding the role of the press's harassment of public figures. In that piece, Alan Clark, Member of Parliament for Kensington and Chelsea, directly blamed the media's harassment for the suicide of Lady Green and Lady Caithness, and the death of Labour Member of Parliament Gordon McMaster. Clark wrote that if the press were able to film the death of Princess Diana, it would be the "ultimate trophy."

Thoughts of death were the furthest thing from the happy couple's mind. The public had openly embraced Dodi as a proper suitor for the Princess, some going so far as to say it was good for the Royal image. The public opinion poll came out near the beginning of August, around the same time that Will Carling, the rugby captain with whom Diana had been formerly paired, stated that the press had "massively exaggerated" his friendship with Diana two years ago. In a radio interview, Carling expressed his concern and bewilderment at the continual hounding of Diana at the hands of the media.

"Sometimes I don't quite understand the obsession with her and I think an awful lot of people are incredibly bored with the obsession. I think it's a shame from her point of view. I don't think a number of people understand what she has been through or what kind of life she leads and can cast all these theories or criticisms.

"Maybe if some of us had been through a little bit of it then we might live our lives a bit differently," Carling stated.

It was obvious that feelings were of no concern to the vicious paparazzi, so Diana and Dodi decided to cut short their Sardinia holiday in order to escape the constant harassment. They decided to return to Paris for a romantic weekend at the Ritz, where their privacy would be guaranteed.

Anxious as always to be reunited with her sons, she planned to meet up with them a few days early, on August 31, to spend time with them before their return to school. Diana also had a hectic schedule planned for the month of September.

The *Times* reported that Princess Diana would be traveling to the Far East in an AIDS campaign, and that she would begin a new role as champion for victims of asthma and Down's Syndrome. Along with a number of London-based engagements, Diana planned to attend an AIDS charity gala dinner in Singapore on September 23. This event would have been a landmark occasion for the Royal Family, as she would be the first to visit Hong Kong since the former British colony was given back to China. Her final engagement for the month would be to return to the new children's unit at the Northwick Park and St. Mark's Hospital in London.

Diana's very real ties to her causes became even more evident when, in the midst of this blossoming romance with Dodi, Diana visited the children's unit at St. Mark's London hospital for two hours on July 21. She insisted on speaking to each child, and was seen to be warm, compassionate and caring. Al Fayed's spokesman, Michael Cole, said, "It was an extraordinarily happy day."

Following the "excessive and abusive attentions" in Italy, Diana and Dodi went to the Olbia airport, where the private Harrods jet was waiting, and set off to find some happy, private moments on board the luxury airliner before beginning their unplanned weekend in Paris. It was August 29th, the beginning of the end.

Chapter 10

The Tragedy

The fragments of Lady Diana's last day are difficult to piece together. Stunned, saddened and unprepared for the news that the "people's princess" had died, media outlets worldwide stumbled into action looking for a story. A tidal wave of theories and speculations flooded news outlets; only a few held any merit. Conflicting reports and conspiracy theories abound but many facts have been confirmed. They offer little comfort, however, for a world mourning the loss of Princess Diana.

Lady Diana and Dodi Al Fayed reportedly shortened their Mediterranean holiday because of harassment by Italian Paparazzi. The Harrods' jet they were traveling on landed at Le Bourget Airport, just outside of Paris, on August 30, 1997, at 3:20 p.m. There was already a group of photographers waiting for them when they arrived in Paris from Sardinia. The Princess and Dodi were accompanied by Dodi's bodyguard, Trevor Rees-Jones, and they were met at the airport by Henri Paul, assistant director of security at the Ritz. They intended to visit Villa Windsor, one of the many jewels in the Al Fayed business crown.

As they journeyed to the Villa Windsor, Lady Diana, Mr. Al Fayed, Trevor Rees-Jones and an Al Fayed driver, Phillipe Dourneau, were in a large Black Mercedes 600 series. Henri Paul followed at a short distance in a black Range Rover.

There are reports that during the journey to Villa Windsor, paparazzi riding in a car, positioned their vehicle directly in front of the Mercedes and attempted to slow the limousine. This would have enabled the photographers on motorcycles to get close enough to the Mercedes to snap pictures of Diana and Dodi.

Reports indicate that it was at this time that Diana expressed concern for the safety of the motorcycle-driving photographers. She felt that the motorcycles were driving too close to the speeding Mercedes and Land Rover, and she feared that there was a chance someone might be seriously injured or even killed if the chase continued. Fortunately no one was hurt, and Diana and Dodi managed to evade the photographers with some clever thinking and evasive maneuvering by the drivers. Phillipe Dourneau accelerated and passed the photographers. Henri Paul also passed, and then he slowed the Land Rover, thereby blocking the pursuing photographers and allowing the Mercedes to speed away toward Villa Windsor.

Dodi and Diana arrived at the Villa Windsor, in the Bois de Boulogne Windsor, at approximately 3:45 p.m. Upon arriving at the Villa, Dodi gave Diana a tour of the stately property and the surrounding gardens.

Shortly thereafter, Dodi and Diana made their way toward the Paris Ritz, where by 5:30 p.m. a number of photographers were already awaiting their arrival. They decided to enter the Ritz through the rear entrance in the Rue Cambon rather than deal with the paparazzi. Once inside the Ritz, the couple relaxed for a time in the luxurious $2000-a-night Imperial Suite.

Around 6:00 p.m., Phillipe Dorneau drove Diana and Mr. Fayed to his apartment, arriving at 6:15 p.m. Again photographers were awaiting their arrival and departure.

Diana and Dodi were later harassed by photographers while shopping on the Champs Elysees at 8:30 p.m. Presumably, because they had so many problems with the photograph-seeking press, they decided to forgo their dinner reservations at Benoit, a very trendy bistro located in Rue Saint-Martin.

The couple headed back to the serenity of the Ritz where they could enjoy some semblance of order. On their way back to the hotel, they were pursued by approximately ten photographers on motorbikes.

Dodi and Diana arrived back at the Ritz at 9:50 p.m. and were faced with another mob of perhaps forty photographers. It was reported that Dodi snapped at the photographers as he entered the hotel. The couple started their dinner at the Ritz's famous seafood restaurant, L'Espadon, a Michelin 2-star rated eatery. Diana ordered scrambled eggs with wild mushrooms, and asparagus, as well as filet of sole tempura. Dodi ate turbot. They found it impossible to dine unnoticed in the restaurant. Because of the stir their presence was creating, after only ten minutes in L'Espadon, they decided to finish their meal in the Imperial Suite.

It has been suggested that during the meal Dodi presented Diana with a very expensive gift: a diamond solitaire ring. He had ordered the ring several days before from one of the most respected and exclusive jewellers in Paris, Alberto Repossi. There is some disagreement as to the value of the ring, but Mr. Al Fayed likely paid somewhere between $200 000 and $300 000 for the gift. Diana had previously given Dodi a pair of cufflinks that had belonged to her father, the Earl of Spencer. Shortly following the tragedy, Mohammed Al Fayed found a gold cigar cutter in Dodi's Paris apartment inscribed with the words, "With Love From Diana." Mohammed Al Fayed also reported finding a silver plaque under Diana's pillow inscribed with a love poem written by Dodi.

While Diana and Dodi dined in the relaxed atmosphere of the luxurious Imperial Suite, Henri Paul was called back from his apartment on the rue des Petite-Champs.

Two weeks after the accident it was reported that Mr. Henri Paul had, after bringing the couple to the Ritz, his first and second drink of the evening at the hotel: two glasses of Ricard Pastis, "Pernod." There are conflicting reports about exactly where Henri Paul went next. It is thought, however, that Henri, believing he was off-duty for the evening, went to Harry's New York Bar, where he had two or three more drinks before leaving at 9:45 p.m. Paul then went to another Parisian bar, one where he was a regular, and stayed until his cell phone rang at 10:00 p.m. It has been reported that he didn't have a drink after arriving. Presumably the call he received was from the hotel informing him that he was supposed to return to work. Paul arrived back at the Ritz at 10:08 p.m. A Parisian newspaper reported that Paul had drunk more pastis in the hotel bar while waiting for Diana and Dodi and that he staggered when leaving. According to the French paper, Paul had been asked to take part in a ruse to dupe the many photographers still waiting outside the Ritz.

The plan was to have the Black Mercedes S600, and several others like it, as well as the black Land Rover, drive to the front of the hotel. This, coupled with the fact that the vehicles were driven by Al Fayed drivers, made it appear as if Diana and Dodi were about to leave the Ritz through the front door. The drivers were reportedly told to drive toward Mr. Al Fayed's private residence at 16th Arrondisement, again making it appear as if the couple was simply on their way back to Dodi's residence after their evening dinner at the Ritz.

Meanwhile, Henri Paul secretly drove a dark blue Mercedes S280 to the rear entrance, where the couple and Trevor Rees-Jones had been waiting for his arrival for five minutes. The group left the Ritz through the back door at 12:19 a.m.

The ruse was only a partial success, as several of the more wily photographers managed to get pictures of Diana and Dodi entering the Mercedes.

A number of reports following the accident had claimed the Mercedes S280 was in fact a bullet-proof S600. These proved to be false; the car was in fact a three-year-old black S280 without any kind of bullet proofing whatsoever. It had been rented by the Ritz and had at one time been stolen and stripped for parts. It was subsequently rebuilt by Mercedes Benz.

It was also rumored that Henri Paul taunted the photographers saying: "you won't catch us," as he piloted the S280 away from the Ritz.

After leaving the Ritz, the Mercedes headed out onto the rue Cambon, turned right onto the ritzy shop-lined rue de Rivoli by the Jardin des Tuilleries. The car then crossed the one way cobblestone-laden Place de la Concorde, taking a left around the obelisk. At this point the Mercedes had increased its speed dramatically. (Many editorial reports following the tragedy concerned themselves with the folly of trying to outpace a motorcycle when driving a moderately powered sedan. It is, under most conditions, almost impossible for the Mercedes to do so. The sedan has neither the power nor the handling capabilities of the motorcycles. It is possible that Dodi, realizing there was no other way to lose the pack of motorcycles, felt that the two-wheelers would be too unstable when traveling at high speed across the cobbles surrounding the Place de la Concorde.)

It was also reported through the press that the black Mercedes ran through a red light in an attempt to loose the paparazzi. As the Mercedes headed west along the right bank of the Seine, along the Cours de la Reine, then onto the Cours Albert 1st, it continued to accelerate toward the narrow, twisting entrance to the 660-foot tunnel underneath Place de l'Alma.

Henri Paul lost control of the vehicle at approximately 12:25 a.m. as the car approached the second tunnel under Place de l'Alma. There is current speculation that another car travelling ahead of the Mercedes may have been involved in the accident. This idea is under investigation. What is known, however, is that the Mercedes touched the central barrier, then careened across the road, crashed into the right wall, and crossed the road again hitting the 13th central pillar. The car then flipped and struck the right wall again, spun around and stopped, facing the same direction from which it had come. The car finally stopped halfway through the underpass.

The S280 left 53-foot skid marks and its estimated speed at impact ranges anywhere from 80 mph to over 120 mph. The normal speed limit at the entrance to the tunnel is 30 mph. Police officials said the speedometer was frozen at 196 kph or 121 mph. This was later proven to be an inaccurate indication of the vehicle's speed at impact for several reasons. The wheels on the Mercedes could very likely have spun freely when the vehicle was rolling, thereby recording a higher reading on the speedometer. Furthermore, experts say that the S280 speedometer will either move to 0 or 120 mph when the power shuts off. A phenomenon called "needle slap" is a more reliable indicator. Needle slap occurs when the force of the vehicle's impact forces the speedometer needle into the glass, leaving a small mark that indicates the vehicle's speed at impact. However, this phenomenom is not evident in all accidents.

Dodi Al Fayed and Henri Paul died instantly in the crash. Eyewitnesses reported that Dodi Al Fayed's body lay across the back seat, while Paul's corpse was thrown through the windshield. The radiator of the Mercedes was pushed into Paul's body, which lay crushed against the horn, causing it to wail incessantly. Trevor Rees-Jones, the only one of the foursome who was wearing a seatbelt, suffered extreme facial and chest injuries. Lady Diana was lying between the rear of the front seat and the base of the rear seat.

Some reports state that shortly after the accident, the cameramen who were pursuing Diana and Dodi arrived at the scene. There are conflicting reports as to their exact number, and their actions in those few minutes before and after the accident. It is known that at 12:27 a.m. an eyewitness called the French Emergency Service, and the Fire Brigade arrived at 12:40 a.m. Shortly thereafter, the police contacted the British Embassy, informing them the Princess of Wales has been in an accident. Charles, who was vacationing with the Royal Family at Balmoral, received the news at 12:45 a.m.

In the melee of activity surrounding the crash site, several photographers began taking pictures of the crash and the dying Princess rather than trying to help her. One cameraman was, reportedly, beaten by the crowd that had gathered around the crash site. Another apparentlly reached into the wreckage, took Diana's pulse, and started taking pictures of her as she lay near death. Meanwhile, a French doctor, Frederic Maillez, arrived at the scene. He proceeded quickly to the crashed Mercedes, assessed the situation and, returning to his vehicle, called for help. There are however, conflicting reports about who placed the first call to emergency services. When Dr. Maillez returned to the wreckage, an off-duty volunteer firefighter was giving first aid to Trevor Rees-Jones. Maillez shifted his attention toward the woman in the back seat and "helped free her respiratory tract." It wasn't until the next morning that he discovered the victim was Princess Diana. In a statement given later, the doctor mentioned noticing "about 10 or 15 of them [photographers] and they were snapping away at the car non-stop." He did, however, also say that, "one cannot say that they hampered my work." Nonetheless, the police would eventually arrest six paparazzi and one driver on the night of the crash and another three photographers in the following weeks. The police also confiscated all their film. Not all the papparazzi who witnessed the gruesome scene were, however, arrested. One photographer, speaking anonymously to the German media, said he had been at the scene and had taken pictures of Lady Diana as she lay dying.

It took the fire crew an hour to cut Diana free of the mangled wreckage. Twenty minutes later, at 2:00 a.m., Trevor Rees-Jones was also freed.

Diana, suffering from massive chest injuries and internal bleeding, was rushed to La Pitie-Salpetriere hospital, arriving there at 2:00 a.m. At 2:20 a.m., she had a massive heart attack and, when doctors performed an emergency thoracectomy (the removal of part or all of the rib cage), they discovered Diana had suffered major damage to her left pulmonary vein (the vital vein carrying blood from the lung to the heart). After closing the wound, doctors performed internal and external heart massage, at times using their hands in a desperate attempt to get Diana's heart beating again. She continued to receive heart massage until 4:00 a.m. Diana, the Princess of Wales, was pronounced dead at 4:00 a.m. on August 31, 1997.

The French Ambassador telephoned the Queen, who was also on holiday at Balmoral, and informed her private secretary that Diana had died. Prime Minister Tony Blair, a confidante and friend of the Princess, was also informed of Diana's death. When Charles received the news, he woke both William and Harry and told them of their mother's tragic death.

At 4:21 a.m. the Press Association prepared to make an announcement. The British Foreign secretary, Robin Cook also prepared to make an announcement from Manila.

Twenty minutes later, the Press Association announced to the world: "Diana, Princess of Wales, has died, according to British sources, the Press Association learned this morning."

At 4:57 a.m., the official announcement of Diana's death was made from the hospital by French Interior Minister Jean-Pierre Chevenement.

At 5:05 a.m., Robin Cook confirmed the announcement from the airport in Manila. This was followed at 5:09 a.m. by the Queen's Buckingham Palace announcement that she and the Prince of Wales were, "deeply shocked and distressed by this terrible news." Tony Blair stated that he was, "utterly devastated." The British Broadcasting Corporation and many other media outlets the world over discontinued regular broadcasting and concentrated solely on the tragedy of Diana's death.

At 11:30 a.m. Queen Elizabeth, the Queen Mother, the Duke of Edinburgh, the Prince of Wales, and Prince William and Prince Harry arrived at the church in Crathie near Balmoral for a private service. The service ended at 12:55, and the Prince of Wales spoke briefly to Rev. Robert Sloan.

Later, at 2:10 p.m. Sunday, August 31, Prince Charles joined Diana's two sisters, Lady Jane Fellowes and Lady Sarah McCorquodale, at Aberdeen Airport. They flew to Paris to bring Diana's body back to England. They arrived at La Pitie Salpetriere hospital at 4:40 p.m. where they met President Chirac and his wife, Bernadette, before proceeding to the room where the coffin was kept. A half-hour later the dead Princess, in a coffin draped with the royal standard, was taken in a hearse to an airport near Paris and flown back to England.

By 6:00 p.m. Tony Blair had arrived at RAF Northolt. At 6:51 p.m., aboard a Royal Squadron BAe 146 aircraft, Princess Diana was repatriated to her homeland. Her coffin, still draped in the royal standard, was accompanied by the Prince of Wales and Diana's sisters. Also in attendance were George Robertson, the Defense Secretary, the Lord Chamberlain, head of the Queen's household, and the Lord-Lieutenant of London.

The coffin was removed from the aircraft and carried by bearers from the Queen's Color Squadron of the RAF to a hearse that was waiting on the tarmac. The hearse spirited the coffin to a private mortuary in London, and from there, shortly after midnight, it was taken to Chapel Royal in Saint James's Palace.

Meanwhile, Dodi Al Fayed's body was being flown to Surray, England to Regent's Park mosque. Dodi was buried within 24 hours of his death, in accordance with Muslim tradition. His final resting place is Brookland Cemetery in Surray. The body of Henri Paul underwent a series of tests to determine his condition on the night of the accident.

In the days immediately following Lady Diana's death there was a great deal of speculation and controversy surrounding Mr. Henri Paul. It was initially reported that Mr. Paul, aged 41, was a single man and a trusted employee who had worked for the Ritz hotel for thirteen years. Michael Cole, a spokesperson for Mohammed Al Fayed, said that Henri was a, "conscientious and responsible member of the staff." Henri was supposed to have taken two special driving courses at Mercedes Benz in Stuttgart, Germany. As well, he was supposedly trained in anti-terrorist techniques. Other sources, however, cast doubt on Henri Paul's driving ability. The press quoted one chauffeur who regularly services clients at luxury Parisian hotels as saying, "I have never seen the guy among the group of 10 or 15 drivers who hang around waiting for work at the Ritz." There were reports that Henri was not licensed to drive a limousine. These reports, however, proved to be a red herring. In France, anyone with a regular operator's license can legally operate a limousine.

Henri was raised in the Lorient, a fishing port on the southwestern coast of Brittany. It was initially reported that, during his mandatory military service, he had risen to the rank of captain while in the French Air Force. These rumors were later contradicted by the French Air Force.

The first test results released to the media Monday, September 1 showed Henri Paul was very drunk the night of the accident: he had 175 milligrams of alcohol per 100 milliliters of blood in his body. To get a reading this high, Henri would have to have consumed the equivalent of one bottle of wine and two glasses of beer or ten shots of whiskey. (In France it is a minor offence to operate a motor vehicle if you have more than 50 milligrams of alcohol per 100 milligrams of blood. More than 80 milligrams per 100 milligrams of blood is a criminal offence. In such cases the driver is not allowed to drive again until they have had a hearing.) There was a great deal of concern from the Al Fayed family that the initial test results were not accurate because there had been so much blood at the accident scene, making it plausible that Henri's blood was tainted or mixed with someone else's. They released to the media the hotel security video in an attempt to show Mr. Paul was not drunk on the evening of August 30, 1997. The video was inconclusive, but a second blood test, conducted on September 4, with the investigating magistrate standing by, confirmed the result of the earlier blood test. The eyeball fluid confirmed Henri was drinking on the night of the accident and that he had only a slightly lower rate of alcohol per liter of blood than the earlier test revealed. This test also showed that Henri was also under the influence of two prescription drugs: fluexetine, the generic form of the antidepressant Prozac, and tiapride, a drug used for treating alcoholism and aggressive behavior. The level of fluexetine in Henri's body was, according to the official prosecutor's statement, "therapeutic" and the tiapride was "sub-therapeutic." Persisting, the Al Fayed family asked for a third test, contending that not enough different individual tissue or blood samples had been taken to produce accurate results. This test provided similar results to the first two, but it was not determined if it was performed on a separate sample from the original. It wasn't until two weeks after the tragedy that the investigating magistrate released Henri Paul's body to his family for burial. Henri Paul was buried in his home town of Lorient, Brittany.

It had been reported during the weeks following Diana's fatal crash that she had whispered her last words to a doctor as he placed an oxygen mask over her mouth shortly after the accident. Those words, "Leave me alone," were subsequently published in major newspapers and periodicals. Other reports claimed, however, that Lady Diana's Spencer's last words were spoken to an Al Fayed aide at the La Pitie-Salpetriere hospital in Paris shortly before Diana's death. These last words were then told to Mohammed Al Fayed, and he passed them on to the individual for whom they were intended.

In the days immediately following the return of Diana's body to Great Britain, there was an enormous outpouring of grief from England and around the world. Over a million flower bouquets were left at the three London Palaces and several other locations throughout the city, including Harrods, where a memorial for Diana and Dodi had been built. Traders in London stood for a moment's silence to pay respect to the dead Princess. Londoners queued for up to 12 hours for the chance to sign a condolence book for the family. Similar books of condolence were prepared in most parts of the world, where similar queues were reported. On Monday, September 1, many countries in the Commonwealth and elsewhere paid tribute to Princess Diana by flying official flags at half-staff.

Two nations were notable exceptions to the overwhelming show of respect and grief for Lady Diana: Libya and Iran. The national Libyan news agency broadcast one of the first and most outlandish conspiracy theories: they accused Britain of assassinating Diana because she was having a relationship with an Arab. Iranian Government television referred to Diana as the "moral disgrace" of the British Court.

On Wednesday, September 3, 1997, the British Broadcasting Corporation announced it would televise the funeral live to 187 countries and that the service would be translated simultaneously into 43 different languages. This would be the largest live broadcasting event the BBC had ever undertaken in its 75-year history, with an estimated worldwide audience of 2.5 billion.

The week after Diana's death, the British public grew somewhat discontented with the overly stoic appearance of the Royal Family. While the nation seemed dumbstruck by sadness and loss, "The Royals," as the press aptly put it, "had not mirrored the public pain." Buckingham Palace had not lowered the Union Jack on Monday, September 1, when flags around the world were lowered. There had not even been an official message from the Queen since Thursday the 4th of September.

The following evening, the day before the funeral, the Queen spoke to the nation, and the world, live from the Chinese Dining Room at Buckingham Palace. She looked directly into the camera and delivered her first live public television address since the early days of her 45-year reign:

"Since last Sunday's dreadful news we have seen, throughout Britain and around the world, an overwhelming expression of sadness at Diana's death. We have all been trying in our different ways to

cope. It is not easy to express our sense of loss, since the initial shock is often succeeded by a mixture of other feelings: disbelief, incomprehension, anger—and concern for others who remain.

"We have all felt these emotions in these last few days. So what I say to you now, as your Queen and as a grandmother, I say from my heart. First, I want to pay tribute to Diana myself. She was an exceptional and gifted human being. In good times and bad, she never lost her capacity to smile and laugh, nor to inspire others with her warmth and kindness.

"I admired and respected her—for her energy and commitment to others, and especially for her devotion to her two boys.

"This week at Balmoral, we have all been trying to help William and Harry come to terms with the devastating loss that they and the rest of us have suffered. No one who knew Diana will ever forget her. Millions of others who never met her, but felt they knew her, will remember her.

"I, for one, believe that there are lessons to be drawn from her life and the extraordinary and moving reaction to her death. I share in your determination to cherish her memory.

"This is also an opportunity for me, on behalf of my family, and especially Prince Charles and William and Harry, to thank all who have brought flowers, sent messages, and paid your respects in so many ways to a remarkable person. These acts of kindness have been a huge source of help and comfort.

"Our thoughts are also with Diana's family and the families of those who died with her. I know that they too have drawn strength from what has happened since last weekend as they seek to heal their sorrow and then to face the future without a loved one.

"I hope that tomorrow we can all, wherever we are, join in expressing our grief for Diana's loss and gratitude for her all-too-short life. It is a chance to show to the whole world the British nation united in peace, and may we, each and every one of us, thank God for someone who made many, many people happy."

The public finally witnessed a monarch whose grief was similar to theirs, a monarch who was also a grandmother and who, like them, "admired and respected" Diana. It also seemed to the British people that somehow, in death, the tensions between Diana, Princess of Wales and Queen Elizabeth II had abated. The same day, the Queen and Prince Philip met with the grieving public at both Buckingham Palace and St. James's Palace. Prince Charles, William and Harry mingled with mourners who came to deliver flowers and give their condolences outside Kensington Palace. The next morning, on the day of the funeral, the Union Jack above Buckingham Palace flew at half-staff for the first time in history, as the funeral cortege passed. Public support for the Queen and the Royal Family increased markedly on the strength of the Queen's message and this gesture.

The day before the funeral, Diana's body was moved at 8:00 p.m. from St. James's Palace to Kensington Palace in West London. Prince Charles and the two boys rode behind the hearse in a black limousine. Massive crowds, estimated in the hundreds of thousands, stood in the rain as the body of the woman who might have been Queen of England was driven slowly past them, en route to Kensington Palace, to spend one last night in her former home.

The decision to move her body to Kensington Palace more than tripled the length of the funeral procession to a new distance of three miles. This was done in anticipation of the millions expected to pay tribute to Diana on the day of her funeral. Many had lined the streets from Kensington Palace to Westminster Abbey—more had camped overnight to ensure they would have a view of the procession as it passed. There were 16x12-foot-high television screens set up in Hyde Park and six other venues around the city, and loudspeakers outside of the Abbey so the masses could view and hear the funeral live.

The procession to Westminster Abbey on Saturday the 6th began at 9:08 a.m. The casket, draped in the Royal Standard and mounted on a gun carriage pulled by six black Irish draught horses, was topped with three wreaths of white lilies and a large white card stenciled with the word "Mummy." The wreaths were from her brother, the Earl Spencer, and her sons, Prince William and Prince Harry. The King's Royal Troop, wearing their brilliant red uniforms and tall black bearskins, accompanied the coffin and carriage. The Earl Spencer, Prince Charles and the two young Princes, William and Harry, and the Duke of Edinburgh joined the procession as it drew closer to Westminster Abbey. Five representatives from each of the over 100 charities that Diana had represented later joined the procession as it moved slowly toward the abbey. Many of those paying their respect along the route wept, cried out Diana's name and threw flowers in the path of the carriage.

The 2 000 invited guests who waited for Diana's coffin to arrive at Westminster Abbey were a mix of celebrities and average citizens— Tom Hanks, Luciano Pavarotti, Sting, Tom Cruise and Nicole Kidman, Hillary Rodham Clinton, Margaret Thatcher, as well as many foreign dignitaries. Also in attendance were individuals Diana had known through her charity work and friends of the Spencer family.

As the guests waited and the cortege made its way from Kensington Palace to the Abbey, the Tenor Bell rang every minute. They listened to organ music pieces by Mendelssohn, Bach, Dvorak, Vaughan Williams and Elgar.

After the cortege entered the Abbey through the Great West Door, the congregation sang the National Anthem and remained standing as the Dean of Westminster, the Very Reverend Dr. Wesley Carr, said the Bidding, before singing the hymn "I Vow to Thee, My Country."

The first reading of the funeral was by the Princess's eldest sister, Lady Sarah McCorquodale:

> *"If I should die and leave you here awhile,*
> *Be not like others, sore undone, who keep*
> *Long vigils by the silent dust, and weep.*
> *For my sake—turn again to life and smile,*
> *Nerving thy heart and trembling hand to do*
> *Something to comfort other hearts than thine.*
> *Complete those dear unfinished tasks of mine*
> *And I, perchance, may therein comfort you."*

This was followed by the British Broadcasting Corporation Singers, accompanied by soprano Lynne Dawson. They sang extracts from Verdi's *Requiem*, one of Diana's favorite pieces.

Verdi's *Requiem* was followed by a reading from Diana's other sister, Lady Jane Fellowes:

> *"Time is too slow for those who wait,*
> *too swift for those who fear,*
> *too long for those who grieve,*
> *too short for those who rejoice,*
> *but for those who love, time is eternity."*

"The entire congregation then stood and sang "The King of Love My Shepherd Is", followed by a reading from 1 Corinthians: 13 by British Prime Minister, the Right Honorable Tony Blair:

"Though I speak with the tongues of men and of angels, and have not love, I am become as sounding brass, or a tinkling cymbal."

This reading was followed by a very special moment in the funeral. Rock star Elton John, who'd had his customized Yamaha grand piano brought into the Abbey for the funeral, sang a special arrangement of his song "Candle In The Wind." It had been rewritten for the somber occasion by John's longtime collaborator, Bernie Taupin.The press reported that it was during this moving segment of the ceremony that the two young Princes lost their composure and wept.

Elton John's song was followed by the eulogy and the tribute read by the Earl Spencer. In this emotional and telling piece, the Earl seemed to give voice to the world's grief for Diana. In the third paragraph, the Earl of Spencer implicitly criticized the Royal Family by saying that Diana "needed no royal title." This was a reference to Buckingham Palace act of stripping away from Diana the title "Her Royal Highness" only months before (Buckingham palace later offered to restore the title postmortem, but the Spencer family declined the offer). The Earl also commented on the constant media harassment Diana had endured; he noted that Diana's "genuinely good intentions were sneered at by the media." The Earl pledged that his "blood" family would continue "the imaginative and loving way" in which she was steering the two young Princes. This speech was perceived by onlookers as a diatribe against the Royal Family. Most in the Abbey, and those observing the funeral from outside, erupted into spontaneous applause and cheers when the Earl had finished his eulogy. The press reported that the young Princes, William and Harry, also clapped for their uncle, while Prince Charles quietly brought his hand to his knee.

The Earl Spencer's final eulogy in its entirety is as follows:

"I stand before you today, the representative of a family in grief, in a country in mourning, before a world in shock.
"We are all united, not only in our desire to pay our respects to Diana, but rather in our need to do so, for such was her extraordinary

appeal that the tens of millions of people taking part in this service all over the world, via television and radio, who never actually met her, feel that they too lost someone close to them in the early hours of Sunday morning. It is a more remarkable tribute to Diana than I can ever hope to offer her today.

"Diana was the very essence of compassion, of duty, of style, of beauty. All over the world she was a symbol of selfless humanity, a standard-bearer for the rights of the truly downtrodden. A very British girl who transcended nationality. Someone with a natural nobility who was classless, and who proved in the last year that she needed no royal title to continue to generate her particular brand of magic.

"Today is our chance to say thank you for the way you brightened our lives, even though God granted you but half a life. We will all feel cheated, always, that you were taken from us so young and yet we must learn to be grateful that you came along at all. Only now you're gone do we truly appreciate what we are now without and we want you to know that life without you is very, very difficult. We have all despaired at our loss over the past week and only the strength of the message you gave us through your years of giving has afforded us the strength to move forward.

"There is a temptation to rush to canonize your memory. There is no need to do so. You stand tall enough as a human being of unique qualities not to need to be seen as a saint. Indeed to sanctify your memory would be to miss out the very core of your being. Your wonderfully mischievous sense of humor with a laugh that bent you double, your joy for life transmitted wherever you took your smile and the sparkle in those unforgettable eyes, your boundless energy which you could barely contain.

"But your greatest gift was your intuition and it was a gift you used wisely. This is what underpinned all your other wonderful attributes and if we looked to analyze what it was about you that had such a wide appeal, we find it in your instinctive feel for what was really important in all our lives.

"Without your God-given sensitivity, we would be immersed in greater ignorance of the anguish of AIDS and HIV sufferers, the plight of the homeless, the isolation of lepers, the random destruction of land mines.

"Diana explained to me once that it was her innermost feelings of suffering that made it possible for her to connect with her constituency of the rejected. And here we come to another truth about her.

For all the status, the glamour, the applause, Diana remained, throughout, a very insecure person at heart, almost childlike in her desire to do good for others so she could release herself from deep feelings of unworthiness of which her eating disorders were merely a symptom. The world sensed this part of her character and cherished her for her vulnerability whilst admiring her for her honesty.

"The last time I saw Diana was on July the first, her birthday in London, when typically she was not taking time to celebrate her special day with friends, but was guest of honor at a fundraising charity evening. She sparkled, of course.

"But I would rather cherish the days I spent with her in March when she came to visit me and my children in our home in South Africa. I am proud of the fact that apart from when she was on public display meeting President Mandela, we managed to contrive to stop the ever present paparazzi from getting a single picture of her. That meant a lot to her.

"These were days I will always treasure. It was as if we had been transported back to our childhood when we spent such an enormous amount of time together, the two youngest in the family. Fundamentally, she hadn't changed at all—from the big sister who mothered me as a baby, fought with me at school, and endured those long train journeys between our parents' homes with me at weekends.

"It is a tribute to her level-headedness and strength that despite the most bizarre life imaginable after her childhood, she remained intact, true to herself. There is no doubt she was looking for a new direction in her life at this time. She talked endlessly of getting away from England, mainly because of the treatment that she received at the hands of the newspapers. I don't think she ever understood why her genuinely good intentions were sneered at by the media, why there appeared to be a permanent quest on their behalf to bring her down. It is baffling. My own and only explanation is that genuine goodness is threatening to those at the opposite end of the moral spectrum.

"It is a point to remember that of all the ironies about Diana, perhaps the greatest was this: A girl given the name of the ancient goddess of hunting was in the end, the most hunted person of the modern age.

"She would want us today to pledge ourselves to protecting her beloved boys, William and Harry, from a similar fate and I do this here, Diana, on your behalf. We will not allow them to suffer the anguish that was used regularly to drive you to tearful despair.

And beyond that, on behalf of your mother and sisters, I pledge that we, your blood family, will do all we can to continue the imaginative and loving way in which you were steering these two exceptional young men so that their souls are not simply immersed by duty and tradition but can sing openly as you planned. We fully respect the heritage into which they have both been born and will always respect and encourage them in their royal role but we, like you, recognize the need for them to experience as many different aspects of life as possible to arm them spiritually and emotionally for the years ahead. I know you would have expected nothing less from us.

"William and Harry, we all care desperately for you today. We are all chewed up with sadness at the loss of a woman who wasn't even our mother. How great your suffering is. We cannot even imagine.

"I would like to end by thanking God for the small mercies He's shown us at this dreadful time. For taking Diana at her most beautiful and radiant, and when she had joy in her private life.

"Above all, we give thanks for the life of a woman I am so proud to be able to call my sister—the unique, the complex, the extraordinary and irreplaceable Diana, whose beauty, both internal and external, will never be extinguished from our minds."

This was followed by the hymn "Make Me a Channel of Your Peace," based on the prayer of St Francis of Assisi.

Prayers were then led by the Archbishop of Canterbury, the Most Reverend and Right Honourable Dr George Carey, beginning with the following prayer for Diana, Princess of Wales:

"We give thanks to God for Diana, Princess of Wales; for her sense of joy and for the way she gave so much to so many people.

"Lord, we thank you for Diana, whose life touched us all and for all those memories of her that we treasure. We give thanks for those qualities and strengths that endeared her to us; for her vulnerability; for her radiant and vibrant personality; for her ability to communicate warmth and compassion; for her ringing laugh; and above all for her readiness to identify with those less fortunate in our nation and the world.

"Lord of the loving: hear our prayer."

Then followed prayers for the Princess's family, for the Royal family, for all in mourning and for the Princess's life and work:

> *"The Princess will be especially missed by the many charities with which she identified herself. We recall those precious images: the affectionate cuddle of children in hospital; that touch of the young man dying of AIDS; her compassion for those maimed through the evil of land mines—and many more.*
> *"Lord, we pray for all who are weak, poor and powerless in this country and throughout the world; the sick, among them, Trevor Rees-Jones; the maimed and all whose lives are damaged. We thank you for the way that Diana became a beacon of hope and a source of strength for so many. We commend to you all those charities that she supported. Strengthen the resolve of those who work for them to continue the good work begun with her.*
> *"Lord of the suffering: hear our prayer."*

The prayers concluded with the offering of a prayer for the congregation, after which the choristers sang "An Air From County Derry" before the Archbishop led the recitation of "The Lord's Prayer." After "The Lord's Prayer," the Archbishop said the blessing.

The congregation then sang the great Welsh hymn "Guide me, O Thou Great Redeemer," following which the Dean of Westminster said "the Commendation":

> *"Let us commend our sister Diana to the mercy of God, our Maker and Redeemer.*
> *"Diana, our companion in faith and sister in Christ, we entrust you to God. Go forth from this world in the love of the Father, who created you; In the mercy of Jesus Christ, who died for you; In the power of the Holy Spirit, who strengthens you. At one with all the faithful, living and departed, may you rest in peace and rise in glory, where grief and misery are banished and light and joy evermore abide. Amen."*

The congregation remained standing as the cortege left the Abbey, while the choir sang extracts from Shakespeare's *Hamlet* and the Orthodox Funeral Service, set to music by John Taverner:

"Alleluia. May flights of angels sing thee to thy rest. Remember me O Lord, when you come into your kingdom. Give rest O Lord to your handmaid, who has fallen asleep. The choir of saints have found the well-spring of life, and door of paradise. Life: a shadow and a dream. Weeping at the grave creates the song: Alleluia. Come, enjoy rewards and crowns I have prepared for you."

At the west end of the Abbey, shortly after midday, the cortege halted for a minutes silence that was observed by the whole nation, before leaving the Abbey for the journey to Althorp.

Althorp, the 300-hectare Spencer family estate, is located just one hour from London in the green rolling countryside of Northamptonshire, near the small town of Great Brington.

In the days following Diana's death, Great Brington had been inundated by throngs of visitors who had come to pay their respects to Diana. They queued outside of St. Mary's church to get a look at the historical Spencer Family Chapel, where 20 generations of Spencer's are buried. Great Brington has a population of only 150 and the town was not prepared for the onslaught of visitors and media attention Diana's death brought. Because of the attention tiny Great Brington was receiving, the Spencers decided to bury Diana on the Althorp Estate, on a tiny secluded island surrounded by an ornamental man-made lake, rather than in the Spencer Family Chapel. The lake called "the Oval" and referred to as the pleasure garden was designed by Samuel Lapidge of Capability Brown. The island is nestled in an arboretum where Diana and her sisters had planted trees.

Diana, the Princess of Wales, was laid to rest on Saturday, September the 6th. The trip from Westminster Abbey to Althorp took three and a half hours. According to the British press news agency, there were only ten people at the final ceremony: Diana's brother, the Ninth Earl of Spencer; Diana's sisters: Lady Sarah McCorquodale and Lady Jane Fellowes; their husbands, Sir Robert Fellowes and Neil McCorquodale; Prince Charles; Prince William; Prince Harry; Diana's mother, Frances Shand Kydd; and Diana's personal butler, Paul Burrell.

Chapter 11

Greater Causes

On Dec. 4, 1993, an audience of volunteers gathered in London at a luncheon on behalf of Headway, the national head injuries association, to hear an address by their patron and fundraising champion Princess Diana Spencer. The crowd was larger than usual and anticipation was high as the moment of her speech arrived. Diana approached the podium, surveyed the crowd, and began. The speech contained the usual assortment of praise for the work of volunteers, and her sense of fulfillment for her own involvement with Headway, but nothing could have prepared the audience for what was to come. Diana's voice cracked with emotion as she tried to explain her reasons for stepping down as patron of Headway, as she tried to explain why, in the coming year, she would be severely limiting her public role with the 114 charities with which she was presently involved. People were staggered. Immediate reactions from the crowd were mixed: sadness, apprehension and disappointment were some of the emotions felt. Diana wanted to concentrate on raising her two sons, and she wanted to focus on her own life without living in the bright glare of the media spotlight. It had only been 11 months since her very public separation from her husband. Who could begrudge her the time and space for which she was asking?

In the days following, hundreds of newspaper columns around the world would be devoted to the consequences of Diana's announcement.

Charities and causes from every corner of the world had benefited directly and indirectly, financially and spiritually, from Diana's involvement, and now they would have to do without their emotional center.

Diana's absence from "the work," as she called it, wasn't long. She had never intended to discontinue charitable work altogether, and it was less than a year before she and her two boys were slipping in the back door of a London homeless shelter to visit and comfort the residents. But her overwhelming desire to continue her benevolent ways should come as no surprise when one considers just how deep were the roots of her commitment to compassion, caring and healing.

The Royals have always been a charitable institution, and Princess Diana was, in particular, a giving individual. A vast majority of the Royals' time is spent appearing at or hosting charitable functions. Most official occasions are on behalf of one organization or another. Presently the Royals patronize more than 3000 charities, universities and other organizations. But since entering public life, Diana had been the undisputed champ-royal at raising awareness, publicity and funds. It was once calculated that a charity function in London could charge as much as £200 for a charitable evening with the Princess in attendance, the same amount as could be charged with the presence of the Queen. In Washington D.C., socialites who initially balked at paying $3500 a ticket for a fundraising dinner with Diana in 1990 were lining up to pay $7000 a plate seven years later to be near the Princess at a fundraising gala. The incalculable amount of money Diana raised was dwarfed by the immense attention she could generate for a social cause with nothing more than a simple gesture. In a famous 1987 incident at the height of international paranoia concerning the contraction of HIV, Diana, while opening a new purpose-built AIDS ward at the Middlesex Hospital, shook hands, sat on beds and chatted with AIDS sufferers while also refusing to wear gloves or other forms of "protection." One patient agreed to be photographed with the Princess, though only from behind, for fear of being identified. That photograph was universally praised by researchers, activists and HIV sufferers alike for dispelling myths concerning casual contact with AIDS patients. After a similar 1991 incident in Canada at a Toronto hospice, renowned author and hospice founder June Callwood wrote, "In my view, pictures of Diana nestled close to a man with AIDS gave more information about HIV transmission than a trillion public-health brochures."

As a young woman Diana was happy when involving herself in social service. Once a week she would visit homes for the elderly and sit quietly with patients, or she would spend an afternoon playing with handicapped children. Her good deeds didn't go unrecognized, and in 1977, when she was leaving school, she received a special award for her community service. These, however, were the carefree days of a young girl of privilege whose sense of responsibility was directed by her parents, peers and school. Even throughout the formative years of her marriage and the whirlwind of charitable luncheons, galas, concerts, and banquets that would require so much of her attention, she was still forming a sense of where her personal obligations should lie. As well, there is a very strict protocol laid down by Buckingham Palace concerning the charitable work of the Royal Family. The job of palatial advisors is to foresee any possible criticism that could arise from the Royal's association with a particular charity and, in their best interests, advise them so as to protect the image of the Royal Family. It isn't surprising, then, that it took an entire year into her marriage for Diana to finally decide on the five charities she would take on as Royal Patron. The Welsh National Opera (a nod to her title), the Royal School for the Blind, the Malcolm Sargeant Cancer Fund for Children, the Pre-School Playgroups Association, and the Albany, an East London community center. All of these became benefactors of the young Princess. At this point in her new life Diana hadn't yet developed the skills or commitments that would eventually thrust her into the arena of international charity.

The events she patronized in those early years reveal the interests of a young wife and mother. Soon after the birth of William she attended a luncheon in aid of Birthright, the appeal arm of the Royal College of Obstetricians and Gynecologists. Even with her relatively recent appearance on the charitable stage, Birthright garnered considerably more publicity by her support. Soon other stars of stage and screen came on board and boosted the image and coffers of the organization. Eventually, in 1984, she was asked to become the charities patron. Her commitment to the organization went well beyond fundraising: Diana toured one of Birthright's research clinics while she was eight months pregnant with Harry.

Diana and her husband had diverse interests. Charles was concerned with causes such as the preservation of historic architecture and the effects of urban planning. These esoteric interests were far removed from Diana's love of children and the elderly. However, the two were able to work together on a few occasions. In particular, Charles had created the

Prince's Trust, an organization that worked toward helping underprivileged young people start their own businesses. Regular rock concerts were the primary mode of raising funds. An avid fan of modern music in those days, Diana was personally involved in putting several of these spectacles together. The royal couple's appearance at several of these concerts endeared Diana even more to the young audience. Her obvious excitement and pleasure at the concerts, which were broadcast on MTV and included stars like Bryan Adams, Phil Collins and Eric Clapton, proved she was just another young lady; someone with whom people could relate. This approachable and unsophisticated quality in her character would pervade her charitable work for the rest of her life.

In 1984, Diana was asked to become the president of Dr. Barnardo's, Britain's largest children's charity, a role which she relished. Of course, Dr. Barnardo's affiliation as a children's charity was of paramount interest to Diana, yet there was something more. Diana had learned something from watching her more experienced husband during his charitable work. He could speak with passion and intelligence on a subject and people would take notice. The papers would print parts of his speech or the television news would carry footage of him speaking. People would talk about the things with which her husband was concerned. Diana knew that her age and relative inexperience put her at a disadvantage in the public forum. She realized her role sometimes consisted of being nothing more than a fashion plate for the cameras, but the focus on her image was something she was intent on changing. Dr. Barnardo's offered her the opportunity to share publicly her feelings concerning the treatment of children and the central importance of the family, as the first line of defense against social malaise such as drug addiction and prostitution. Here was her chance for more than just a photo opportunity.

Diana seized every opportunity to present awards at banquets, to help organize fundraisers on the behalf of Dr. Barnardo's and finally, in 1988 she was rewarded. Addressing the charity's annual conference in London, Diana, who had written her own speech, spoke forcefully about the problems facing modern parents and the benevolent work of Dr. Barnardo's: providing foster homes and residential care for young people who couldn't live with their families. By emphasizing how organizations like Dr. Barnardo's stepped in to pick up the pieces of suffering children's lives, Diana was, at this time, in fact, beginning to spearhead a campaign that would see a radical shift in attitudes toward Dr. Barnardo's. The charity was attempting to shrug off the image of a Victorian style orphanage and let people know about the work it did with physically and mentally handicapped children. Diana got this message across to the masses. Royal watchers and the media noticed the change in Diana's persona. She was drawing attention because of what she said, not just because of who she was.

With this newfound attention came some unwanted criticism, particularly when Diana began to take up causes that were more controversial than new birthing techniques or foster homes. The 1987 incident at the Middlesex Hospital AIDS ward brought international recognition to what was then considered an unspeakable disease which was restricted to social degenerates, homosexuals and drug abusers. It seemed easy to question Diana's motives. Here was a very public, headline-grabbing display of the Princess at work. People were outraged at the thought of Diana transmitting HIV—which many at the time thought could be caught through a hug or a kiss—to her two young sons. She was threatening the future King of England with a dramatic act strictly to boost her own image. This, however, was simply not the case, as the coming years would prove, although Diana did find it difficult to deal with the criticism. Angela Serota, a good friend of Diana's, has been reported as saying, "She finds it very hurtful. It's very undermining for her, but she believes it is usually out of ignorance. She knows that people doubt her motivation. I've heard people suggesting she's just doing it for the publicity. The point that must not be forgotten is that Diana does all this knowing that people are misjudging her, but she's got the strength and compassion to follow her own inner beliefs."

It was difficult for anyone to create sympathy for AIDS sufferers in the mid-eighties with the rampant ignorance that surrounded the disease, but Diana managed to do so. Her advisers warned her that by being publicly associated with AIDS, she could be harming her future position as Queen of England. Diana had to argue incessantly just to get tacit permission from Buckingham Palace to even start aligning herself with AIDS charities. She investigated the disease personally by contacting other organizations and researchers. Studies were produced at Diana's request showing the growing number of babies and young mothers who were contracting the disease without any homosexual or intravenous drug activity. In spite of the criticism, Diana persevered and finally the visit was made and the famous photograph was taken. Enlightened people around the world joined in praising her courage. A journalist at the time commented, "shaking hands with an AIDS patient is the most important thing a Royal has done in 200 years." However, the criticism of the Princess did not stop. In 1991, James Pickles, a former judge-turned-newspaper columnist wrote, "I believe her constant, high-profile, all-embracing support for AIDS victims is both wrong and damaging to her. Caring for blameless victims was all right, but it was dangerous for her to express the same concern for men who got the disease by indulging in sleazy, unnatural sex with other so-called gays." In the face of this sort of opposition Diana only struggled harder against ignorance.

One theory put forward to account for Diana's interest in AIDS stemmed from her social circles where the disease seemed to strike most predominantly. Fashion, dance and theater have all witnessed the devastating effects of HIV, and since many of Diana's friends were involved in the arts, she may have unfortunately become acquainted with the disease on a personal level. So involved was Diana in the cause that, besides opening AIDS wards around the country, she took an intense scientific interest in the disease, trying to increase her own awareness. A 1988 trip to France included a learning tour of the research laboratory of the Institut Pasteur, where some of the most intensive AIDS research in the world was being conducted. Proffessor Luc Montagnier, one of the discoverers of the AIDS virus, praised Diana's personal involvement. "It is very important that those in the public eye are seen to be involving themselves in supporting the campaign against AIDS and efforts on behalf of AIDS patients," said Montagnier. Regardless of her reasons for associating herself with the disease, the Princess became a tireless worker on behalf of the cause. Much of her work and many of her visits took place without an entourage or notice by the media. The author Nicholas Davies relates a story in his book, *Diana: A Princess and Her Troubled Marriage*, of the Princess's frequent and unannounced visits to the Mildmay Mission, an AIDS hospice in East London. Helen Taylor-Thompson, chairman of the hospice, told the story to Mr. Davies. "The phone rang one day and to my astonishment it was Buckingham Palace asking if it would be alright if Princess Diana paid an unofficial, private visit. They gave us only a few days to prepare, which I understand is very unusual. The day she arrived she was suffering from the aftermath of flu, but she was wonderful, absolutely charming, and asked us so many questions about the place and the patients. She also asked if there was any way she could help." All of Diana's visits had positive and surprising affects on people, but this visit was particularly poignant, as one young patient named Martin found the courage, because of the Princess's visit, to tell his family he was HIV positive and didn't have long to live.

Diana's common sense and compassion are obvious in her public statement that "HIV does not make people dangerous to know, so you can shake their hands and give them a hug. Heaven knows they need it." Diana would seek out those who were not only sick but who were ostracized for other reasons. In 1989, when the Princess visited a newly built AIDS hospital for children in Harlem, New York, she was challenging a whole assortment of pre-established societal biases and myths. However, it would turn out one young AIDS sufferer would be shattering myths of her own. Diana toured the hospital and was particularly taken with one little girl named Monica, who wasn't expected to live much longer. The two chatted and played together, but the time came when the Princess had to leave. Emotionally drained, the Princess never forgot young Monica. As it turned out, unbeknownst to Diana at the time, the little girl lived much longer than expected, and six years later the pair had a poignant reunion in the same hospital.

Diana was rewarded for her tireless efforts in 1991, when she was asked to become the patron of the National AIDS Trust. But the honor was tainted by the loss of a close friend to the HIV infection in the same year. Adrian Ward-Jackson was a prestigious London art dealer who was also a stalwart AIDS fundraiser and deputy chairman of the AIDS Crisis Trust. When Diana learned that Ward-Jackson was close to death, she interrupted her family holiday in Scotland to be by his side. She maintained a vigil by his hospital bed and stayed with his family after his eventual passing. The incident served to deepen Diana's commitment to her fight against AIDS.

Diana made several trips to US hospitals and, eventually, she was able to employ the profile of another well-known public figure, America's former First Lady Barbara Bush. The pair visited with patients on both sides of the Atlantic, forging a friendship and a powerful alliance in the struggle against ignorance of HIV. It has been said that Diana's commitment to AIDS was the making of her. Her compassion and devotion to the sick and dispossessed suddenly became a topic of global conversation. She could have chosen from any number of worthwhile causes and received bountiful publicity without any of the backlash. Instead, Diana chose an awesome burden in AIDS and found her calling in the world of public opinion.

Diana was certainly aware of the more traditionally disreputable aspects of some of the victims' lives. The Royals soon learned that the Princess could be a tenacious champion of those who otherwise would have been ignored: she rejected the idea that people who suffered because of their own actions should alone bear the full weight of their own suffering. She proved her real-life understanding of pain and struggle by taking on the cause of addiction. Turning Point, Britain's largest national charity, was involved with the treatment of alcoholics, drug abusers and mental health outpatients. In 1987 Diana agreed to become Turning Point's patron. As she had already proved with her other endeavors, Diana did not want to be merely a figurehead. She tackled the thorny issues of alcoholism and drug addiction head-on. Foregoing the high-level bureaucrats of the organization, she rolled up her sleeves and began the difficult and often frightening task of visiting offenders in prisons, locked treatment wards and rehabilitation clinics. Visiting these centers and prisons offered her immense opportunity to fraternize with victims of addiction. The Princess slowly began the process of becoming a staunch and vocal supporter of research into the compulsions and nature of addiction. She would spend lengthy periods with incarcerated men, often running over the time that was officially allotted. By discussing their troubles and experiences, Diana gained valuable insight into these troubled souls, prompting more than a few comments as to how knowledgeable she was on the subject of addiction. Similar to her desire to comfort the very ill, she also sought out some of the most destitute addicts, offering her compassion to them.

In Nottinghamshire a special hospital was erected where almost all the patients were locked up for their own or the public's safety. At the time that Diana went there, she was the only Royal to have ever visited the institution. Diana was brave enough, and caring enough, to have contact with inmates kept locked up in their wards. The Princess even took part in open group discussions with patients. This behavior, coupled with her trips to prisons, was creating turmoil at Buckingham Palace. Diana was becoming more independent, and more of a challenge to the traditions surrounding her.

The Princess refused to take escorts with her on some of her private visits because she feared their presence would create a wall between her and the addicts. Though her advisors chastised Diana for taking such risks, the Princess continued unfazed. They needn't have been so worried. Counselors and other professionals were amazed at the ease with which she could strike up a rapport with even the most hardened addicts. Regardless, Diana continued to attract the criticism of some officials. She was the most forward-thinking of all the Royals, and she would often run into opposition from the staid establishment of Buckingham Palace. Bob Houston, the editor of *Royalty Monthly* magazine, in 1988 said, "She has been tremendously privileged but her early experience is far broader than that of the Royal Family. She is bringing a fresh perspective to social problems." It was this "fresh perspective" that showed itself on a 1984 visit to Broadway Lodge, an alternative rehabilitation center in Weston-Super-Mare Avon. Her visit to the clinic drew protest from the local community Health Council who chastised Diana for not visiting the government sanctioned NHS treatment center. The Lodge's philosophy is based on a different method of treatment, employing some of the practices of Alcoholics Anonymous that were developed in the US It was reported that a member of the community Health Council said, "Her visit gave the royal seal of approval to the 'Minnesota method', which is shunned by most doctors and the government."

Controversy followed Diana beyond local health councils. By 1990 Diana had decided to take on government policy, a definite no-no for members of the Royalty. During the conservative reign of Prime Minister Margaret Thatcher, a policy called "Care in the Community" was adopted. The policy would see former inmates of mental institutions who weren't considered a threat to society returned to their communities. Diana spoke simply and directly against the strategy. "Those rosy words 'Care in the Community' do not, I believe, convey the harsh reality faced by the mentally ill when they are released from hospital," she said. Vocal protest from Members of Parliament could not silence Diana as she refused to retract her statement. Because of her high profile activities and vast knowledge of the subject, Diana was a sought-after speaker for many social and political gatherings. At an international congress on alcohol and drug abuse in Glasgow, 700 delegates from 54 countries turned out to hear the Princess's call for more funding for addiction research. She again spoke pointedly about her feelings: "Sadly many people still regard addiction as a moral weakness," she said, "a number of these self-appointed moralists even choose to make such judgements from behind a cloud of cigarette smoke. Presumably they regard cigarette smoking as morally neutral and non-addictive." However, it was still the addicts themselves who mattered to Diana. She was not a clinician. She was not looking for statistical material to prove a thesis. She was just an overwhelmingly compassionate person who could lend a helping hand. Caring was her strength and improving people's lives was her goal. The faces of the many young people she knew she could help inspired her to continue her work.

After the Princess toured the drug addiction unit of White Church Hospital in Cardiff, one young addict said, "the princess is very courageous coming to a place like this. A lot of people would rather forget about people like us." Forgetting is the one thing of which this Princess seemed incapable.

It wasn't just the sexy, high-profile causes that captured the Princess's attention in those years. Her work with the Child Accident Prevention Trust, where she was seeking to raise awareness about accidents in the home and the safety of toys, was evidence of her committment to help not to create an image. The Marriage Guidance Organization also became a favorite of Diana's. It is reported that Diana did not take part in any of the marriage guidance sessions but that she was a valuable asset when she sat in on therapy for young couples. Not suprisingly, people were willing to discuss their problems with Diana. With all of the publicity surrounding her work and her private life, people began to feel as if they actually knew the Princess intimately. This feeling of intimacy was likely one of Diana's greatest assets when it came to working with others: people felt they could relate to her. In much of Diana's charitable work she was photographed caressing someone's hand or putting a smile on a child's face. Generally when she spoke, particularly in the later years of her marriage, she would be very self-referential, referring to her own problems or her own situation whenever it related to the topic. Her openness and warmth endeared her to the public in a way that no other Royal before her had done.

Her dedication was also evident in some of the things for which she didn't get much publicity. After visiting with children from the British Deaf Association, she told them she would learn sign language before her next visit. True to her word, she took up the difficult task of learning how to sign, and the next time she visited she used her new skills with an appreciative audience.

Diana also had a talent for fusing her social life with charitable functions. Not only was this a fantastic public relations tactic but a great way to expose those charities which might not otherwise get a chance to appreciate the arts. After touring a center that cares for children with cerebral palsy and launching a national appeal for the Foundation for Conductive Education—of which she was patron—Diana sat with the afflicted children and watched a performance by the Birmingham Royal Ballet. By turning an essentially social function into a charitable event, Diana could gain sympathy for a cause, not only among the rich and powerful, who could afford to attend the gala events, but with those who would see the glamorous photos in magazines and newspapers thereby keeping the greater cause in the public eye.

Throughout her marriage, Diana fulfilled the busy travel schedule of a monarch. Trips abroad dominated her royal itinerary. But Diana would punctuate all of the officially sanctioned events by seeking out charitable organizations in different countries, hoping to have a few minutes with the people whom they helped.

Leprosy became one of Diana's causes when she was asked to be patron of the Leprosy Mission, an organization that works in more than 33 countries. The effects of leprosy may not be evident in the UK or other developed countries, but many underprivileged nations still know the devastation it can cause. Similar to AIDS, leprosy sufferers must endure the harsh ignorance surrounding the contraction of the disease. So trips to countries where the mission was working would inevitably include a visit from Diana. In 1989 she visited the Sitanala Leprosy Hospital in Indonesia. This was Diana's first time in contact with people who suffered from the disease, but with her usual straightforwardness she plowed ahead and began shaking hands with each and every patient, many of whom were children. A few months later she was visiting Nigeria and went about the same task. In full view of the camera, Diana endeavored to touch—making that all-important human contact—as many of the lepers as possible.

Trips abroad also offered the opportunity to meet dignitaries from around the world. Generally bored with these sorts of official occasions (Diana much preferred the company of the needy she was trying to help), there were some people she met on such occasions who would have a profound affect on the Princess. In particular, Mother Teresa, whose hospice Diana had visited on a trip to Calcutta became an important figure in Diana's life. Unfortunately, Mother Theresa was not in Calcutta during Diana's first visit to the motherhouse. Saddened by not meeting Mother Teresa personally, Diana flew to Rome, where the nun was recuperating from a heart attack. She and Mother Teresa prayed together for the world's poor and hungry. These portraits serve as an interesting foreshadowing of Diana's future, as international charitable organizations and causes would soon dominate the Princess's agenda.

By December of 1992 the demise of Diana's marriage had taken a very public turn. Many of her personal struggles had become the topic of water-cooler conversations around the world. It became increasingly difficult for Diana to attend or patronize any sort of charitable event without the media focusing attention on her private affairs. She was no longer allowed to direct attention to a cause without having the distraction of her personal life shadow the event.

Undaunted, the Princess continued her good works for as long as she possibly could. Reassuring a conference of volunteer workers in London, Diana said, "Your patron has never been happier to see you. Whatever uncertainties the last few weeks have brought, I want you to be certain of this: our work together will continue unchanged." True to her word, Diana continued with her charity work. She even began to take on newer and more personal issues by publicly speaking out at a conference on eating disorders, a topic of which she had an intimate understanding. Unfortunately, Diana could endure the public spotlight no longer and in 1993 she made that tearful announcement to the Headway conference. Drained of energy, Diana began the slow and painful process of separating herself from the work that had sustained her for nearly twelve years. The following is the full text of the speech the Princess gave at the Headway National Head Injuries Association luncheon. It is easy to discern the anguish the Princess was experiencing:

"It is a pleasure to be here with you again, sharing in your successes of the past year. Headway has grown into an organization which is improving the quality of so many lives. I am so proud of the work you have achieved. In the past 12 years, I can honestly say that one of my greatest pleasures has been my association with people like you. During those years I have met many thousands of wonderful and extraordinary people, both here and around the world—the cared for and the carers. To the wider public, may I say that I have made many friends. I have been allowed to share your thoughts and dreams, your disappointments and your happiness. You also gave me an education, by teaching me more about life and living than any books or teachers could have done. My debt of gratitude to you all is immense. I hope in some way, I have been of service in return. A year ago I spoke of my desire to continue with my work unchanged. For the past year I have continued as before. However, life and circumstances alter and I hope you will forgive me if I use this opportunity to share with you my plans for the future, which now indeed have changed. When I started my public life 12 years ago, I understood that the media might be interested in what I did. I realized then that their attention would inevitably focus on both our private and public lives. But I was not aware of how overwhelming that attention would become, nor the extent to which it would affect both my public duties and my personal life, in a manner that has been hard to bear. At the end of this year, when I have completed my diary of official engagements I will be reducing the extent of the public life I have led so far. I attach great importance to my charity work and intend to focus on a smaller range of areas in the future. Over the next few months I will be seeking a more suitable way of combining a meaningful public role with hopefully, a more private life. My first priority will continue to be our children, William and Harry, who deserve as much love, care and attention as I am able to give, as well as an appreciation of the tradition into which they were born. I would also like to add that this decision has been reached with the full understanding of the Queen and the Duke of Edinburgh, who have always shown me kindness and support. I hope you can find it in your hearts to understand and to give me the time and space that has been lacking in recent years. I could not stand here today and make this sort of statement without acknowledging the heartfelt support I have been given by the public in general. Your kindness and affection have carried me through some of the most difficult periods—and always your love and care have eased that journey. And for that I thank you from the bottom of my heart."

An editorial in the *London Times* referred to Diana's announcement as, "A mature decision that deserves respect," and this sentiment seemed to pervade public opinion. Most people realized the great price Diana had paid for her role as champion of the sick and weak.

The Princess's work continued, to a lesser degree, as she had requested. However, a trip somewhat later to the homeless shelter with her two boys was the beginning of what seemed to be a significant return to her public duties. Diana visited the sight of a gruesome and fatal racist attack in London in order to make a plea for an end to racism. She also made a decidedly unglamorous trip to Japan and visited with several organizations concerned with the elderly, sick and disabled. A small evening reception at the British Embassy was the only social event on her agenda. The British Red Cross was making overtures at this time for Diana to become their president, stepping up her previous appointment as vice president. The Princess even flew to New York, where she accepted an award for her charity work from the United Cerebral Palsy Foundation. It seemed as if Diana were returning to her old ways of dividing herself amoung well over 100 charities all over again. The time off must have recharged her batteries, for it appeared she was ready to get going again. But Diana had other things in mind. She wasn't just stepping back into her old role, she was creating herself anew.

Diana had been planning for the day when she would no longer have the title "Her Royal Highness." She knew it was going to be part of her divorce agreement and she was ready to accept the inevitability of that day. It seemed that Diana was planning for this by beginning to concentrate her efforts toward three distinct international causes: cancer and heart research, AIDS patients and research, and the plight of the homeless. She knew that without her title her name would be less useful to the multitude of charities to which she belonged. Even though she would be under far less pressure without the title, she realized that she might not receive the same recognition in some countries that she had before, thereby making her efforts to work internationally less fertile. To stand down from her royal charities was a difficult decision, but it was one that had to be made.

On July 15, 1996, Diana erased all doubt as to what new role she envisioned for herself. In one swift move, Diana resigned official support from 93 charities in which she was still involved. This time it was official, and there was no going back. Diana now wasn't backing away to look for time and space; she was reshaping herself into the unfettered international humanitarian she seemed to be working toward in the months previous to her decision. The Princess informed the 93 charities in a personally signed letter sent from Kensington Palace. As you can see from the text of the letter there is a definite shift in tone from 1993. That letter is as follows:

"It has been a great privilege for me to serve as your patron and it has always been my wish that I should do so wholeheartedly and to the best of my ability. Therefore it is with great sadness that I write to you in order to explain matters which have now become apparent. As you know, my personal circumstances, in particular my marriage to the Prince of Wales, have been the subject of detailed conjecture in recent months, and this will soon be formalized in the normal legal manner. Although I am embarking upon the future with hope, I also do so with some trepidation since there are a number of matters which I will need to resolve. It is for this reason that I am writing in order to resign my current role as patron with you. As I seek to reorganize my life, it will not be possible for me to provide you with the level of commitment that I believe you deserve. I feel that someone in the Royal Family may now be better suited to support your tremendous endeavors. I want to express heartfelt thanks for the many opportunities that you have provided me with for serving the people of this country. I will always retain a keen interest in everything that you do and trust that we shall have reason for our paths to cross in the not too distant future."

The seven charities Diana continued her allegiance with were Centerpoint, the English National Ballet, the Leprosy Mission, the National AIDS Trust, the Hospital for Sick Children, Great Ormond Street, and the Royal Marsden Hospital. Speculation as to the reasons for Diana's decision ranged from her suffering the effects of patronage burnout to a more overt political stab at Buckingham Palace. The reasons for her decision seem obvious, however, when you consider the huge list of organizations she was leaving behind and the great level of commitment needed to serve them. This partial list gives some idea of the Princess's former level of involvement:

Association for Spinal Injury Research, Rehabilitation and Reintegration
Australian Council on Smoking and Health
Australian Junior Red Cross
British Deaf Association
Ninth Congress of the European Society for Child and Adolescent Psychiatry
Malcolm Sargeant Cancer Fund for Children in Australia
National Council for Child Health (Child 2000)
College of Physicians and Surgeons of Glasgow (royal patron and honorary member)
Dystrophic Epidermolysis Bullosa Research Association
British Lung Association
Huntingdons Disease Association
Parkinson's Disease Society
National Rubella Council
Institute for the Study of Drug Dependence
International Spinal Research Trust
British Sports Association for the Disabled
College of Obstetricians and Gynaecologists (royal honorary fellow)
National Hospital for Neurology and Neurosurgery Development Association
Faculty of Dental Surgery of the Royal College of Surgeons of England (honorary fellow)
National Meningitis Trust
Royal School for the Blind
New Zealand Foundation for the Blind

Anglo-European College of Chiropractice
Barnardo's (president)
Benesh Institute of Choreology
Commonwealth Society for the Deaf
Disablement Independence Association (president)
General Council and Registry of Osteopaths (president)
Help the Aged
Leukemia Research Appeal
Northern Ireland Pre-School Playgroups Association
St. Mary's Save the Baby Fund

Fatigue, set off against the opportunity to now pursue whatever cause she chose, seems the most likely reason for her departure from these many organizations.

Naturally, the charities left behind were concerned about their futures. Dominic Jenkins, chief executive of the Ty Hafan hospice, wrote to Diana asking her to reconsider her decision. He told the *London Times*, "the support of the Princess has been vital. I am absolutely certain the people of Wales would wish her to carry on. It is the Princess as a person, not the HRH title, that we want." There could have been no finer testament to Diana's new and expanded role. People were finally recognizing her work outside of the realm of royalty. As difficult, however, as it must have been for Diana to sever ties with those organizations, she knew it was absolutely necessary if she was going to pursue her new agenda. And her new agenda was going to become increasingly apparent to the world in the following months.

In her most public fundraising maneuver since exiting the Royal Family, Diana decided to auction off 76 of her old ball gowns for charity. The event proved to be a $3.3 million financial windfall for the organizations Diana supported.

In January of 1997, Diana made her first publicized visit abroad as an ex-member of the Royal Family. Not surprisingly, the trip was planned to meet with victims of another sort of plague. In the African nation of Angola, Diana would meet people who had lost limbs, senses and family members to the ravages of anti-personnel landmines. She was photographed walking through treacherous mine fields and speaking with the victims of landmine explosions. There was, however, an official tinge to the visit, since it was on behalf of the British Red Cross's campaign to eliminate the use of land mines. The British Red Cross, in an international partnership with other organizations around the world, was attempting to have all of the countries who use or produce landmines to sign a treaty banning their use. The initiative had its beginnings at an Ottawa conference in 1996, where Canadian Foreign Affairs Minister Lloyd Axworthy challenged the participants to return to Ottawa one year later to sign the all-encompassing treaty. The initiative was running into all sorts of political opposition. The Democratic government in the US and the Conservative government in the UK were said to be stalling the process asking for provisions in the treaty that would essentially make the initiative impossible. As well, two key landmine-producing countries, Russia and China, weren't interested in signing a comprehensive treaty of any description. It is reported that there are more than 100 million anti-personnel mines scattered around the world with the same amount in various military inventories. It is estimated that 26 000 civilians, most of them women and children, are killed or maimed each year by the mines. Furthermore, these mines render thousands of acres of farmland useless and make it next to impossible for civilians to return to a normal life after the bombs of war have stopped falling.

Diana was approached by the British Red Cross to be a part of the treaty process. They needed someone who could command great attention, someone who could highlight the devastation these weapons caused, someone people would respond to; Diana was an obvious choice. In her lifetime Diana had never chosen the easy causes. She continually took on the role as defender of those who couldn't defend themselves. With her decision to lend support to the issue of eliminating landmines, Diana faced a challenge far greater than that of eliminating ignorance or offering a comforting hand to an inflicted individual. Her new struggle was a global struggle, one that would require her efforts not only in the fields with victims but in the offices and halls of governments and legislators. It would also see a return to the media spotlight, a spotlight toward which Diana felt, at best, ambivalent.

After being approached by the Red Cross and watching videotapes that showed the destruction of landmines, Diana agreed to lend support even though she had officially severed ties with the charity six months previous. As was always the case, Diana was not interested in simply throwing a fundraising gala and making a big splash—she truly believed that survivors could be helped by her presence. With little idea what she was getting into, Diana again decided to meet, personally, the victims of these horrible blasts. Diana went to Angola and began offering hope to the people living in that war-ravaged country.

A cause or charity with Diana at its helm was subject not only to public interest but also to public criticism. For her work overseas Diana was chastised publicly by a junior minister of the British parliament for contravening the policy of the government of the period. Stripped of her title, Diana was now able to say things and align herself with causes that she would have been unable to speak for had she still been a Royal. She was able to respond publicly to these criticisms without fear of reprisal from Buckingham Palace. Diana brushed off the criticism with her usual common-sense approach, saying that attacking her motives was useless. As far as the Princess was concerned, the goal of banning the landmines was what was important, and it wouldn't be achieved by arguing over whether or not she was sincere.

The attacks were a sort of recognition of Diana's new power. During the dispute a columnist for the *London Times*, Magnus Linklater, wrote, "If Diana is lured further into this area she could find herself taking on not just the odd junior minister, but the full weight of the British arms industry. Whether this is a suitable battle for a Princess whose experience has so far consisted largely of comforting AIDS victims and visiting terminally ill patients in hospital is questionable. But no one should doubt that if she wants to take it on, she could mount a powerful and effective campaign."

A "powerful and effective" campaign is exactly what Diana launched for her newfound cause. Several fundraising dinners were held. An American Red Cross fundraiser brought in almost a million dollars for artificial limbs to be distributed to landmine victims.

Princess Diana was very vocal about her opposition to the use of landmines. At a $7000 a plate fundraiser in Washington, Diana aimed some remarks directly at the Clinton administration. "In the name of humanity, ban landmines," said Diana.

Diana's next trip abroad was three weeks before her untimely death. This time she wanted less publicity. She was looking for a more private environment where she could meet, converse with and comfort survivors with less ceremony than had previously taken place. The back roads of Bosnia were her next destination. She chose the organization Landmine Survivors Network to host her trip to the turmoil-ridden country. Diana was delighted by the idea of landmine survivors helping others rid the world of the indiscriminate devastation of these weapons. Diana spent her time meeting families and children, victims who had survived and the loved ones of those who hadn't. Jerry White, co-founder and director of LSN, accompanied Diana on the trip to Bosnia and worked closely with her in the effort to ban the mines. In a glowing tribute in the *Christian Science Monitor*, White wrote, "She didn't have to risk her life visiting the minefields of Angola in January, or Bosnia in August. But she did because she cared deeply about the consequences of man's inhumanity to man and was determined to reach out to the victims." This was to be Diana's final trip in aid of the landmine ban.

Diana is credited with adding a new sense of urgency to the landmine cause. After her trip to Angola, Britain's new Labor government accepted full participation in the ban initiative, and the Clinton administration came forward to discuss the issue. Ironically, on the day of Diana's death, delegates from over 100 countries were assembling in Oslo, Norway to discuss a treaty to ban landmines. The assembly observed a minute's silence in honor of the Princess. Discussions are presently underway to name after Princess Diana the document that comes out of the next meeting of countries concerning anti-personnel mines.

Tragically, Diana's last official charitable engagement was in support of a cause that dwelt as close to her heart as any other. On July 21, Diana visited the new children's unit at the Northwick Park and St. Mark's Hospital in London.

Diana's charitable schedule for the weeks following her untimely death had been crammed full. She was supposed to have been launching, within a few days after the accident, an appeal to help children with asthma and Down's syndrome. She had also been scheduled to attend a luncheon as guest of honor in support of several Jamaican children's charities. Overseas, she was to have visited Singapore for a gala in support of AIDS.

Even in death Diana was a powerful force for good. The Diana fund, a memorial fund established soon after her death to benefit charities the Princess promoted, was reported to have received $240 million within weeks of commencing. Telephone donations were coming in at a rate of 350 an hour.

No one can say what the world might have been like had Princess Diana not been taken. The shunned and sick of this world were fortunate to have had such a staunch defender on their behalf. The greater public can only marvel at what she accomplished in her all-too-brief lifetime. Her memory challenges everyone to achieve a greater dignity for all inhabitants of the planet. Perhaps it is fitting to let Diana's own words be her greatest tribute. In an interview from Angola, with the *London Times*, Diana said, "I am not a political figure. The fact is I'm a humanitarian figure, always have been, always will be."

Chronology

1506

The Spencers come into possession of Althorp, a 1500-acre estate in Northamptonshire, where they build the stately residence known today as Althorp.

1603

Sir Robert Spencer, said to be the richest man in England, is made Baron Spencer.

1948

14 November: Prince Charles Philip Arthur George is born, first child of Princess Elizabeth and Prince Philip and, upon the death in 1952 of his grandfather, King George VI, heir to the British throne.

1954

May: The Queen returns home from a world tour; though she hasn't seen her son in six months, she greets Prince Charles, then five years old, with the smoothing of a collar and a cold handshake.

1961

1 July: Diana Frances Spencer is born at Park House near Sardingham, Norfolk; she is third daughter of Viscount and Viscountess Althorp. Her father Edward John (Johnnie) Spencer will later become the eighth Earl Spencer; her mother, Frances Ruth Fermoy, is the second daughter of the fourth Baron Fermoy. They had been married in Westminster Abbey, with the Queen and 1700 guests in attendance. Lady Diana is also a direct descendant of King Charles II. When Diana's future son, William, becomes King, he will be the first monarch since King James II with mostly British blood.

30 August: Diana is christened in a local church in Sandringham. Diana is raised at her father's Park House, on the Queen's Estate at Sandringham, and later at Althorp.

1967

Diana's mother, Frances, falls in love with Peter Shand Kydd and abruptly leaves Johnnie Althorp and the children for a flat in Cadogan Place in London. The two older girls, Sarah and Jane, are especially shocked by the separation. Diana is six years old and her younger brother Charles is three. In London, Diana attends day school. At Christmas, the Spencer family spends their last Christmas together, at Park House.

1968

June: Diana is a pupil at Silfield School in King's Lynn (she was there for two years) when her mother sues Viscount Althorp for divorce on the grounds of cruelty. He countersues on the basis of adultery and wins custody in a long and bitter court battle.

1 July: Diana's birthday surprise is camel riding for twenty children on a camel named Bert (borrowed by her father from the Dudley Zoo). Earlier in the year she had won first prize in the Fur and Feather section of the Sandringham Farm for her guinea pig Peanuts.

1969

April: The divorce of Diana's parents becomes final. Frances marries Peter Shand Kydd within a month. The Diana and Charles begin to commute on weekends and holidays to their house at Itchenor, on the Sussex coast, where Diana learns to swim and sail.

1 July: Created Prince of Wales in 1958, Prince Charles is invested into that office at Caernarvon Castle, Wales. He seems to win over many hostile Welsh by speaking their tongue. It is also Diana's eighth birthday; she and her school friends watch the ceremony on television.
The previous evening, the documentary " Royal Family" is televised in Britain and the Commonwealth. It is the first time that the public sees royalty as human beings going about their private lives.

1970

At age nine, Diana enters Riddlesworth Hall in Norfolk, a school only two hours from home. Her favorite hymn is "I Vow To Thee My Country" (later to be sung at her wedding and her funeral). At the end of the first year she wins the Legatt Cup for helpfulness.

Mary Clarke becomes a nanny to the Spencer family, for two years. Much later, Clarke remarks of Diana, "I remember her saying: 'I shall only get married when I am sure I am in love, so that we will never be divorced.'" As well, she describes her at this period as "beautiful, obsessive, every bit an actress, astute, devious, strong-charactered, nonetheless sympathetic, genuine and sensitive, in tune with ordinary folk."

1972

Prince Charles first meets Camilla Shand, born 17 July 1947 to Major Bruce and Rosalind Shand. Camilla's father is a member of the Queen's household, her mother is a cousin of Lord Ashcombe, head of the wealthy Cubitt family, which built Belgravia. Camilla informs Charles that she is the great-granddaughter of Mrs. Alice Keppel, the favorite mistress of Edward VII, then goes on to say, apparently, "So how about it, then?"

1973

14 November: On her brother Charles's twenty-fifth birthday, Princess Anne marries, Captain Mark Phillips, son of a director of the Wales Food Company and an equestrian with an Olympic gold medal. Anne is European three-day-event champion of the year. Later, the couple has two children, Peter (1977) and Zara (1981).

1974

Diana is thirteen when Raine Dartmouth, daughter of novelist Barbara Cartland, enters her father's life. The four children dislike her immediately, calling her "Acid Raine" and singing "Raine, Raine, go away." She seems to make Johnnie happy, but she becomes even more unpopular with the girls later when, determined to set the estate on a sound financial basis, she sells off many of the artistic treasures of Althorp to pay debts of £2.4 million.

1976

14 July: Johnnie Spencer and Raine Dartmouth are married. Spencer (now the eighth Earl Spencer) and Dartmouth (having been divorced by the Earl Dartmouth, Spencer's old friend, for adultery, and having lost custody of the four children) are quietly married. None of their children are present.

1977

6 June: To celebrate the Queen's Jubilee year, bonfires are lit across the kingdom. The next day, a public holiday, the Queen proceeds through London in the State Coach to St. Paul's Cathedral. The festivities, with parties in the streets, amount to a second coronation by the people.

November: Prince Charles, now twenty-nine, is a weekend guest at Althorp for a shooting party. He has been dating Sarah Spencer, but he notices Diana and begins to see her as a possible mate while they are in Nobottle Wood, a field in the Althorp estate.

December: Diana fails her "O" levels for the second time. She decides to leave West Heath, but before she does, Principal Ruth Rudge presents her with the Miss Clarence Award for service (she helped old women in the neighborhood, as well as handicapped children).

1978

Diana attends her last school, but only for six weeks, the Institut Alpin Videmanette in Rougemont, Switzerland. Homesick and unable to speak the required French, she returns to England, her school days over. She moves into her mother's four-story house in Chelsea; later she is joined by Laura Grieg, a schoolmate from West Heath, and Sophie Kimball, whom she had befriended at the Swiss school.

April: Diana's sister Jane marries Robert Fellowes, the Queen's assistant private secretary. The Queen Mother attends. The reception is at St. James's Palace. They live in a grace-and-favor apartment at Kensington palace, courtesy of the Queen.

September: Earl Spencer suffers a brain hemorrhage at Althorp, lapses into a coma and is near death. When he recovers four months later, he credits his wife Raine with miraculously saving him by sheer will power; the three daughters become more accepting of her as a result of her obvious dedication to their father.

1979

May: Diana's sister Sarah marries Neal McCorquodale, a cousin of Raine. Diana's mother pays for the wedding and allows Raine to sit with Earl Spencer. The bridal bouquet is caught by Diana.

August: Lady Sarah Armstrong-Jones, daughter of Princess Margaret and a bridesmaid at Sarah Spencer's wedding, invites Diana along for a few days on the royal yacht *Britannia*, during Cowes Week; Prince Charles will be aboard. Afterwards, Charles sends Diana a dozen roses and an invitation to Balmoral, the royal estate in Scotland.

1980

Through binoculars, a reporter sees Charles and Diana embracing by the River Dee at Balmoral.

14 November: The press reveals that Diana has spent Charles's thirty-second birthday with him privately at Sandringham House. Diana is now seen as his potential future wife.

1981

January: Charles finally proposes to Diana during a weekend at Highgrove, while they share a bottle of champagne. She accepts.

24 February: On the day of the official announcement of the engagement, a reporter asks whether they are in love. Charles replies, "Yes ...whatever love means"; Diana, anxiously looking at him, says, "Of course."

18 May: A long-distance telephone conversation between Charles (in Australia) and Diana (in Britain), having apparently been tapped, is printed in *Newsweek* (after first being published in the German magazine *Die Aktuelle*). Referring to the fact that thousands of people are with him and she is not, Diana says, "I really miss you, darling... I'm really jealous." Charles replies, "Yes, I know. It's too bad, but in a couple of years you might be glad to get rid of me for a while." Diana insists "Never."

29 July: The spectacular royal wedding is celebrated in St. Paul's Cathedral. An heir to the throne has not married an Englishwoman for three hundred years. Some 600,000 people line the route from Buckingham Palace to the cathedral; the television and radio audience worldwide is estimated at at least 750 million.
Eleven years later, in his book *Diana: Her True Story,* Andrew Morton writes that a few days before the wedding, while opening gifts, Diana mistakenly opened one that contained a gold bracelet with the initials "F&G" engraved on it ("Fred and Gladys," Charles and Camilla's pet names for one another). During the honeymoon on the royal yacht

Britannia, Morton reports that photographs of Camilla fell out of Charles's diary. At a dinner with President Anwar Sadat of Egypt, Charles wore gold cufflinks in the shape of two Cs.

1982

17 May: Having lived in Buckingham Palace until now, the royal couple move into refurbished apartments in Kensington Palace. Diana, eight months pregnant and suffering serious morning sickness, is much relieved.

21 June: Diana gives birth to Prince William Arthur Philip Louis ("Wills") at St. Mary's Hospital in Paddington, London (traditionally, royal babies have been born at Buckingham Palace). Soon after, Diana overhears Charles in the bathtub speaking on a mobile phone. He is telling Camilla that he will always love her. Later, postpartum depression sets in; Diana loses weight and is thought to be afflicted with anorexia nervosa. Servants begin to hear noisy arguments; Charles wants to go off alone, but Diana wants him there, with her and the baby.

September: Diana makes her first solitary official visit, representing the Queen at the funeral of Princess Grace of Monaco.

11 November: Diana and Charles engage in a shouting match when he insists that she accompany him as planned to the Annual Festival of Remembrance in memory of the war dead at the Royal Albert Hall. Diana, exhausted from sleeplessness, refuses and bursts into tears. Angry, Charles storms out. At the ceremony he explains to those present, including the Queen, that Diana is ill and cannot attend. Shortly afterwards, having realized her mistake, she appears at the hall. Rumors of problems in the marriage begin to spread.

It is thought that a skiing holiday in Liechtenstein will be a "second honeymoon" and a respite from all of Diana's problems. But when Charles entreats her to allow photographs, she will not. In tears, she says she misses the infant William.

1983

The Prince and Princess of Wales successfully make an official visit to Australia and New Zealand. Tradition dictates that very young children of the Royal Family are left at home on such occasions, but Diana staunchly resists pressure from the Queen and her husband and brings along Prince William, who is still less than one year old. A few months later, on a similar trip to Canada, William remains back in Britain. Diana is saddened to miss his first birthday on 21 June.

1984

Charles becomes president of Business in the Community (BiC), founded in 1981 by businessmen to lobby for corporate donations to projects that will result in new business and jobs.

15 September: Diana gives birth to "Harry," Prince Henry Charles Albert David, born, like his brother, at St. Mary's Hospital, Paddington. The royal couple now have two sons (jocularly known as the "heir and a spare"). There will be no further royal issue.

1985

Diana's brother, Viscount Charles Althorp (later the ninth Earl Spencer), turns twenty-one. He reportedly spends £250,000 on his birthday party.

The royal couple tours Italy; William and Harry join them near the end of the visit.

1986

23 July: Prince Andrew, the second son of the Queen and Prince Philip, marries Sarah Ferguson ("Fergie") in a lavish spectacle at Westminster Abbey. Her father is Major Ronald Ferguson, Prince Charles's polo manager (when Fergie was fourteen, her mother left the Major for Hector Barrantes, an Argentinian polo star). Unlike Diana, Sarah Ferguson has a "past" (including a liaison with Paddy McNally, twenty-two years her senior.) Before the wedding, Andrew and Sarah openly share a bedroom at Buckingham Palace.

November: Inspired by Bob Geldof's Band Aid, Inner City Aid is established with Charles as patron. Its purpose is to raise £10 million to rehabilitate inner cities; in the first year, a mere £33,000 is amassed; after the second year, virtually ignored by the Prince, it ceases operations, having achieved little.

During a painful year, Charles is again seeing Camilla Parker-Bowles, while Diana develops bulimia nervosa. What was once the fairy-tale romance and marriage now consists of separate lives in private.

1987

13 June: After returning from visits to the Third World as patron of the Save the Children Fund, Princess Anne is rewarded for her contributions by receiving the title Princess Royal from the Queen. Although Anne is widely perceived as being genuinely concerned, the title also has the merit of distinguishing Diana and Sarah Ferguson from the two other princesses.

December: Prince Charles delivers his so-called "Luftwaffe" speech in which he claims that the London skyline has suffered more damage from British planners than from Nazi bombs in World War II. The negative reaction from architects is tumultuous; they are further incensed when Charles has his own candidates named in place of other architects previously appointed to building projects. More than one career is ruined.

1988

May: The tabloids gleefully report that Major Ronald Ferguson has been seen exiting the Wigmore Club, a Soho "massage parlor."

Fergie flies to Australia to join Prince Andrew, without her infant daughter Beatrice; her popularity in Britain is plummeting.

1989

The Buckingham Palace press office states that Tim Laurence, the Queen's military equerry, was the author of "intimate" letters taken from Princess Anne's briefcase. Laurence offers to resign but is supported by the Queen. Later in the year, Anne's husband, Mark Phillips, is said to have fathered a "love child" in New Zealand. Anne requests a formal separation.

1991

Notable milestones during the year include the Queen's sixty-fifth birthday and Prince Philip's seventieth. Though it is Charles and Diana's tenth wedding anniversary, there is little reason for celebration. In a minor occurrence, perhaps a portent of things to come, the Queen requires three stitches in her leg when she is bitten by one of her ubiquitous and beloved corgis.

10 February: Developing the fact that none of them were serving in the Persian Gulf Wars, then raging, The *Sunday Times* takes the young Royals to task over their seemingly frivolous lifestyle while the war rages. The newspaper criticizes how these young people's lives are "parading a mixture of upper-class decadence and insensitivity which disgusts the public and demeans the monarchy."

3 June: Now eight, Prince William is accidentally struck by a schoolmate's golf club. His skull fractured, he undergoes emergency surgery at Great Ormond Street Hospital, where Diana maintains a bedside vigil all night. Charles, however, goes to the opera. The public is appalled at his seeming insensitivity. The episode is a watershed in Charles's declining popularity; Diana finds more and more public sympathy.

1 July: Charles is absent for Diana's thirtieth birthday. Rumors concerning his absence are published in the day's newspapers.

2 July: A columnist in the *Daily Mail* cites friends of Prince Charles as saying that Charles offered to throw a birthday party for her, but Diana declined.

25 December: On one of the television networks, the Queen's traditional Christmas Day address is inserted as an actual interlude "watched" by characters in *Coronation Street*, Britain's oldest soap opera. In addition to references to Eastern Europe and a Commonwealth meeting in

Zimbabwe, the Queen states that she will not abdicate in favor of Charles. Ratings for that network's broadcast of the speech double over the previous year.

1992

16 January: The *Daily Mail* reports the existence of compromising photographs of the Duchess of York, Sarah Ferguson, with Steve Wyatt, a Texas oilman, while on holiday in Morocco. Found by a cleaner in Wyatt's Mayfair flat, the photos are turned over to the police and not published, though the tabloids describe them explicitly.

6 February: It is forty years since the Queen acceded to the throne. A BBC documentary is shown, and the Palace looks forward to a year of celebration. That same day, however, the press are challenging the Queen's exemption from income tax and the Civil List subsidies of the Royal Family. As well, a sex scandal involving Paddy Ashdown, leader of the Liberal Democratic Party, is reported.

11 February: The Prince and Princess of Wales are on a visit to India. It is widely known that Charles has long promised to accompany Diana to the Taj Mahal, but now-famous photographs show Diana alone at the Moghul monument to love; Charles stays behind in Delhi to meet novice journalists. They have separate suites and depart India separately. The trip is a disaster for the marriage.

19 February: Diana meets Mother Teresa

19 March: During the first week of the British general election, Buckingham Palace announces that discussions of the separation of the Duke and Duchess of York have begun. Later, Charles Anson, the Queen's press secretary, pillories Fergie as "unsuitable for royal and public life."

29 March: Diana's father, the eighth Earl Spencer, suddenly dies; she hurriedly returns from a skiing holiday. On arrival in Britain, Diana drives alone from London to Althorp. At the actual funeral, Prince Charles comes in late and then departs early to have tea with the Sultan of Brunei.

19 April: Taking her two children out of school, Fergie departs for a five-week holiday in the Orient with her "financial advisor," John Bryan.

23 April: Buckingham Palace affirms that the divorce of Princess Anne and Captain Mark Phillips is now final. The next week, she is observed in public with Tim Laurence for the first time.

16 May: On an official visit to Egypt, Diana is photographed alone, again, at the pyramids, while Charles makes a private trip to Turkey. The same day, rumors circulate in London about a book describing Charles's infidelity.

7 June: The *Sunday Times* publishes the first of five weekly extracts from Andrew Morton's book *Diana: Her True Story*, which states that Diana attempted suicide five times as a result of a failed marriage and jealousy over another woman. the *Times* easily breaks it circulation record; in book form, *Diana: Her True Story* is eventually a massive best seller in Britain and America, both in hard cover and paperback. Coincidentally, on the same day, the Queen invites Camilla Parker Bowles to the royal enclosure at the Windsor horse show.

12 June: Enthusiastically welcomed to Southport, Lancashire, Diana weeps in public.

15 June: At the annual Garter ceremony at Windsor Castle, the Queen summons Charles and Diana. Diana makes it clear that she wants to be quit of the marriage and the Royal Family and to continue her charity work. The Queen and Prince Philip offer her a large allowance and her own official residence; she will also have custody of the children and return the title Her Royal Highness.

17 June: As the Royal procession is entering the Ascot Meet, Fergie and her children are seen to wave to it from the crowd. The Queen invites Andrew Parker-Bowles, Camilla's husband, to the royal box; Diana is also in attendance. Charles and Diana are seen leaving together in a limousine, but one mile down the highway they separate and drive off in their own vehicles.

22 June: It is reported that Charles has expressed to his parents his belief that he will never become King. Six days later, newspapers state that he has discussed divorce with them.

1 July: Charles is absent from Diana's thirty-first birthday.

6 July: Friends of Prince Charles begin a campaign to discredit Diana in the press, through a series of "leaks." Articles in *Today* by Penny Junor portray Diana as a neurotic who turned the children against their father and is herself the cause of the marriage's failure. *Diana: A Princess and Her Troubled Marriage* by Nicholas Davies is in bookstores at the same time as Andrew Morton's book. Davies later describes his book as a counterweight to Morton, noting that he portrays Diana as hysterically argumentative and profane, spoiled and demanding, and herself responsible for the breakdown.

13 July: According to a Harris Research Centre poll published in the *Daily Express*, most Britons blame Charles. Queried about the most popular royal, 34% named Diana, 11% the Queen, 11% Princess Anne, 9% Charles.

26 July: Charles and Diana do not celebrate their eleventh anniversary together.

20 August: the *Daily Mirror* prints photographs of Sarah Ferguson, topless, frolicking with Johnny Bryan in France, her children present. That same day Fergie abruptly leaves Balmoral, presumably banished forever.

25 August: "Squidgygate": the *Sun* prints a transcript of an intimate telephone conversation (illegaly obtained almost three years earlier) between James Gilbey and a woman he calls "squidgy" (purportedly Diana); he repeatedly professes his love for her. the *Sun* states that a seventy-year-old retired bank manager made a tape of the conversation in his garden; later, experts dispute the claim, pointing out that because of the sophistication of the tape, it had to have been an "inside job." The newspapaer also makes avaliable to the public a telephone line which carries the conversation. More than 60,000 people pay over £100,000 to hear it; the money is supposed to go to the National Society for the Prevention of Cruelty to Children, but it is declined.

1 September: The press publishes what appears to be an internal memo, printed on Buckingham Palace stationery, discussing how Diana has damaged the monarchy; it is proved to be a fake. Also, the *Sun* claims that Diana has had a "physical" relationship with Major James Hewitt, William and Harry's riding instructor.

2 September:Hewitt announces that he is suing the *Sun* for libel. Meanwhile, the *London Evening Standard* writes that James Gilbey and Diana rendezvoused secretly at a "safe house" in Norfolk.

4 September: The *Daily Mail* says that Diana talked her police bodyguards into absenting themselves while she had six secret meetings with Gilbey in Norfolk. The next day, Scotland Yard issues a denial, seemingly at the wish of the Palace.

6 September: Diana accompanies Wills back to school. Charles is present for Harry's first day.

16 September: "Black Wednesday": The government is forced to spend billions defending the pound sterling; even so, the pound is devalued by twenty percent.

21 September: The sterling crisis has provoked anti-German feelings. Diana relinquishes her £72,000 Mercedes, switching to British cars from the Palace car pool.

25 October: Charles and Diana attend the gala at Earl's Court in celebration of the Queen's fortieth year as monarch. The next night, for the first time in three years, they are seen together again, at the Royal Opera House, where Placido Domingo is playing Othello. The press expresses optimism about their future.

2 November: The royal couple travels to South Korea for an official visit. Over the next few days, phototgraphs of them in the British tabloids show all too clearly that they are at odds, distant and alienated. At the end of the five-day tour, Diana returns home alone. A statement issued by Kensington Palace on 6 November states that the Princess wishes to disassociate herself from criticism in the press of the Queen and Prince Philip: "the suggestion

that they have been anything other than sympathetic and supportive is untrue and particularly hurtful."

13 November: the *Daily Mirror* affirms the existence (though not the contents) of what is later known as the "Camillagate" tape.

14 November: Charles spends his forty-fourth birthday at Highgrove. Diana is in Paris, where she has a forty-five minute audience with President Mitterand.

17 November: In London, Diana delivers the long keynote speech for European Drug Prevention Week. If parents love their children, she says, young people will be unlikely to turn to drugs: "hugging has no harmful side effects."

21 November: The Queen is passing her forty-fifth wedding anniversary at Windsor Castle (Prince Philip is in Argentina) when fire breaks out and devastates the historic edifice. The next day, without consulting Parliament, Peter Brook, Secretary of State for National Heritage, says that the government will pay the estimated 60 million pounds worth of damage. A fierce debate in the press centers on whether or not the public should foot the bill during a devastating recession.

24 November: The Queen delivers her famous "annus horribilis" speech: "1992 is not a year on which I shall look back with undiluted pleasure."

26 November: Prime Minister John Major announces in the House of Commons that the Queen will voluntarily pay income tax and cover part of the Civil List Expenses.

9 December: Major announces in the House of Commons that the Prince and Princess of Wales are separating "with regret."

11 December: At a dinner for European leaders on the royal yacht *Britannia*, the Queen seats Diana at the top table with herself, and between President Mitterand and Douglas Hurd, the British foreign secretary. At the third table are Prince Charles and John Major.

12 December: In an overshadowed ceremony at Crathie Kirk on the Balmoral Estate, Princess Anne is married to Tim Laurence, only two weeks after her divorce.

15 December: Diana states that as far as her many charities are concerned, it will be "business as usual."

30 December: After six days apart from them at Christmas (which they spent with the royal party at Sandringham), Diana and her sons fly to the island of Nevis in the Caribbean. There she is hounded by the paparazzi. On the flight over, she travels economy class with her friends, while Wills and Harry are in first class (keeping with protocol).

1993

14 January: "Camillagate": an Australian magazine publishes the transcript of a most explicit telephone conversation between Prince Charles and Camilla Parker-Bowles. Five days later it is reprinted in Britain by the *Sunday Mirror* and *The People*. Charles is heard to say, "I want to feel my way all along you, all over you, and up and down you and in and out. I fill up your tank! I need you several times a week." In response to another embarrassingly memorable wish by the Prince, young women begin referring to tampons as "Charlies."

24 January: The front page of the *Sunday Times* states: "leading members of the Establishment have decided that the cause of monarchy will be best served by extolling Charles and denigrating Diana."

26 January: the *London Evening Standard* quotes "one of Charles' circle" as saying that Diana is in "a familiar state of nervous excitement" and is "very dangerous"; he refers to her "neurotic tyranny."

3 February: the *Times* reports that as a government campaign to promote the wearing of seatbelts is launched, both the Princess of Wales and the Prime Minister are observed not wearing them.

6 February: In an interview with the *Daily Mail*, Mary Clarke, Diana's former nanny, states that "Diana became ill because of the anger and

hurt of finding out "she wasn't loved" by Charles, who she referred to as "a spoilt little boy wallowing in self-pity." Clarke is referring to Diana's struggle with bulimia nervosa.

16 February: While Charles is meeting farmers in Mexico, Diana gives a speech on AIDS in London. She refers to "a narrowness of mind and a sad lack of common humanity" exhibited by many commentators on the topic.

2 December: According to a poll in the *Daily Express*, twice as many people blamed Charles for the collapse of the marriage as blamed Diana; fifty-seven percent "sympathized most" with Diana, and only twelve percent with Charles. When asked who had "done most to improve the standing of the Royal Family over the last two years, 50 percent indicated Diana, 29 percent the Queen, and 14 percent Charles.

3 December: Diana states that she will no longer have a public life.

1994

29 June: In an interview on British television, Charles acknowledges that he became an adulterer after the breakdown of his marriage.

July: On the twenty-fifth anniversary of his investiture as Prince of Wales, Charles is to be re-presented for the approval of the public.

August: Diana denies published reports that she has been constantly phoning Oliver Hoare, only to ring off when his wife comes on the line.

3 October: Anna Pasternak's "Princess in Love" states that Diana and James Hewitt were lovers for five years. This is confirmed the following year by Diana.

1995

3 March: Camilla and Andrew Parker-Bowles are divorced.

August: It is reported that Diana is involved with Will Carling, captain of the English rugby team. On 29 September, he and his wife Julia agree to separate.

20 November: In a BBC interview, Diana admits to the affair with James Hewitt but rejects the suggestion that she and Charles should divorce.

24 November: The Palace announces that the Royal Family's Christmas gathering as Sandringham will include Diana.

18 December: Diana will not be at Sandringham, at her own request, though her sons will be going.

20 December: Buckingham Palace announces that the Queen has urged Charles and Diana to divorce.

1996

28 February: Calling it "the saddest day" of her life, Diana finally says that she has agreed to a divorce from Charles.

May: The Duke and Duchess of York are divorced.

4 July: After weeks of negotiation, lawyers offer the terms of divorce to Diana.

12 July: Charles and Diana agree on the terms of their divorce. Reportedly, she will receive a settlement of 17 million pounds but will lose the title "Her Royal Highness." The next day, a tearful Diana is seen in public.

15 July: Charles and Diana are granted a decree nisi, the first step toward the divorce, having been separated for over two years.

16 July: Citing the fact that she can no longer be called "Her Royal Highness," Diana resigns as patron of some one hundred charities, which, she says, would be better served by new royal patrons. However, she continues on as president of two hospitals (the Royal Marsden Hospital and the Great Ormond Street Hospital for Children), and remains the patron of the National AIDS Trust, the Leprosy Mission, the English National Ballet and Centrepoint.

28 August: After over fifteen years in the world's most famous marriage, the Prince and Princess of Wales are granted a decree absolute, officially ending their union. Diana will continue to live at Kensington Palace, still a member of the Royal Family due to her capacity as the mother of William and Harry.

September: In Washington, Diana breakfasts at the White House with Hillary Clinton and attends a fund raiser in aid of breast cancer research.

November: On a visit to Australia, Diana visits patients at the Victor Chang Cardiac Research Institute in Sydney. Also during this month she attends a charity dinner in Buenos Aires

10 December: Diana attends a conference on leprosy in London. She later flies to New York for the Metropolitan Museum of Art's Costume Institute Ball.

1997

13 January: The Princess of Wales arrives in Angola to publicize the British Red Cross's campaign to ban land mines. At an orthopedic center in Luanda, she meets some of those who have been maimed by mines. After inspecting a minefield, she is termed "the Princess of Peace" by Angolans. A BBC documentary of the visit is shown on 11 February.

24 February: The *Express on Sunday* is to be sued for libel by Diana for stating that she would retain half of the money raised for AIDS and cancer research by the auction of eighty of her gowns at Christie's on 25 June. On 2 March, she receives an apology and an agreement to settle for a large but undisclosed sum, which Diana donates to charity.

1 April: Returning from a workout at a gymnasium, Diana is assisted by a passerby in retrieving the film from the camera of an intrusive photographer. The incident is recorded by another member of the press and the scuffle is front-page news.

25 June: Christie's charity auction realizes over $3.2 million (US) from the sale of Diana's gowns. Also in June, she addresses the Royal Geographic Society regarding the proposed ban on the manufacture and use of land mines.

18 July: Camilla Parker-Bowles turns fifty; Prince Charles throws a lavish party for her at his Gloucestershire residence of Highgrove.

6 August: The world first begins to hear about Diana's new love interest, Emad (Dodi) Al Fayed, son of Egyptian billionaire Mohamed Al Fayed, owner of Harrods, *Punch* magazine and the Ritz Hotel in Paris.

8 August: In Bosnia, Diana continues her campaign against land mines.

9 August: The *Sunday Mirror* publishes the first photos of Diana and Dodi kissing in the Mediterranean, which reportedly cost £400 000 to purchase. The accompanying text luridly proclaims "Princess Diana has finally found a man who makes her feel like a REAL woman."

Mid-August: Model Kelly Fisher launches a lawsuit against Dodi for allegedly breaking their engagement.

30 August: Diana and Dodi have dinner at the Ritz in Paris. Around midnight, the official car is sent off as a decoy for the thronging paparazzi.

31 August: Diana and Dodi, accompanied by bodyguard Trevor Rees-Jones, leave the hotel. Henri Paul, deputy head of security for the hotel acts as their driver. At approximately 12:35 a.m., the Mercedes they were travelling in slams into a support pillar of an underpass. Dodi and Paul are killed instantly, Diana is mortally wounded, and Rees-Jones is critically injured. After being freed from the wreck, the two survivors are rushed to hospital.

4 a.m.: Diana, Princess of Wales, is declared dead by attending physicians. Later that day her body is returned to Britain, accompanied by Prince Charles and Diana's sisters. Dodi Al Fayed is buried in England.

5 September: The Queen breaks with tradition and delivers a special television address.

7 September: After following a five-and-a-half kilometer route which began at Kensington Palace, Diana's body arrives at Westminster Abbey for the funeral service. Afterwards, the casket is transferred to Althorp for private burial on a small island in a lake on the grounds.

Bibliography

Adler, Jerry and Peterson, Daniel:"Diana's Battle Royal" (*Newsweek:*, 11
    March 1996)

Alderson, Andrew & Swain, Jon: "...the Wales's rumored truce is a sham"
    (*Sun*: 8 November 1992)

Alderson, Andrew: "How Diana wrecked palace PR offensive"(*London Times*:
    8 November 1992)

Buckingham Palace Statement: "It is announced...with regret" (*London Times*:
    10 December 1992)

Barbash, Fred: Princess Di Admits to an Affair (*Washington Post* Foreign
    Service: Tues, 21 November 1995)

———: Britain Feeling the Royals' Pain (*Washington Post* Foreign
    Service: Wed, 5 October 1994)

Barry, Stephen P.: *Royal Service: My Twelve Years as Valet* to Prince Charles
    (New York: MacMillan Publishing Co., Inc., 1983)

Best, John: "Princess Carries on After Fainting Fit" (*London Times*: 8 May, 1986)

Blackhall, Susan, & Blundell, Nigel: *Fall of the House of Windsor* (Chicago:
    Contemporary Books Inc., 1992)

Borders, William: "For 'Hounding' a Friend of Charles, Press is Chided" (The
    New York Times, 15 December 1980)

Brendon, Piers & Whitehead, Phillip: *The Windsors: A Dynasty
    Revealed* (London: Hodder and Stoughton Ltd, 1994)

Callwood, June: "Reaching out in T.O." (*Macleans*, 15 September 1996)

Campbell, Lady Colin: *Diana in Private: the Princess Nobody Knows*
    (New York: St. Martin's Press, 1992)

Chua Eoan, Howard: "Princess Diana, 1961–1977: In Living Memory" (*Time*
    Magazine, Commemorative Issue, 15 September 1997)

Davies, Nicholas: *Diana: A Princess and her Troubled Marriage* (New York: Bantam Books/ Carol Publishing Group, 1993)

"Di's Private Battle" (http://pathfinder.com.people: 3 August 1992)

"Diana absent from Charles's side at wedding" (*Sunday Times*: 1 November 1987)

Diana: the BBC *Panorama* interview in full (Transcripts: http://www.pa.press.net princess/interview.html Mon, 20 November 1995)

Downie Jr., Leonard: "The Royal Wedding: Conversation Pieces" (Washingtonpost.com:International Report: 29 July 1981)

Duff, Martha: "Fractured Fairytale" (*Time*: 11 March 1996)

Elliot, Michael and Petersen, D.: "I Won't Go Quietly" (*Macleans*: 4 December 1995)

Fairley, Josephine: *The Princess and the Duchess* (New York: St. Martin's Press, 1989)

Friedman, Dennis: *Inheritance: A Psychological History of the Royal Family* (London: Sidgwick & Jackson, 1993)

Gledhill, Ruth: "Archbishops urge compassion and understanding" (*London Times*: 10 December 1992)

Green, Michelle and Denworth, Lydia & Wright, John: (*People* Online. 18 December 1995.)

Green, Michelle & Smith, Terry & Wright, Margaret: "True Confessions"(http:/ pathfinder.com/people: 4 December 1995)

Green, Terry & Healy, Sanderson, Laura & Smith, Michelle & Wright, Margaret: "Diana Under Fire" (http://pathfinder.com/people: 14 September 1992)

Green, Terry & Thorpe–Tracey, Rosemary & Smith, Michelle & Wright, Margaret: "Love on the Rocks…" (http://pathfinder.com/people: 29 June 1992)

Grigg, John: "Marriage of rare qualities" (*London Times*: 1991)

Hall, Trevor: *Charles and Diana, the Prince and Princess of Wales* (Don Mills, Ontario: Collins Publishers, 1982)

Hamilton, Alan: "Palace is silent on royal anniversary" (*London Times*: 29 July 1991)

Hamilton, Alan & Pitman, Joanna: "Koreans keep smiling through royal gloom" (*London Times*: 5 November 1992)

Hamilton, Alan & Wood, Nicholas: "Princess sends best wishes, but may not go to wedding" (*London Times*: 11 December 1992)

Hamilton, Alan: "Parting no barrier to throne" (*London Times*: 10 December1992)

Hamilton, Alan & Wood, Nicholas: "Separation but no divorce for Prince and Princess" (*London Times*: 10 December 1992)

Healy, Laura Sanderson & Thorpe–Tracey, Rosemary & Kaufman, Joanne: "Seven–Year Hitch" (http://pathfinder.com/people: 1 August 1988)

Healy, Laura Sanderson & Johnson, Bonnie & Smith, Terry: "Autumn of their Discontent" (http://pathfinder.com/people: 9 November 1987)

Holden, Anthony: *King Charles III* (New York: Weidenfeld & Nicolson, 1988)

Holden, Anthony: *The Tarnished Crown: Diana and the House of Windsor* (New York: Random House, 1993)

"I Would Like to Marry Soon, says Lady Diana" (The *Guardian* 29 November 1980)

Junor, Penny: *Charles* (London: Sidgwick & Jackson, 1987)

Keel, Paul: "Charles Hunts as Lady Di goes to Ground" (The Guardian, 15 November 1980)

"Lady Diana Denies meeting Prince on Royal Train" (The *Times*, 29 November 1980)

Lague, Louise & Smith, Terry & Wright, Margaret: "Questions for an Absent Father" (http://pathfinder.com/people: 17 June 1991)

Latham, Caroline & Sakol, Jeannie: *The Royals* (New York: Congdon & Weed, 1987)

Leete–Hodge, Lornie: *The Country Life Book of Diana, Princess of Wales* (Toronto: The Hamlyn Publishing Group Ltd, 1982)

Lillis, David K.: "British press flirts with a princess...and angers a queen" (London: *The Christian Science Monitor*, 21 January 1983)

MacLeod, Alexander: "Critics See Frank Biography of Prince as a Possible Signature of Abdication" (London: *The Christian Science Monitor*, 19 October 1994)

Magrino, Susan: *Harper's Bazaar*. 26 June 1997.

Martin, Ralph G.: *Charles & Diana* (New York: G.P. Putnam's Sons, 1985)

Morton, Andrew: *Diana: Her New Life* (New York: Simon & Schuster, 1994)

————: *Diana: Her True Story* (New York, NY: Pocket Books, 1992)

————: "Diana to leave 'gilded cage' home at Kensington Palace (The *Sunday Times*: 5 December 1993)

————: "Rivals" (The *Sunday Times*, 12 May 1991)

————: "Truce" (the *Sunday Times*: 7 July 1991)

Murray, Ian: "Charity duties will take centre stage" (*London Times*: 11 December 1992)

Obituary: "Diana, Princess of Wales" (*The Economist*, 6 September 1997)

"Palace regrets couple's parting" (*London Times*: 10 December 1992)

Phillips, Andrew: "Diana's Story" (*Macleans*: 15 June 1992)

————: "Royal Fire Storm" (*Macleans*: 30 November 1992)

————: "Icon for All Seasons" (*Macleans*: 15 September 1997)

Pimlott, Ben: *The Queen: A Biography of Elizabeth II* (London: HarperCollins Publishers, 1996)

Parris, Matthew: "Domestic drama proves chilling news for peers" (*London Times*: 10 December 1992)

"The M.V.P." (http://pathfinder.com.people 10 October 1990)

The Prince and Princess of Wales' Wedding Day (Agincourt, Ontario: Methuen
    Publications, 1981)
Roberts, Roxanne: "State of the Union, Ten Years After" (Washingtonpost.com:
    International Special Report: 28 July 1991)
Smith, Michelle Green Terry & Wright, Margaret: "The Outsider" (http:/
    pathfinder.com/people: 6 December 1993)
Spink, Katherine: Invitation to a Royal Wedding(Toronto: Collins
    Publishers, 1981)
Spoto, Donald: The decline and Fall of the House of Windsor (New York: Pocket
    Books—a division of Simon & Schuster, 1995)
Staff Reporter: "Palace Ends Clash with Newspaper Over Prince" (The *Times*,
    24 November 1980)
Stewart, Malcolm: "Queen Attacks Story on Charles" (The *Guardian*,
    22 November 1980)
Thornton, Philip: Charles' Other Woman: (PA News: Mon, 20 Nov., 1995)
Wade, Judy: Inside a Royal Marriage (Angus & Robertson Publishers, 1987)
Walker, Martin: "Palace Stays Mum on 'Delightful' Diana" (The *Guardian*,
    11 November 1980)
Wallace, Bruce: "Diana Princess of Wales: 1961–1997" (*MacLeans*:
    8 September 1997)
White, Jerry: Travels with Diana: A Landmine Survivor's Tale (*Christian
    Science Monitor*, 3 Setember 1997)
Whittaker, James: *Settling Down* (London: Quartet Books Limited, 1981)
"Who's on Trial—the Press, the Palace, or Lady Diana?" (The *Guardian*,
    3 December 1980)
Witherow, John: "Lady Diana Gives All Her Hunters the Slip"(The *Times*,
    15 November 1980)
Witherow,John: "Harassed Lady Diana Remains Calm and Polite" (The *Times*,
    26 November 1980)

Diana: A Commemorative Biography

With special preface by Dame Barbara Cartland

ORDER FORM

Available at your local bookstore or use this page to order.

❏ 1-55197-846-6 –DIANA: A COMMEMORATIVE BIOGRAPHY-
$14.95 U.S./$16.95 CAN/£7.95 UK

Send to: COMMONWEALTH PUBLICATIONS INC.
9764 - 45th Avenue
Edmonton, Alberta, CANADA T6E 5C5

Please send me the items I have checked above. I am enclosing $_____ (please add $2.50 U.S. per book to cover postage and handling). Send check or money order, no cash or C.O.D.'s, please.

Mr./Mrs./Ms._____

Address_____

City/State_____ Zip_____

FAX ORDERS: (403) 432-9409

CREDIT CARD ORDERS CALL TOLL FREE: 1-888-877-3865

Please allow four to six weeks for delivery.
Prices and availability subject to change without notice.

Diana: A Commemorative Biography

With special preface by **Dame Barbara Cartland**

ORDER FORM

Available at your local bookstore or use this page to order.

❏ 1-55197-846-6 –DIANA: A COMMEMORATIVE BIOGRAPHY-
$14.95 U.S./$16.95 CAN/£7.95 UK

Send to: COMMONWEALTH PUBLICATIONS INC.
9764 - 45th Avenue
Edmonton, Alberta, CANADA T6E 5C5

Please send me the items I have checked above. I am enclosing
$_____ (please add $2.50 U.S. per book to cover postage and
handling). Send check or money order, no cash or C.O.D.'s, please.

Mr./Mrs./Ms._____

Address_____

City/State_____ Zip_____

FAX ORDERS: (403) 432-9409

CREDIT CARD ORDERS CALL TOLL FREE: 1-888-877-3865

Please allow four to six weeks for delivery.
Prices and availability subject to change without notice.